T0414146

Teacher Management in China

Education has long been highly valued in China and it continues to be highly valued, both by the state, which appreciates the value of education for maintaining China's economic rise, and by parents, who, affected by the One-Child Policy, devote a large proportion of their incomes to their one child's education. This book explores current systems of teacher management in China and assesses their effectiveness. It charts the development of China's education system, outlines present day human resource management methods in Chinese schools, including practices for recruitment and selection, training and development, performance appraisal, and rewards, both pay and non-financial rewards, and describes recent changes and innovations. The book concludes that a high performance work system, enhanced by traditional paternalistic humanised management and by pragmatism, predominates, with important consequences for teachers' jobs and performance and for the quality of students' school life.

Eva Huang is a Lecturer at George Brown College, Canada.

John Benson is a Professor and Head of the School of Business at Monash University, Malaysia, and an Adjunct Professor in the Department of Management at Monash University, Australia.

Ying Zhu is a Professor and Director of the Australia Centre for Asian Business at the University of South Australia.

Routledge Contemporary China Series

Teacher Management in China
The transformation of educational systems

Eva Huang, John Benson and Ying Zhu

Routledge
Taylor & Francis Group

LONDON AND NEW YORK

First published 2016
by Routledge
2 Park Square, Milton Park, Abingdon, Oxon OX14 4RN

and by Routledge
711 Third Avenue, New York, NY 10017

Routledge is an imprint of the Taylor & Francis Group, an informa business

© 2016 Eva Huang, John Benson and Ying Zhu

The right of Eva Huang, John Benson and Ying Zhu to be identified as authors of this work has been asserted by them in accordance with sections 77 and 78 of the Copyright, Designs and Patents Act 1988.

All rights reserved. No part of this book may be reprinted or reproduced or utilised in any form or by any electronic, mechanical, or other means, now known or hereafter invented, including photocopying and recording, or in any information storage or retrieval system, without permission in writing from the publishers.

Trademark notice: Product or corporate names may be trademarks or registered trademarks, and are used only for identification and explanation without intent to infringe.

British Library Cataloguing in Publication Data
A catalogue record for this book is available from the British Library

Library of Congress Cataloging in Publication Data
Names: Huang, Eva, author. | Benson, John, 1948- author. | Zhu, Ying, 1961- author.
Title: Teacher management in China : the transformation of educational systems / Eva Huang, John Benson and Ying Zhu.
Description: Abingdon, Oxon ; New York, NY : Routledge, 2016. | Series: Routledge contemporary China series ; 146 | Includes bibliographical references and index.
Identifiers: LCCN 2015040249| ISBN 9781138910850 (hardback) | ISBN 9781315693040 (ebook)
Subjects: LCSH: Teachers--Training of--China. | Teachers--Recruiting--China. | Teachers--Rating of--China. | School personnel management--China. | Educational change--China.
Classification: LCC LB1727.C5 H83 2016 | DDC 371.1020951--dc23
LC record available at http://lccn.loc.gov/

2015040249

ISBN: 978-1-138-91085-0 (hbk)
ISBN: 978-1-315-69304-0 (ebk)

Typeset in Times New Roman
by Sunrise Setting Ltd, Paignton, UK

MIX
Paper from responsible sources
FSC
www.fsc.org   FSC® C013604

Printed and bound by CPI Group (UK) Ltd, Croydon, CR0 4YY

Contents

Illustrations

Preface

The Chinese education sector is the largest globally, with over 200 million full-time students and close to 15 million teachers. Education is seen as part of one's personal development and it is often viewed as the only way to change one's destiny for a better life. This tradition was strengthened by the introduction of the One-Child Policy, which took effect in the late 1970s. Parents are now extremely ambitious for their only child and they are often willing to sacrifice whatever they can afford to give their child the best opportunities and educational success. Thus, educational expenses represent an ever-increasing proportion of income expenditure for households. With admission to the World Trade Organization in 2001, and the further opening of the Chinese domestic market, the Chinese education sector has been, and will continue to be, an attractive business proposition for international educational institutions in the near future.

Echoing people's high expectation for education, the Chinese government also perceives education as a critical way to build a sustainable and prosperous country. As early as the late 1970s, the Chinese eminent leader, Deng Xiao-ping, advocated the fundamental role of education in achieving the national goals of the 'Four Modernisations': industry, agriculture, science and technology. Since 1993, the Chinese government has prioritised the strategic development of education and instituted a series of on-going educational reforms. The acknowledgement of the critical role of education in state development led the government to place considerable emphasis on teacher management. Such intervention is not new, with teacher management going through several phases: from an emphasis on Chinese elements (prior to 1840s), through a Western elements dominant era (1900s to 1940s), an anti-tradition and anti-Western period (1950s to 1970s), and finally, to the present model involving both Chinese and Western elements (from 1980s to the present).

The objective of this book is to offer insights into the transformation of the educational system and teacher management in China. Applying an institutional approach, this book traces the education changes from the Late Qing Dynasty, when the modern education system was first introduced from developed countries, through to the contemporary educational system, which is claimed by the Chinese government to be a modern system 'with Chinese characteristics'. In doing this, the book addresses several important questions that have so far remained largely unexplored in the literature including ascertaining the key contextual factors that have shaped the present education system and practices, the adoption of strategic approaches to teacher management and whether such HRM practices lead to higher teacher performance and improvements in the quality of student life.

By addressing these questions, we hope this book will enrich our understanding of the historical development of the Chinese education system as well as providing a contemporary analysis of the present, albeit continually evolving, education system and teacher management in China.

Eva Huang, John Benson and Ying Zhu
1 September 2015

Acknowledgements

We would first and foremost like to thank all those who participated in the study: staff of the education bureaus, school principals, classroom teachers and students. Without their patience and understanding, this book would not have been possible. We would also like to acknowledge and thank the various people, both in China and elsewhere, who readily provided their insights and criticisms of the study and this monograph. Finally, but not least, we would like to thank the University of South Australia for their ongoing support of the project.

Abbreviations

CCP	Chinese Communist Party
CFA	Confirmatory factor analysis
CFI	Comparative fit index
GDP	Gross domestic product
HPWS	High performance work systems
HR	Human resources
HRM	Human resource management
IRB	In-role behaviour
OCB	Organisational citizenship behaviour
OECD	Organisation for Economic Cooperation and Development
PA	Performance appraisal
PM	Personnel management
POS	Perceived organisational support
PRP	Performance related pay
QSL	Quality of school life
RMB	Renminbi – the official Chinese currency
RMSEA	Root mean square error of approximation
SHRM	Strategic human resource management
SRMR	Standardised root mean square residual
TLI	Tucker-Lewis fit index
WTO	World Trade Organization

1 Introduction

Since the open door policy and economic reforms commenced in the late 1970s, dramatic and substantial changes have occurred in China. The reforms have turned the country from an agricultural-based, backward, manual and isolated society into a fast-growing, industrial-based economy (Wang and Wang 2006). China today has one of the fastest economic growth rates in the world, averaging around 10 per cent annually over the past 2 decades (Zheng and Lamond 2009; Zhu *et al*. 2010). It has become the largest contributor to world economic growth since 2007 and the second largest economy in the world, surpassing Japan in 2010 (Fukumoto and Muto 2012). It is foreseen that China will be the world's largest economy in the next 1 to 2 decades if the rapid growth can be maintained (Fukumoto and Muto 2012). Compared with the growth of the overall world economy, China's economic development is often regarded as a miracle (Lin *et al*. 1996; Yeung *et al*. 2008; Zheng and Lamond 2009). China's economic reforms have been an unprecedented achievement, prompting some to comment: 'never has the world seen a major economic power emerge in such a short time span and attain such a weight in the total world economy' (McNally 2007: 177).

Due to the increasingly competitive global market, the Chinese Government, however, recognises that relying solely on its previous 'world factory' developmental model cannot achieve a sustainable prosperous society (Gu 2010; Ministry of Education 2010). In order to build a sustainable and prosperous society, education is regarded as a key tool (Lewin and Hui 1989). The significance of education in the society has been highlighted by the government's *Outline of Education Reform and Development in China*, which stresses that 'a strong nation lies in its education and a strong education system lies in its teachers' (Central Committee of the Chinese Communist Party and State Council 1993: 8). Moreover, accompanying its exponential economic growth, China faces a myriad of challenges including regional development disparities, a widening gap between rich and poor, uneven and unfair wealth distribution and a growing dislike of government officials and the rich (The World Bank 2013). These issues, if tackled inappropriately, could result in social unrest and turmoil (Han 2008; The World Bank 2013). To address these challenges, the provision of quality and equitable education has been deemed critical (Central Committee of the Chinese Communist Party and State Council

1993; Han 2008). Accordingly, developing education has been a priority at various levels of governments (State Council 2005, 2006). The need to build a highly qualified teaching workforce has been highlighted and reforms to teacher management have been undertaken (Central Committee of the Chinese Communist Party 1985).

Traditionally, Chinese people have been highly appreciative of the role of education in their personal development, which was often viewed as the only way to improve one's life and opportunities. This tradition was strengthened by the introduction of the One-Child Policy that took effect in the late 1970s. Parents now have ambitious expectations for their only child and are often willing to sacrifice whatever they can afford to give their child the best opportunities and educational success (Romanowski 2006). Thus, educational expenses comprise an ever-increasing proportion of income expenditure for households (Zhu *et al.* 2010). For example, the typical parent in most cities spends at least one-third of their household income on their children's education, and, in some cities, the proportion can account for up to half of the household income (Mok *et al.* 2009). With China's admission to the World Trade Organization in 2001 and the further opening of the Chinese market, the Chinese education sector has been, and will continue to be, an attractive business proposition for international educational organisations in the near future.

The education sector in China is the largest globally (Forrester *et al.* 2006; Robinson and Yi 2008), for example, there were 14,589,394 full-time teaching staff in 2013 (National Bureau of Statistics of China 2014). This large number of teaching staff, if managed well, will arguably have a positive influence on the 209,905,483 full time students (National Bureau of Statistics of China 2014) and subsequently would benefit the stability and further development of the country. By contrast, if teachers are not managed well, the whole country could suffer, as demonstrated by the Cultural Revolution Movement (for details of the destructive impact of the Cultural Revolution Movement, see chapter 2). As China now stands at a crossroads (Zhang and Chen 2012; Lane 2013), improved teacher management is particularly critical and urgent.

Research gaps, theoretical foundations and key questions

Despite the significance of education, human resource management (HRM) research in this sector has been largely neglected (Ouchi *et al.* 2005; Cooke 2009; Pil and Leana 2009). Research on HRM is often conducted in industry, particularly in the manufacturing industry (Batt 2002; Sun *et al.* 2007; Liao *et al.* 2009), where it has improved our general understanding of the various HRM practices and the relationship between people management and performance. Nevertheless, the features of schools are considerably different from the characteristics of the manufacturing sector and the profit-driven service sector (Cochran-Smith and Fries 2001; Berry 2004). Consequently, the management approaches generated from other sectors might not be directly applicable to the education sector. The lack of HRM research in the public sector in China, for example, in the education sector, has resulted in 'a significant gap in our understanding of the key changes to, and challenges facing, human resource management in the country as a whole' (Cooke 2009: 18).

Furthermore, most HRM studies investigating transitional HRM in China only 'offer general descriptions without showing the nature of current Chinese HRM' and have 'failed to explore how and why these changes happened' (Zhu *et al.* 2012: 3965). Details of these studies are provided in appendix 1. Adopting the approach of Benson and Zhu (1999), transitional HRM in this study is defined as the process of the transformation and development of HRM practices in response to the changing institutional contexts. Exploring contextual factors in HRM research is important, as they play a significant role in shaping the transformation of HRM (Warner and Rowley 2011). While investigating contextual factors, 'more sophisticated analytical tools to fully understand specifically how and precisely why HRM has evolved to the particular forms we find it in today' are called for (Warner 2009: 2183). Institutional theory achieves this goal by conceptualising the complex process of social changes (Warner *et al.* 2005) and by providing a framework to comprehend radical changes in response to contextual influences (Greenwood and Hinings 1996). Consequently, this study addresses this gap by utilising institutional theory to investigate the influences of contextual factors on HRM.

In addition, even though the significant role of HRM for organisational effectiveness has been noted (Huselid 1995; Kehoe and Wright 2013), this relationship has recently been challenged (Wall and Wood 2005; Wright *et al.* 2005; Paauwe 2009). It is suggested that the HRM–performance link 'should be treated with caution' (Wall and Wood 2005). One reason for this ambiguous link is that the common organisational performance indicators, such as financial results, are also influenced by factors other than HRM issues (Orlitzky *et al.* 2003; Paauwe 2009). As a result, to understand better the HRM–performance link, better performance indicators are called for (Richard *et al.* 2009; Guest 2011). We argue that the education sector is an excellent place to test the HRM–performance relationship given that the education sector has a more direct relationship between employees and organisational effectiveness.

To overcome these deficiencies, this study is designed to explore the contextual factors shaping HRM policy and practice, to identify the current HRM practices, to test a conceptual model that relates HRM to teachers' job performance and students' quality of school life, and to examine the transitional HRM model in Chinese schools. Specifically, this study has four aims:

1. To explore the contextual factors shaping HRM policies and practices. Past research has shown that contextual factors play a significant role in the transformation of HRM in a radical transitional period, for example, Tsui *et al.* (2004), Zhu *et al.* (2007, 2012) and Warner (2011). This aim is addressed by the research question: *How have contextual factors shaped HRM policies and practices?*
2. To explore transitional HRM models in Chinese schools. This aim furthers our understanding of HRM transformation in a transitional economy. Previous

research has shown a convergence and divergence between traditional and Western people management models. For example, Benson and Zhu (1999) identified three paradigms of people management in transition: minimalist, transitional and innovative. Ding *et al.* (2001) identified a transitional convergent model moving further from personnel management to Western HRM with fewer Chinese characteristics. Zhu *et al.* (2012) presented paternalistic, transactional and differentiated models, while Zhu *et al.* (2007) in an earlier study identified a hybrid model that had both Chinese and Western elements. This study investigates whether Chinese schools are adopting a hybrid people management model. This aim is addressed by the research question: *How can the current HRM system in Chinese schools be best characterised?*

3. To identify current HRM practices, specifically, recruitment and selection, training and development, performance appraisal and reward management. These four HRM functions represent the most explored issues in the literature (Boselie *et al.* 2005) and reflect the main objectives of key strategic HRM programmes (Paauwe 2009). Focusing on these functions can answer the call from Cooke (2009) for a more in-depth understanding of the particular aspects of HRM practices. Accordingly, the research question underpinning this goal is as follows: *How is HRM conducted in terms of recruitment and selection, training and development, performance appraisal and reward management?*

4. To test a conceptual model that links HRM to teachers' job performance and students' quality of school life. This goal contributes to our understanding of the HRM–performance link that is still uncertain in the literature. This goal is addressed by the research question: *Does the adoption of a strategic HRM approach lead to higher levels of teachers' job performance and students' quality of school life?*

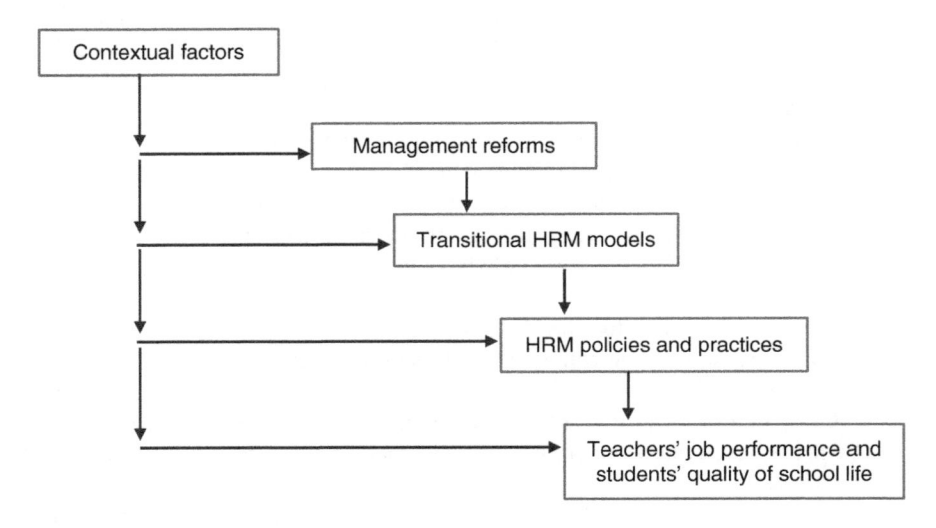

Figure 1.1 Research framework

In summary, this study is conceptualised by the research framework presented in Figure 1.1. First, it identifies the contextual factors and their impacts on management reforms and then it explores the influence of both the contextual factors and management reforms on the transformation of HRM practices. The transitional HRM model in the Chinese school system is subsequently presented and discussed. The focus then shifts to the investigation of HRM policies and practices in the school system through case study analysis. Finally, the impact of the HRM model on teachers' job performance and their students' quality of school life is subsequently examined. By doing so, this study will make a significant theoretical and practical contribution to Chinese educational management and the wider HRM literature.

Summary of research methods

The research was conducted in three administrative districts (districts 1, 2 and 3) in Guangdong province. As one of the few regions that have received large shares of capital inflow and investment, Guangdong province is one of the most developed areas in China (Zhu *et al.* 2010). Among the most developed areas in Guangdong province, districts 1, 2 and 3 have played a significant role in undertaking educational experimentation that, if shown to be successful, will spread to other parts of the country. These districts represent the latest developments in teacher management in the country. A profile of these three research sites is provided in Table 1.1.

Based on the objectives and nature of this research, a sequential mixed-method approach was adopted. People management models, namely, personnel

Table 1.1 A profile of the research sites

Characteristics	District 1	District 2	District 3
Area (km²)	154.7	1073.8	806.1
Number of subordinate towns	4	8	10
Population	1,100,000	2,600,000	2,460,000
Number of kindergartens	126	301	281
Number of kindergarten students	35,236	61,506	58,323
Number of kindergarten teachers	4,819	5,040	4,765
Number of PJM schools	86	175	194
Number of PJM school students	111,798	223,108	223,568
Number of PJM school teachers	5,535	9,962	10,237
Number of SMV schools	13	26	32
Number of SMV school students	20,614	67,449	69,421
Number of SMV school teachers	1,447	3,584	3,726

Source: interview data (2011, 2012). PJM, primary and junior middle schools; SMV, senior middle and vocational schools

management, HRM and strategic HRM, are well established in Western literature. However, given that the research setting is in China under different institutions, Western management theories may not be fully applicable (Tsui 2009; Warner 2011) as has been demonstrated in previous studies, for example, Rowley and Benson (2002) and Zhu *et al.* (2007, 2012). In addition, limited HRM has been conducted in the education sector worldwide (see Ouchi *et al.* 2005; Cooke 2009; Pil and Leana 2009; Jimmieson *et al.* 2010). Consequently, rich, detailed and explorative data are first needed to understand the current HRM practices and the prevailing HRM models as well as the relevance of various people management models in Chinese schools. This approach is consistent with the suggested theory building process for indigenous research in China as outlined in Wang (2012), namely, to investigate distinct Chinese phenomena by inductive indigenous research. Following this exploration, a survey design is necessary to test and to generalise the impacts of the HRM model that is identified in the first stage of the qualitative research. As such, a mixed-method two-stage sequential design was employed (see Table 1.2).

At stage one, semi-structured interviews were conducted with nine educational officers and 42 school principals to explore present practices and changes in HRM in Chinese schools. To capture the changes in HRM policies and practices, two rounds of data were collected. The first round of data was gathered in early 2011, while the second round was collected 18 months later in late 2012. Data analysis was undertaken by thematic analysis and the frequency of occurrence of the thematic codes with NVivo was used to explore HRM practices and to determine the extent to which practices coincided with what are generally referred to as high performance work systems (HPWS).

Based on the findings of stage one interviews, which suggested that HPWS were prevalent, a questionnaire was undertaken at stage two (see chapter 4). The survey was conducted with 1,051 teachers and their supervisors as well as 5,022

Table 1.2 Research design of the current research

Sequential mixed methodology		Data collection method	Data analysis method
Stage 1	Qualitative method (two rounds)	Semi-structured interview (n = 51) 1 director of the city education bureaus 8 HR managers of town education bureaus 42 principals of various schools	Thematic analysis Frequency of occurrence Nvivo software
Stage 2	Quantitative method	Structured questionnaire (63 schools) 1,051 class teachers and their supervisors 5,222 students	Assessment of multivariate normality Confirmatory factor analysis Analysis of variances Multilevel SEM with Mplus

students in 63 schools of different types. The questionnaire asked teachers to rate HPWS practices and perceived organisational support (POS), supervisors to rate teachers' job performance and students to rate their quality of school life. Each teacher questionnaire was matched to his/her supervisor and five students who had completed a questionnaire. Participants were informed about the nature, procedure and data analysis methods of the study. Confidentiality and anonymity was guaranteed, as was their right to withdraw from the study at any time. Multilevel structural equation modelling was undertaken to test whether HPWS improves organisational effectiveness in terms of students' quality of school life via teachers' perception of organisational support and job performance.

Outline of the book

The book contains seven chapters. Chapter 1 provided the rationale for HRM research in Chinese schools pointing out its significance to Chinese industrial development. Research gaps, aims and questions were discussed. A brief research method section and information on the contributions of this research were presented.

Following this introductory section, chapter 2 provides an overview of the transformation process in China and its impacts on education. As experiences and institutions have enduring impacts on current institutional choices (Boas 2007), this chapter provides a historical overview of the transformation in China in terms of its societal and educational systems. It begins with an outline of societal changes and educational reforms in the Late Qing Dynasty (1840 to 1910). This is followed by an elaboration on the historical background, key aims of education, educational and HRM policies and practices and their impacts in three different periods: the republican era (1911 to 1949), the central planned economy era (1949 to 1978) and the economic reform era (1978 to present).

Building on the previous discussion, chapter 3 investigates the evolution of HRM in the Chinese school sector. A theoretical framework incorporating institution theory is adopted to guide the analysis as it offers an approach to understanding radical changes and explaining the contextual dynamics for organisational adaptations (Greenwood and Hinings 1996). It also accounts for the what, why and how questions with regard to organisational responses to institutional factors (Scott 2004). As such, this chapter starts by outlining institutional theory. Guided by this theoretical perspective, the second section addresses the issue of the evolution of HRM in Chinese schools. This section is divided into two parts: the contextual factors and the management reforms in the Chinese school sector. By adopting this approach, chapter 3 answers the first research question: *How have contextual factors shaped HRM policies and practices*?

Chapter 4 examines the transitional HRM models in the Chinese school sector based on the findings of chapter 3 and addresses the second research question: *How can the current HRM system in Chinese schools be best characterised?* The chapter commences by reviewing the literature on the transformation of people management models: personnel management, HRM and strategic HRM (i.e. HPWS). It then focuses on the common management models in the Chinese context: humanised management, paternalistic management and pragmatic management. Based on these reviews and the research data, a new management model was identified: the pragmatic integrated transitional management model. This model is characterised by high performance work systems, which are facilitated and enhanced by traditional paternalistic humanised management. This integrated model is underpinned by pragmatic management.

Chapter 5 then addresses the third research question: *How is HRM conducted in terms of recruitment and selection, training and development, performance appraisal and reward management?* This chapter presents the results from the two rounds of interviews conducted in 2011 and 2012. This chapter provides detailed contextual information on these HRM practices.

The penultimate chapter, chapter 6, extends the findings of chapters 4 and 5 by addressing the fourth research question: *Does the adoption of a strategic HRM approach lead to higher levels of teachers' job performance and students' quality of school life?* It does this by exploring the impacts of HPWS on teachers' job performance (in-role performance and organisational citizenship behaviours) and students' quality of school life. It begins with the literature review on the relationships between HPWS and job performance. It then shifts to the elaboration on the uniqueness of the education sector and hypothesis development. An overview of the research methods and data analysis approach is then provided, which is followed by an elaboration of the research findings.

The final chapter, chapter 7, highlights the significance of education as one fundamental element of a society, in national economy and development as well as national stability and competitiveness. In China, education has played, and will continue to play, a critical role in its transitional process. This final chapter illustrates both theoretical and practical implications of this research and discusses the on-going challenges and future development of the Chinese education system.

2 The evolution of Chinese society and changes in education

Introduction

Experience and institutions exert an enduring impact on current institutional choices (North 1990; Boas 2007). Without a full understanding of the historical events, it is difficult to sufficiently comprehend the institutions and systems (Scott 2008b). As such, this chapter provides a detailed account of the evolution of the current educational system and HRM in the Chinese education sector. Such transitions in Chinese society will provide the backdrop to how and why the current educational systems and HRM models have evolved.

China is one of the world's oldest civilisations. Its history is full of vicissitudes and turbulences with 'its recurrent ups and downs' (Warner 2009: 2169). China has experienced three key social transitional models, namely federalism, capitalism and socialism (Goncalves 1996). Federalism was present in China for approximately 2,400 years encompassing over 12 dynasties. From 1912 to 1949, China entered a republican era under the domination of the Kuomintang (Nationalist) Party. The period between the late federalism and the republican era was chaotic as China witnessed a number of wars with various Western countries, saw the collapse of the Imperial Order, experienced division of the country and wars among warlords, had a resistance war with Japan and witnessed a civil war between the Kuomintang Party and the Chinese Communist Party (CCP). With the establishment of the People's Republic of China in 1949 under the regime of the CCP, economic recovery was put on the agenda. The economic recovery, nevertheless, did not occur smoothly. The catastrophic Great Leap Forward Experiment and the Cultural Revolution Movement led China to turbulence and isolation from the rest of the world. Following the Cultural Revolution, economic reforms were conducted and brought an unprecedented growth and development that has reshaped the economy in terms of behavioural, institutional and organisational outcomes (Warner and Rowley 2011). Within the past three decades, China has transformed from rural and agricultural to urban and industrialised, from rigidly state-controlled to market-oriented and from self-contained to an internationally oriented economy (Wang and Wang 2006).

Consistent with the economic and social changes, the education system also experienced shifts to meet new institutional requirements. During the 2,400 years of federalism, the dominant education system was Confucianism, which served as tools to cultivate obedient citizens and to consolidate the social status of the ruling class (Gan 2002). The core of this education system was the Imperial Examination System (*keju zhidu*) that selected the best candidates to be government officials (Gan 2002). The examination system was open to all regardless of social status, wealth and age, and thus, provided a fair system for the selection of government officials (Shi 2013). However, the system over-emphasised understanding and memorisation of Confucianism (Dang 2001). As a result, it failed to cultivate officials who would effectively govern the country and regions to meet the developmental needs of the country (Gan 2002; Shi 2013).

In the turbulent republican period, Western educational models were perceived to be advanced and a powerful force in building a strong and independent nation. As a result, Western educational models were prevalent and their impact can still be found in contemporary China. After the establishment of the People's Republic of China, the previous Western educational models were deemed capitalist and were thus abandoned. Scholars and teachers were accused of having a capitalistic nature and were required to be retrained and remoulded. Many Western educational approaches were abolished. It was not until 1978 when China began to undertake a series of political and economic reforms that education became a priority. Since then, the so-called socialist education system with Chinese characteristics has been slowly evolving.

This review begins from the republican era (1911 to 1949) when the modern education system was formally established and developed. The modern educational system in China, however, was first introduced as early as 1862 when the Qing Dynasty set up the School of Combined Learning (*jingshi tongwenguan*) (Yang 2001). Since then, a series of educational reforms based on Western systems and practices were implemented which had a significant impact on the formation of the educational system under the republican era. Consequently, to have a better understanding of the educational system between 1912 and 1949, it is necessary to examine the societal changes and educational reforms in the Late Qing Dynasty.

Social and educational changes in the Late Qing Dynasty (1840 to 1910)

Until the First Opium War with the United Kingdom (UK) in June 1840, China had been a feudal and independent society. During that time, China was the most populous country in the world with almost one-third of the entire world's population (Zhou 2001). As recently as the 1820s, China contributed 30 per cent of the entire world's gross domestic product (GDP) (Yan 2001; Zhou 2001). The country's economy was based on the combination of small-scale farming and cottage industry. Education, at this time, was dominated by the Imperial Examination System. Freedom of speech and thought were constrained as books that were against the interests of the ruling class were destroyed. Furthermore, people with thoughts that were different from those of the ruling class were persecuted or even killed (Li 2004). Three separate kinds of schools, namely, the government sponsored (*gongxue*), the private sponsored (*sixue*) and academy of classic learning (*shuyuan*), aimed to educate and develop government officials. The teaching content focused on the Four Books (*sishu*) and the Five Classics (*wujing*), which outlined the principles of society and government as well as codes for personal conduct. Science and technology were totally ignored. The education system was mainly for the elite, as most people could not afford the high expense of schooling. As a result, most Chinese people were illiterate.

After the First Opium War (May 1840 to August 1842), the Qing dynasty was moving towards a semi-colonised and semi-feudal society when China became involved in a series of wars. They were with the UK and France (the Second Opium War, October 1856 to October 1860), Russia (1858 to 1864), Japan (the First Sino-Japanese, July 1894 to April 1895) and the Eight Nation Alliance (the UK, France, Germany, the USA, Japan, Russia, Italy and the Austro-Hungarian empire, May 1900 to September 1901). Each time, when China was defeated, it signed treaties that allowed the annexation of territories, provided huge indemnities and gave away trade privileges. The wars changed the Qing dynasty from a strong, powerful, prosperous and independent country to a nation of poverty, weakness and a semi-colonial, semi-feudal economy. The decades of defeat prompted the Qing dynasty to realise that a substantial gap existed between China and Western countries in terms of social, education, military and technology systems and citizens' overall living standard. To rejuvenate the nation, the Qing dynasty decided to learn from Western countries to improve its capabilities to resist these advanced countries (*shi yi zhi changji yi zhiyi*). Three gradual reforms, the Westernisation Movement (or the Self-Strengthening Movement) (*yangwu yundong*), the Hundred Days Reform (*Bairi Weixin*) and the New Deal of the Late Qing Dynasty (*qingmo xinzheng*), were thus implemented and marked the start of the modern educational system in China.

The Westernisation Movement (1861 to 1895) planned to build a strong nation (*qiu qiang*) by establishing military factories and to develop a prosperous country (*qiu fu*) through market-oriented civil industry. The establishment of new factories and increasing international trade required a significant number of skilled people. As the previous educational system failed to cultivate the required workforce, the Qing dynasty was obliged to adjust its educational system and create new Western-style schools. At the same time, the government established organisations to translate Western books, particularly those in social and applied sciences (Yang 2001). The Qing dynasty also dispatched students (aged 13 to 20) using government funds to the US, the UK and France to learn advanced science and technology (Xu 1996; Feng 2001).

The Westernisation Movement concluded when China lost the First Sino-Japanese War (1894 to 1895). Defeated, the Qing dynasty had to cede Taiwan and pay 230 million tales of silver, which was about four and a half times Japan's annual national revenue (Deng 2006). The loss of the war caused disillusion in the Chinese dream of building a strong nation by military and technology. More profound reforms, for example, in the political system and educational system, were therefore called for.

Inspired by Japanese successful reforms (the Meiji Reforms), the Qing dynasty implemented the Hundred Days Reform and the New Deal of the Late Qing Dynasty. Educational reforms were perceived to be one of the most significant factors in revitalising China (Yang 2001). Therefore, a series of educational reforms were implemented and a number of education policies were issued. A significant number of people were sent to Japan to study advanced social and applied sciences. For instance, from 1896 to 1909, around 68,000 Chinese studied in Japan (Li 1982). High-ranked officers were also dispatched to Western countries to explore and learn their advanced political, economic and educational systems (Yang 2001).

The most significant educational policy in the Qing dynasty was the Kui-Mao Educational System or the Zou-ding School Regulations (*zhouding xuetang zhangcheng*) issued in 1904 (Wang 1999). Based on the Japanese educational system and experience of church schools, the Kui-Mao Educational System was the first modern system that had widespread impact in China (Li 2009). The hierarchy of the system is shown in Figure 2.1. This system went from kindergarten through to research academy including different levels of general, vocational and teacher's training schools, colleges and universities. The regulation also promoted a 5-year compulsory education system (Li 2009). Realising the significant role of teachers, this policy had detailed regulations on managing teacher's training schools (Guo 1999). Furthermore, this policy also stipulated rules for managing schools, teaching methods and approaches and school placement regulations for different types of schools (Li 2009).

To oversee the implementation of the new educational policy, a new ministry, the Education Ministry, was established. Educational departments were founded at the provincial levels to promote compulsory education (Li 2009). Encouraging Education Organisations were also set up following the issue of Regulations on Encouraging Schooling by the Education Ministry in 1906 (Guo 1999). In the same year, provinces were granted the autonomy to design and implement educational reforms based on their own situations (Li 2009). The modern educational system had some variation in different provinces to meet local conditions. This system served as the basis for the development of the educational system during the republican period.

The impacts of the educational reforms were profound. In 1905, the feudal examination system that had existed for over 1,300 years was eliminated. Thus, it changed the traditional elite education system in which only a minority of people could attend schools to the compulsory education model in which every child was encouraged and supported to go to school. In less than 10 years, the number of modern schools developed from 769 in 1902 to 59,117 in 1909 with an annual increase of 86% and the number of students rose from 31,428 to 1,639,641 with an annual increase of 76% (Li 2009). Teaching content changed from an art-focus to a combination of social and applied science. The thought of 'democracy and science' was introduced, which had a critical impact on later societal development. Graduates from the modern and overseas schools later became the major force in the collapse of the Qing dynasty (1911), the establishment of the Provisional Government of the Republic of China (1912), the abdication of the *Yuan Shi-kai* Monarch (1916), the outbreak of the May Fourth Movement (1919), the opposition to the

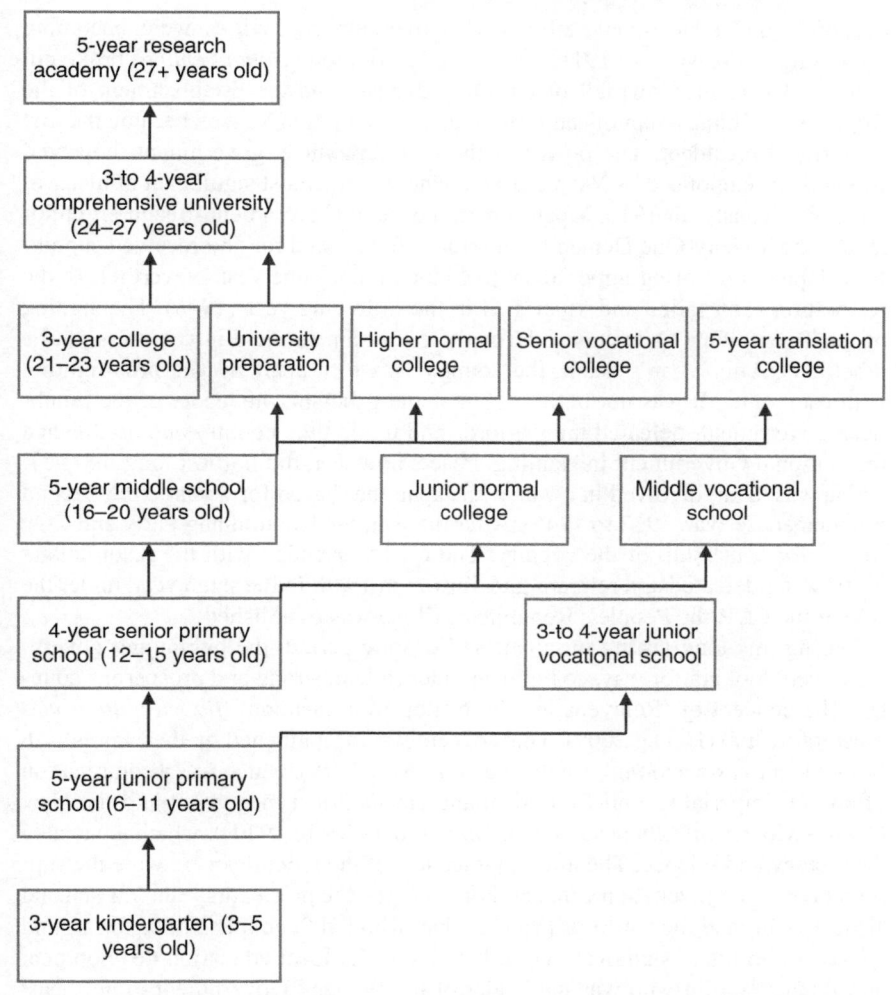

Figure 2.1 The first modern educational system in China: Kui-Mao Education System
Source: Adapted from Li (2009)

dictatorship of the Northern Warlords (1917 to 1927) and the pursuit of democratic process in the 1930s and 1940s (Wang 1999). The educational reforms served as a basis for the development of the educational system in the republican period.

The republican era (1911 to 1949)

From the First Opium War in 1840 until the founding of the People's Republic of China in 1949, the history of China was actually the history of turbulence, chaos and wars. While the Late Qing Dynasty was busily engaged in the political, economic and educational reforms, antigovernment activities were becoming increasingly intensive. In 1911, the *Xinhai* Revolution (*xinhai geming*) broke out and this led to the downfall of the Qing dynasty and the establishment of the Republic of China, a republican form of government. Sun Yat-sen became the first provisional president. The power of the new republican government, however, was soon monopolised by Yuan Shi-kan, who was the most significant minister of the Qing dynasty. In 1915, Japan forced the Yuan Government to sign an unfair treaty: the Twenty-One Demands. In return, Yuan asked for and received support from Japan in restoring imperialism to China in that same year. Nevertheless, the restoration soon failed and Yuan died in the following year (1916). The signing of the Twenty-One Demands and Yuan's restoration resulted in countless public rebellions. After Yuan's death, the country was torn apart by warlords fighting with each other. It was not until 1928 that Jiang Jie-shi, the leader of the republican government, defeated the warlords and unified the country and established the National Government in Nanjing. Peace, however, did not last long. In 1937, China was again involved in a war with Japan that lasted for 8 years (the Second Sino-Japanese War, 1937 to 1945). After the war, the Kuomintang Party and CCP fought for leadership of the country. The civil war ended with the Kuomintang Party being defeated and retreating to Taiwan in 1949. In the same year, under the rule of the CCP, the People's Republic of China was established.

During this long-lasting turbulent and chaotic period, the public and government were looking for ways to build an independent, strong and prosperous country. The concept of 'Rejuvenating the Nation by Education' (*jiaoyu jiuguo*) was most influential (Huang 2009). This concept was strengthened by the May Fourth Movement (*wusi yundong*) (established on 4 May 1919), which was a combination of an anti-imperialist, anti-Confucian and anti-political movement and the New Culture Movement (*xin wenhua yundong*, mid-1920s to 1930s), which advocated democracy and science. The important leaders of the republican era were the supporters of this rejuvenation concept. For example, the presidents (Sun Yat-sen and Jiang Jie-shi) and the warlords (Yan Xi-shan who led Shanxi Province for around 38 years and made significant contributions to the local education development and Zhang Zuo-lin who was the leader of the Beiyang Government in northeast China in 1927). They were willing and enthusiastic about investing large proportions of limited resources into education. The willingness and enthusiasm in education from the top leaders acted as the driving force in educational development.

Guiding principles for education

In general, education serves two functions: to meet societal needs and to meet individual needs (Xu and Mei 2009). Advocators for societal needs propose that education should address the requirements of society while individual needs must be subject to societal needs. As a result, the key aims of education should focus on training the educated to be good citizens and to maintain social stability and development. Supporters of the individual needs approach suggest that education should emphasise the nature of the educated and the individual's personal interest

Table 2.1 Educational guiding principles in the republican era

No.	Year	Document	Key themes
1	1912	The Suggestion on Guiding Principles for Education	To pay attention to moral education based on pragmatic, military and national education To adopt aesthetic education to help individuals achieve morality
2	1922	The Act of School System Reforms	To cultivate a sound personality To develop the republican spirit To establish the democratic principle
3	1929	Guiding Principles for Education and Implementation Methods of the Republic of China	To increase people's quality of life To achieve national survival To develop people's livelihood To aim at national sustainability & people's livelihood To gain national independence To promote democracy To improve people's well-being To promote a world of universal harmony
4	1946	The Constitution of the Republic of China	To promote citizens' culture and autonomy, spirit and morality To build physical capability, scientific and living skills To balance educational development of different regions and promote social education to an ordinary citizen's cultural and educational level

Sources: Chen (2005); Li and Wang (2011); Su and Zhang (2009)

should be placed first. As such, the important goals of education under this perspective are to develop individuals and provide personal satisfaction.

During this historical period, four key documents concerned with the guiding principles for education were issued (see Table 2.1). The first one was drafted in 1912 by Cai Yuan-pei, the Education Minister, when the Republic of China was founded. The second was generated in 1922 by the non-official National Association for the Advancement of Education consisting of around 2,300 educators who were heavily influenced by the May Fourth Movement and the New Culture Movement (Keenan 1974). The third was based on the 'Three People's Principles' (nationalism, democracy and people's welfare/livelihood) proposed by Sun Yatsen, the first president of the Republic of China. The last document was enacted after the Second Sino-Japanese War.

Judging from the four educational documents, education in this period was to serve as a combination of both social and individual functions with individual needs outweighing the needs of society. In terms of social functions, education aimed to build an independent, prosperous and democratic nation. Influenced by the thought of Jean-Jacques Rousseau and John Dewey as well as the May Fourth Movement and the New Culture Movement, activities that focused on the individuals' overall developments were emphasised (Keenan 1974). As such, cultivating individuals' growth and development through moral, physical, intelligent and aesthetic education were targeted.

Educational policies and practices

The Republican governments were faced with serious financial problems due to the turbulent social environment, rebellions and wars. Yet under such a difficult situation, education was a priority and countless educational bills and regulations were issued. Among them, the following policies and practices are worth noting. First, governments spent a relatively large proportion of the annual national revenue on education. The education bills regulated that the governments' education budget should be 4 per cent of GDP (Xiong 1996). Even in the most difficult time when fighting against the Japanese invasion, the republican government adopted a policy of 'education in war time should be conducted in the same way as in peaceful time' and this policy greatly enhanced the development of a stable educational environment (Xie 2008).

Since the 1922 educational reforms, the 6–3–3–4 American Educational system (6-year primary school, 3-junior high school, 3-year senior high school and 4- to 6-year university) had been adopted, replacing the Japanese model established in the Late Qing Dynasty. The senior high schools were further divided into general, normal, commerce, agriculture or other vocational education (Pepper 1996). Detailed laws for different levels of schools in terms of teaching goals, study years, curricula, teaching resources, teaching workforce, administration, exams and graduation were issued (Li and Wang 2011). Private teaching institutions, including Christian and foreign-owned, were encouraged and supported by the government. Furthermore, the government developed a detailed set of financial regulations for the private educational institutions (Pepper 1996). This approach led to a balance between private and public schools, for example, out of 51 recognised universities in 1931, around half were private and half were run by the national or provincial government (Pepper 1996). The educational institutions, either public or private, enjoyed a high degree of academic freedom and autonomy. They were not, largely, subject to political pressure.

A significant achievement during this period was the widespread introduction of compulsory education. Based on the experience from the Late Qing Dynasty, the education department in 1912 published an educational bill, which regulated that 4-year primary schooling was compulsory and the compulsory education was free of charge. In addition to the 4 years of free education, teacher's training institutions also provided free education (including fees, lunch and living allowances) to their students. In many cases, students attending universities could benefit from free education as well as free lunches (Xie 2008). The impact of the compulsory education was significant. For example, by 1930 over 69 per cent of children went to school in Shanxi Province and around 58 per cent in Shanghai (Xiong 1996). Even in war time (1937 to 1945), the republican government continued to develop education and the enrolment rate for school age children reached 76 per cent by 1945 (Li 1997).

Teacher management system

Teacher quality is the key to education quality (Goldhaber *et al.* 2011). As a result, teacher management became critical in achieving educational goals. Since the establishment of the first modern school during the Westernisation Movement period[1], the key role of high quality teachers in the overall quality of education has been recognised by the Chinese government (Li 2009). With the progress of educational reforms and the compulsory education in the republican era, the teacher management system was further developed. The following sections will elaborate on the management of teachers in four key functions, namely, recruitment and selection, training and development, performance appraisal and compensation management.

Recruitment and selection

In terms of teacher recruitment and selection, a principal accountability system (*xiaozhang fuzezhi*) and engagement system were implemented. Principals of public schools were appointed by the relevant educational departments, for example, the provincial government and its education departments. Principals of private schools were named by the board of directors and then approved by the local government and education departments. The appointed principals were then responsible for the appointment of teaching staff. Nevertheless, the principals did not have absolute power of appointment and removal because in most cases the decision rested with the appointment committee formed by various levels of teaching staff of the school (Liu and Qin 2005). Teachers were usually appointed on a 1-year contract basis (Liu and Qin 2005).

Applications for teacher's position were openly invited from home and abroad. The main source of teachers were graduates from teacher training schools and from overseas educational institutions. As students attending normal schools or universities could be exempt from tuition fees as well as free board and food allowances, the normal schools or universities became the only solution for students from poor families to undertake further education (Xie 2008). This approach helped ensure a highly qualified teaching workforce. Degrees and the Teacher Qualification Certificate were the basic recruiting requirements (Zhang 2010). Teachers who wanted to work for primary schools and middle schools were required to undertake training from normal schools and normal universities respectively. Those who wanted to take up a teaching position at a university needed a master's degree (Liu and Qin 2005).

Training and development

Teacher training comprised pre-service and in-service training. Developed from the Late Qing Dynasty, a teachers' pre-service training system in the republican era had been increasingly developed. Many intellectuals who studied in Japan, the US and European countries returned to China and were employed in the tertiary teacher education institutions. They brought in Western educational theories and contributed significantly to the development of modern teacher education. To meet different requirements, there were a variety of teacher's training organisations, for example, normal universities, normal colleges, normal schools, country normal schools and female normal schools (Liu and Qin 2005).

Teacher's in-service training was mainly designed for current teachers who failed to obtain the Teacher's Qualification Certificate. As the criteria were strict, a considerable number of teachers could not get the certificates and therefore had to undertake in-service training (Zhang 2010). They could only take up temporary teaching positions and they were requested to undergo on-the-job training for a certain period (usually 3 years) (Zhang 2010). In addition, they needed certification before finally being transferred to contract teaching positions. This approach, together with the free teacher's training system, significantly enhanced the quality of the teaching staff.

To further develop teachers, the republican government regulated that teachers who reached a certain length of service could get 6 months or 12 months paid leave to undertake further training. For example, in Sun Yat-sen University, professors who had worked for 5 years were eligible for 1-year study or research abroad (Liu and Qin 2005). According to the Middle School Regulations issued in 1933, teachers of middle schools who served over 9 years could get 1-year full-paid leave to conduct study or research (Liu and Qin 2005).

Performance appraisal

In the republican era, the key approach for teacher's job evaluation was through the Teacher's Qualification Certificate system. It specified detailed and strict regulations in terms of the evaluation committee, methods and contents, requirements and criteria. To guarantee the fairness of the evaluation, the committee was made up of between seven and 11 members who represented different interests, for example, the educational officers, educational experts, principals and teachers (Zhang 2010). Testing criteria included degrees, physical conditions, morality, teaching and academic competences and pedagogy (Liu and Qin 2005). Teachers who passed the tests could get the relevant certificates. The results of the evaluation were open to public inspection and linked with teacher training as well as their further employment (Liu and Qin 2005). Rather than a one-off act, the certificates were current for 4 years for primary school teachers and 6 years for middle school teachers (Zhang 2010). Teachers who did an excellent job could receive a new certificate of between 4 or 6 years' duration upon application and approval (Zhang 2010). The rest of the teachers would have to apply and pass the evaluation again in order to get new certificates (Li 2012). Teachers' certificates were also linked to their pay (Ge 2012). In addition to the certificate system, some universities and schools also conducted annual performance appraisals by an evaluation committee to determine their teachers' future employment (Liu and Qin 2005).

Reward management

The republican era also had detailed laws and regulations covering teacher's pay, such as incremental pay scales, pay standards, relevant qualifications, working experience and the minimum and maximum pay (Ge 2012). Teacher's incomes were closely related to their university degrees and teaching competencies (Yan 2006). The design of teacher's minimum pay was based on two standards, namely, teacher's pay should be twice that of the local basic living expenses and should not be lower than that of the local public servants (Yan 2006).

For the majority of the republican era, teachers enjoyed a high social status and an attractive remuneration and benefits package (Ge 2012). Teachers at universities received the highest pay, ranging from 12.6 to 47 times that of an ordinary worker (Yan 2006). The salary for a high-ranked professor was $600 per year, which was equivalent to the income of the ministers of the government (Liu and Qin 2005; Ge 2012). A middle school teacher earned 4.7 times more than ordinary workers, which could sustain the livelihood of seven people (Yan 2006). Even though there were some disagreements in reported research concerning primary teacher's pay, most studies drew the conclusion that a primary school teacher earned around twice as much as an ordinary worker (Yan 2006; Wang 2011). In addition to pay, teachers also had other welfare and benefits, for example, allowances, pension, medical fees and prizes (Yan 2006).

Impact of educational and teacher management systems

Overall, the republican era had a relatively enlightened teacher management system with a rigid entrance standard. The teacher's training institutions provided pre-service training and in-service training to teachers. The Teacher's Qualification Certificate system was the primary means for teacher's job evaluation, which was linked to their further training, employment and pay. The high social status of the profession, together with the attractive remuneration and benefits package, attracted and retained high quality teachers.

Largely, education was separate from government control. It was managed by well-known educators, for example, Cai Yuan-pei, Yuan Xi-tao and Jiang Meng-lin, who were all subsequently appointed as Ministers of Education (Huang 2009). Universities had high levels of independence and teachers enjoyed high levels of academic freedom (Zhou and Shen 2011). Education reforms were a combination of a bottom-up and top-down approaches, as they were mostly initiated by educators and non-government education associations and then were supported and reinforced by the government through laws and regulations (Zhou and Shen 2011).

Two further achievements are worth highlighting. First, the system cultivated a large number of educationists who made significant contributions to the development of education, for example, Cai Yuan-pei, Huang Yan-pei, Tao Xing-zhi, Yu Z-iyi, An Yang-chu, Liang Shu-ming, Lei Pei-hong, Tai Shuang-qiu, Chen He-qin, Hu Shi and Ren Hong-xie. Their influences on social morality and cultural development were more significant than any politician of that period (Bi 2011). Second, in addition to the educationists, the education system also nurtured thousands of education elites in different areas. For example, it raised five Nobel Prize winners. Within only 8 years, during the most difficult war time with Japan, the National Southwest Associated University cultivated over 90 academicians (80 academicians of the Chinese Academy of Science and 12 academicians of the

Chinese Academy of Engineering), two holders of the State Supreme Science and Technology Award and numerous social scientists (Xie 2008). These academic achievements even outweighed those of contemporary China.

The central planned economy era (1949 to 1978)

After defeating Kuomintang, the CCP established the People's Republic of China in 1949. Between 1949 and 1978, China adopted the Soviet model of economic development that was based on central planning and heavy industrialisation. Under the central planned economy, a centralised system of administration and finance was set up. In order to overtake the UK and catch up with the US (*chaoying gainmei*), as well as to manifest the advantages of socialism, Chairman Mao Ze-dong led the Great Leap Forward Experiment (*da yuejin*) from 1958 to 1960. This experiment, however, did not bring prosperity and the expected significant increases in productivity, but rather resulted in serious economic decline. The experiment also led to a 'style of boasting' that has had an enduring negative impact on China, especially in public service organisations. Even though there was a short period of economic adjustment under the leadership of President, Liu Shao-qi, and Central Party Committee Secretary, Deng Xiao-ping, between 1961 and 1965, the leadership was recaptured by Chairman Mao and the Gang of Four (*sirenbang*). They subsequently conducted a 10-year catastrophic Cultural Revolution Movement (*wenhua da geming*). Political ideology rather than economic development was emphasised. People who spoke the truth were persecuted, and even now, many Chinese hesitate to speak publicly, especially in state-owned enterprises and other public sector organisations (Cooke 2009). The movements led to an enlarged gap between China and the outside world. Living conditions and standards were low and people were increasingly unhappy with the inefficient structure of the planned economy.

Guiding principles for education

The guiding principles for education during the central planned economy were politically and ideologically oriented. At the beginning of this era, the individual functions of education were emphasised when Chairman Mao proposed, in the 1957 speech *On the Correct Handling of Contradictions Among the People*, that 'the key principle of education is to cultivate the overall development of young people in terms of morality, intelligence and physicality and help them become the socialist-minded literate workforce' (Zhuo 1994: 100). However, 1-year later, in 1958, the Central Committee of the Communist Party and the State Council issued the Directive on Educational Activities (Zhuo 1994; Tsang 2000). In this document, the educational guiding principles were changed to the view that education must be put at the disposal of proletarian politics and it must combine with productive labour, as well as be subject to the leadership of the CCP (Zhou and Shen 2011). Six key points were highlighted in this document. First, education must serve the proletariat class; second, education must combine with manual labour; third, the CCP leadership over education must be guaranteed; fourth, Marxism-Leninism must be the educational theory; fifth, political and ideological focus over education must be ensured; and sixth, teachers and students should acquire firm and correct political views (Tsang 2000). Individual-based education was not encouraged for fear of undermining social control (Dong 1990). These educational guidelines had a significant impact on educational policies and practices as well as teacher management.

Educational policies and practices

Under the central planned economy, educational policies and regulations were designed by the CCP and the central government and then reinforced by laws and regulations (Dong 1990). To finance education, a centralised public-finance system was adopted where lower levels of government submitted all the tax revenues to the higher-level government who then reallocated these funds (Tsang 2000). Under this system, China's public education became increasingly underfunded. From 1949 to 1985, an average of 2 per cent of gross domestic product was distributed to education (Tsang 2000). This low level of investment ranked China among the lowest in the world for public education (Yang 2005).

Immediately after the establishment of the People's Republic of China, the educational system was reconstructed to ensure a socialist direction and the government's control over education. First, the previous schools, either private (including foreign-owned) or public, were taken over and were all changed to public schools. Marxism and Leninist theory courses were compulsory in every school to cultivate the right political perspectives (socialism) in the educated (Wang and Du 2006). Second, teachers were required to undertake training on Marxism-Leninism philosophy as well as Mao Ze-dong thought before they started work (Zhuo 1994). Third, in order for the CCP to maintain control over education and to meet the needs of socialism construction, higher education institutions were reorganised. A Soviet model that focused on specialised technology, especially in heavy industry, was adopted, replacing the previous Western education system that was considered to represent capitalism. This approach resulted in a considerably diminishing number of comprehensive universities and the development of many specialised colleges. Fourth, to promote widespread mass education to the peasants and workers, agriculture schools were introduced and rapidly expanded (Tsang 2000).

Perceiving a threat to the socialist revolution from the capitalists, Chairman Mao began a 10-year Cultural Revolution in 1966 (Deng and Treiman 1997). The intellectuals who were regarded as capitalists became the key targets (Tsang 2000). To counteract the intellectuals' domination on the education system, schools and universities were soon controlled by teams of Red Guards (mainly young students), soldiers, workers and peasants. Teachers and professors were removed from their positions as Chairman Mao claimed that, 'we no longer tolerate the ruling of bourgeois intellectuals over our schools' (Zhang *et al*. 2007: 632). They were persecuted and oppressed with some being sent to re-education camps and some even being killed. The fortunate teachers were forced to do manual work and reclassified as rural residents (Tsang 2000). The education system was changed to 5–2–2–2/3 (5-year primary schooling, 2-year junior middle schooling, 2-year senior middle schooling and 2- or 3-year college). All primary schools in urban areas were closed for 2 to 3 years at the beginning of the Cultural Revolution (Zhang *et al.* 2007). Graduate schools were abolished for 12 years and admission to undergraduate students was terminated for 6 years. Admission to secondary teacher training schools and the programme of sending students for overseas study and research work were also blocked. In some cases, admission for colleges students were allowed but focused on political merit and even students who finished 2-year junior middle schools could be accepted (Wang and Du 2006). The belief in the strength of practice meant that students were encouraged to learn from factories and farms rather than from the classic curriculum. Consequently, more than 17 million educated youth from urban areas were sent to the countryside for re-education over the period (Zhou and Hou 1999). Overall, education in this period focused on class struggles and students learnt practical skills in fields and factories rather than classic knowledge in the classroom.

Teacher management system

In the central planned economy, teacher's personnel management differed significantly from the republican era.

Recruitment and selection

A job allocation system was implemented. As all schools were public, the government was the sole employer. Major sources of teachers were graduates from teacher's training schools, colleges or universities. The personal files of graduates were sent to the relevant education bureaus where the students' *hukou* (the Household Registration System) was validated. Quite often, graduates were allocated to where they came from. There were some exceptions – excellent graduates who were student leaders and CCP members with 'good' political attitudes were allocated to cities. Under this central allocation system, graduates were not granted the autonomy to choose schools and schools were not able to employ the candidates they wanted (Burns and Wang 2010). All teachers had job security but they were not allowed to change jobs or schools for personal reasons. This allocation system, which fostered favouritism and nepotism, often resulted in low teaching capability, performance and morale (Burns 1987; Tong *et al.* 1999).

Training and development

Pre-service training was conducted by teacher's training institutions. During this period, students could undertake free teacher training like their counterparts in the Late Qing Dynasty and the republican era. Admission to these schools was given to those who had a good family background (peasants and workers) and who had 'firm and right' political attitudes. Political and ideology training was the key focus. As Chairman Mao claimed, 'those who wanted to be peoples' teachers must be the students' of people first' (Bi 2011: 11) and so teachers were required to learn from the working class and peasants. Therefore, they went to the work places, for example, fields or factories to undertake 'socialism remoulding' during the Cultural Revolution era. Teacher's advancement into leadership positions was based on political background. Professional development for teachers was almost non-existent.

Performance appraisal

Teacher's job evaluation, if there was any, was mainly based on political considerations. The results of evaluation were not linked to training, development or reward practices (Sun 2009). Appraisal feedback was seldom provided. Employees usually did not have any power to contest the evaluation results with their supervisors or leaders. Appraisal criteria focused on political attitude and the results were kept on teacher's personal files, which were held by relevant education bureaus.

Reward management

A seniority flat-base pay scale was adopted where teachers were classified as cadres. This led to a rigid 16-grade wage system where competitive, individual and material incentives were discarded in favour of cooperative, collective and moral incentives (Child 1995). Egalitarianism was highlighted and reward differentials within scales were minimal. Pay was largely decided by age, length of service and political loyalty. No actual incentives were provided for teachers to strive for promotion.

Unlike their counterparts in the republican era, teachers had low social status and low pay. At the beginning of the establishment of the PRC, teachers were deemed as the 'capitalist outsiders' to socialism. This situation became worse in the Cultural Revolution period when teachers were regarded as the enemies of the nation (Tsang 2000). Teachers were described as the 'Smelly No. 9' (*chou laojiu*). Intellectual aristocrats were considered to be 'peddl[ing] feudal, bourgeois, and revisionist rubbish in universities' (Deng and Treiman 1997: 399). Thus, they were required to be 'reborn' through continuous criticism and self-criticism as well as to 'tuck their tails, be obedient pupils to the mass' (Deng and Treiman 1997: 400).

Consistent with their social status, teacher's pay was among the lowest (Tsang 1996). Their monthly pay was about the same as a street peddler's one-day income (Buley-Meissner 1991). The low investment by the government led to shortage of school buildings and equipment in poor condition (Tsang 1996). As such, teachers working conditions were poor. Even though schools provided housing, they were limited to one room per family (Buley-Meissner 1991). Teachers had poor health, were burdened with low social status and low pay and stigmatised as failures (Buley-Meissner 1991).

Impact of educational and teacher management systems

Overall, the policies and practices of teacher management differed significantly from the previous periods. It is therefore not surprising that they had a different impact. First, a large adverse influence on societal and economic development occurred. During the Cultural Revolution period, teachers were belittled and forced to leave their jobs. Workers and peasants neglected their jobs and occupied campuses resulting in students leaving their schools. As such, the whole society was in turmoil. Consequently, a decline in production occurred and people's living standards fell. The gap between China and the Western developed countries became increasingly wide. Second, infrastructure, schools buildings and facilities, as well as libraries, were destroyed. Higher education, in particular, suffered tremendous losses with the whole system being almost shut down. Many academics and technicians, professionals and teachers were lost. Third, a whole generation became the victim of a disrupted education system due to the vastly watered-down or non-existent curricula and being deprived of university opportunities (Meng and Gregory 2002). This disruption resulted in a lack of trained talents or skilled workers to meet the needs of the economic reforms. Finally, the low social status and low pay, as well as the poor working conditions, made teaching an unattractive job. This resulted in a serious shortage of qualified teachers (Buley-Meissner 1991), and thus, adversely influenced the human capital of the whole nation. As intellectuals were criticised and harshly persecuted for holding certain scientific perspectives, people developed a habit of not speaking up. All of the above factors were to have a far-reaching impact on the later social and economic development of the country (Zhuo 1994).

The market-oriented economy era (1978 to present)

Commencing in 1978, the national focus shifted from class struggles to economic construction, modernisation and national development. The era of a market-oriented economy had commenced, which was to turn out to be a significant period for China. After the death of Chairman Mao, Deng Xiao-ping, the pragmatist reformer, took power and initiated a series of economic, agricultural, public finance and enterprise reforms to realise the Four Modernisations (modernisation of industry, agriculture, science and technology). The open policies that encouraged learning and borrowing from abroad facilitated foreign investment, trade and technology exchange. The reforms were so successful that China became one of the largest destinations for direct foreign investment (Björkman *et al.* 2008). The dominant role of state-owned enterprises in the central planned economy gave way to mixed ownership comprising foreign-owned, joint venture, village and township, state-owned and private enterprises. Following the admission to the World Trade Organization (WTO) in 2001, China further opened its markets and promoted further international trades and exchange. Having the largest population in the world, China also focused on its domestic market to maintain sustainable economic development.

Consistent with rapid and substantial economic development (see chapter 1), China has also experienced dramatic social changes (Zhu *et al.* 2010). Following the reforms and the 'open door' policies, the transfer of technology, knowledge and culture from Western countries has exerted a substantial impact on people's belief, norms, values and daily lives. Few of the world's nations underwent as many changes in institutional rules, social norms and cultural values (Tsui *et al.* 2004). Warner argues that these changes have 'turned the world of the average Chinese worker upside-down' (Warner 2009: 2169).

Education played a significant role in this successful transformation process. Before commencing the economic reforms, Deng Xiao-ping had stressed the role of education in achieving China's economic, industrial, social and political goals. It was realised that without the modernisation of education, the aims of the 'Four Modernisations' and economic development would not be achieved (Lewin and Hui 1989). Therefore, education reforms have been increasingly aligned, albeit quite slowly, with the needs of the country's industrial and economic development (Forrester *et al.* 2006). For example, in 1997, the 15th National Congress of the Communist Party proposed that the national development strategy should be based on science and education (Xu and Mei 2009). In 2004, *The Action Plan for Invigorating Education 2003 to 2007* issued by State Council suggested that education was critical for China's sustainable development. Hence, it became a strategic priority for the development of the modernisation of the country (Xu and Mei 2009).

Guiding principles for education

Replacing the previous ideological orientation, the guiding principles for education focused on meeting the requirements of developing a market-oriented economy with Chinese characteristics (Tsang 1996). The significant guiding principles of the economic reform era are summarised in Table 2.2. In 1983, Deng Xiao-ping introduced the 'Three Orientations' that proposed that 'education must be oriented to the modernisation, the world, and the future'. The Three Orientations became the guiding principles for later educational reforms (Dong 1992). After the Tiananmen Square Incident in 1989, however, the political focus was again stressed with the issue of the *Outline of Educational Reform and Development in China* (Central Committee of the Chinese Communist Party and State Council 1993). Now, aiming to achieve a sustainable development, China is undergoing a shift from the world-factory processing model to a knowledge- and technology-based development model (Gu 2010). The *Outline of China's National Plan for Medium and Long-term Education Reform and Development (2010–2020)* was thus issued (Ministry of Education 2010). In addition to outlining these detailed principles, the guidelines also set educational development goals for the next 10 years to turn China into a country rich in human resources.

These three regulations emphasised both individual and social needs. However, the social needs are prevalent over individual needs with a focus on building a strong and prosperous nation. It is worth noting that the role of political ideology in underpinning educational reforms is stressed. For example, education

Table 2.2 Educational guiding principles in the market-oriented economy era

No.	Year	Document	Key points
1	1983	Three Orientations	Education must be oriented to modernisation, the world and the future
2	1993	Outline of Educational Reform and Development in China	Education should serve the modernisation construction of socialism in cohesion with production and work To cultivate morally sound, intellectually strong and physically healthy individuals
3	2010	Outline of China's National Plan for Medium and Long-term Education Reform and Development (2010–2020)	To facilitate the goals of building a moderately prosperous society in all respects To put forward the strategic objectives of modernising education To shape a learning society To turn China into a leading country in terms of human resources by 2020

Sources: Dong (1990, 1992); Gu (2010); Wang and Du (2006)

reforms are required to keep the 'Four Cardinal Principles', namely, safeguarding the socialist road, the people's democratic dictatorship, the CCP leadership and Marxism-Leninism and Mao Ze-dong Thought (Liu 1992; Central Committee of the Chinese Communist Party and State Council 1993). To the Chinese government, the Four Cardinal Principles are the baselines for building a stable, prosperous and strong China (Liu 1992).

Educational policies and practices

With the deepening of economic reforms, educational reforms were undertaken to meet the institutional requirements of the various developmental stages. Generally speaking, the educational reforms can be divided into four stages. The first stage was a readjustment period, which aimed to reverse policies and practices of the Cultural Revolution. The second stage initiated educational reforms during the 1980s, while the third stage focused on deepening the educational reforms in the 1990s. The final stage strove to establish an advanced education system.

Immediately after the Cultural Revolution, a wide range of approaches was adopted to counteract the negative impacts of the chaotic and destructive educational system. The role of education was emphasised in the process of national economic development. A teacher's role in education was also recognised. Rather than being the enemies of people, teachers were now considered part of the working class. The national entrance exam was reinstated in late 1977 and it marked the beginning of the restoration of higher education and a series of reforms in the education sector. The education system changed back to the 6–3–3–3/4 model (6-year primary school, 3-year junior middle school, 3-year senior middle school/vocational school, 2- or 3-year college and 4-year university). Initial efforts were made to revocationalise senior middle school education to meet the increasing call for skilled workers. Replacing the previous focus on providing a mass education for peasants and workers, more emphasis was put on education quality and developing key educational institutions. Experimentation in the decentralisation of education management and finance was also undertaken.

The second stage (1980s) marked the prelude of educational reforms to cater for the newly emerging market economy. The *Decision on the Reform of the Education System* issued in 1985 was an auxiliary document that prompted fundamental changes to the structure, financing and administrative management of the education system (Central Committee of the Chinese Communist Party 1985). Nine-year compulsory education was proposed and the responsibility for basic education was transferred to local governments. Vocational and technical education was emphasised and expanded to meet the acute needs for skilled workers, semi-skilled workers and middle-level technicians (Tsang 1996, 2000). Higher education institutions were granted more autonomy. In 1986, the Compulsory Education Law, which set the goal for 9-year compulsory education nationwide, was enacted (The President of PR China 1986). To facilitate this law, *Suggestions on Strengthening and Developing Teacher Education,* which focused on developing teacher's training institutions and training qualified teachers, was issued in the same year (Zhou and Reed 2005).

The third stage (1990s) represented widespread and overall educational reforms that stressed the need to develop quality education to meet the requirements of a developing and prosperous economy. The *Outline of the Educational Reform and Development in China* (1993) was considered a fundamental reference for the educational reforms in the 1990s (Xu and Mei 2009). It placed education at a strategically prioritised position. It contains six parts covering the guiding principle for education, overall educational reforms in the different levels of education institutions and education system reforms. Following the release of the Outline, a number of education reforms were implemented. In 1993, the Teacher Law, which officially classified teaching as a profession was released (The President of PR China 1993). In 1995, the Education Law was issued in order to consolidate the strategic position of priority development of education (The President of PR China 1995). In 1999, facing a serious shortage of qualified teachers, the *Decision on Deepening Educational Reform and Promoting Quality Education in an All-Round Way* (Central Committee of the Chinese Communist Party and Ministry of Education 1999) was issued. In addition to promoting quality education, these two documents also defined directions for the educational reforms and development in the twenty-first century.

The fourth stage of educational reforms, which commenced in the 2000s, focused on achieving the goals of rejuvenating China through science and education, as well as through capable human resources. Emphasis was placed on building a harmonious society by providing quality and equal education to everyone. The *Decision on Further Strengthening Education in Rural Areas* (State Council 2003) and the *Action Plan for Invigorating Education 2003 to 2007* (Ministry of Education 2004) were issued to pay attention to providing quality education in rural areas. Echoing these two documents, the Compulsory Education Law was revised and reissued in 2006 to promote nationwide implementation of nine-years of free education (The President of PR China 2006). To build China into a moderately prosperous society in an all-round way and accelerate the socialist modernisation, the *Outline of China's National Plan for Medium and Long-term Education Reform and Development (2010-2020)* was issued in 2010 (Ministry of Education 2010). This guideline serves as a blueprint for educational development in China, aiming to turn China into a leading country in terms of talent and innovation through the development of a learning society (Gu 2010).

Teacher management system

In response to educational reforms as well as social and economic pressures, reforms in the management of teachers were also undertaken. As soon as the strategic role of education in achieving the Four Modernisations was recognised, improving teacher qualifications and quality became a national goal to modernise the country's education system (Robinson and Yi 2008). Importantly, the teacher's strategic role was recognised in the *Outline for Education Reform and Development in China* (Central Committee of the Chinese Communist Party and State Council 1993). Since the commencement of the reforms in 1978, the Chinese government has focused on building a fully qualified teaching force through a series of guidelines, directives and reforms.

Recruitment and selection

Teacher's staffing has gone through a circular process from centralisation, to decentralisation and to partial recentralisation. The system of unified placement for all graduates in the central planned economy period continued until the end of 1980s (Niu 2009). From the 1990s, the principal accountability system (*xiaozhang zerenzhi*) was undertaken and principals had considerable autonomy in hiring staff. Based on the basic requirements and criteria set by education bureaus, principals defined staffing priorities, selection methods and hiring decisions. The role of education bureaus changed to overseeing the whole process and approving the final hiring decision as well as fulfilling the remaining documentation and filing responsibilities (Niu 2009). Since then, a two-way choice-system (*shuangxiang xuanze*) that granted the right for schools and teachers to choose each other has been practiced. An experimental contract system for teachers was implemented and subsequently put into practice step-by-step. The introduction of teacher contracts put an end to the traditional permanent employment and the 'iron rice-bowl' system (Paine and Fang 2006).

During this period, some official documents proposed a strict teacher's hiring system, for example, the *Decision on Elementary Education Reform and Development* (State Council 2001), the *Implementation of Suggestions on Deepening the Elementary Education Personnel Reform* (Ministry of Personnel and Ministry of Education 2003) and the *Decision on Further Strengthening Education in Rural Areas* (State Council 2003). Despite the issues of these regulations, secrecy and nepotism were manifested in staffing and practices under the principal account-ability system (Niu 2009).

This decentralised hiring approach continued until the issue of the *Temporary Guideline for Open Recruitment and Selection in Public Organization* in 2005 (Ministry of Personnel 2005). Under this guideline, the public sector is required to undertake open public hiring before they could employ staff. Borrowing the experi-ence from the hiring practices of public servants, the open public staffing system for teachers consists of rigorous procedures including open recruitment, job advertise-ment, written exams and assessments, public notifications and physical health checks.

Training and development

Realising the significant role of teachers in education quality, the Chinese gov-ernment was faced with the problem of the poor quality of the teaching force due to the loss of teachers during the Cultural Revolution and a subsequent fail-ure to attract talented people to the teaching profession. For example, in 1988, 40 per cent of teachers in primary schools, 70 per cent in junior middle schools and 60 per cent of senior middle schools were not qualified (Buley-Meissner 1991). Consequently, the Chinese government has exerted considerable efforts to improve teacher quality. During the past 3 decades, over 13 regulations or laws have been issued by the State Council, the National People's Congress or the Ministry of Education concerning teacher-training provisions.

Training in the current system comprises preservice training and in-service training. Providers of preservice and in-service training are different because the former is undertaken by universities and the latter by post-job training institutions (Yang 2012). Before assuming teaching positions, teachers must have relevant preservice training conducted in 4-year teacher training institutions or 3-year teacher training colleges (Lamie 2006). The Teacher Law and the Education Law incorporated teachers' preservice into the national legal system and set out stan-dards and qualifications for hiring trainee teachers. In 1996, the State Education Commission suggested building a teacher education system with Chinese socialist characters that exemplified life-long education ideology (Lamie 2006).

Before 1997, teacher education was free and teacher's training was confined to specific teacher's training schools, colleges and universities (Niu 2009). In 1999, with the issue of the *Decision on Deepening the Educational Reform and Promoting Quality Education in an All-Round Way* (Central Committee of the Chinese Communist Party and Ministry of Education 1999) and the *Suggestion on Restructuring the Teacher Education Institutions* by the Ministry of Education and State Council, other comprehensive universities were encouraged to participate in teacher preparation (Zhou and Reed 2005). In 2002, the *Suggestion on Teacher Education Reform and Development for the 10th Five-Year Plan* calls for the best senior secondary graduates to enter teaching preparation programs (Ministry of Education 2002). This document together with the *Action Plan for Invigorating Education 2003 to 2007* (The Ministry of Education 2004) proposed the estab-lishment of accreditation and evaluation systems of teacher education programs.

In-service training plays a paramount role in enhancing and developing teacher quality and it is an integral part of a teacher's lifelong education (Xu and Mei 2009). In-service training for teachers was given a high priority from the early stages of economic reforms due to the large number of teachers who required training. For example, there were 2.4 million teachers who failed to meet the basic required standards, and so, in-service training was conducted across the country for teachers at all levels in 1985 (Zhou and Reed 2005). To speed up the training of the unqualified teaching force, the *Decision on the Reform of Education* by State Council in 1995 suggested the provision of radio, television and correspondence courses for teachers and teachers were encouraged to undertake professional lifelong learning (Paine and Fang 2006). The *National Programmes for Educational Reform and Development* (1999) urged increased financing for in-service teacher training by all levels of governments (Ministry of Education and Ministry of Finance 1999). In the same year, the *Regulation on Primary and Secondary School Teachers Continued Education* issued by the Ministry of Education outlined in detail the aims, contents and requirements of in-service training (Ministry of Education 1999). Substantial emphasis was placed on training key teachers with the release of the *Action Plan to Revitalise Education for the 21st Century* (State Council 1999). Teacher's in-service training was also triggered by curriculum reforms that specified that teachers must undertake training before they could teach the new curriculum (Paine and Fang 2006). As a result, in 2003, prior to the introduction of the new curriculum, 10,000 key trainers were trained and they, in turn, conducted training for other teachers across the country (Paine and Fang 2006).

Teacher's professional development is a relatively new concept in China and much more linked with in-service training (Yang 2011). Even though teacher's education credentials increased in the early 1990s after a decade of effort, the quality was still unsatisfactory. As a result, the Chinese government proposed to build teaching as a profession to ensure teacher quality (Zhou and Reed 2005). The Teacher Law and Regulation on Teachers Qualification Certificates (Ministry of Education 2000) officially identified teaching as a profession and specified different criteria for different levels of teacher's qualifications. A number of laws and regulations were subsequently issued to stress the development of the teacher's certification system and professional ladder advancement system. For example, the *Decisions on Deepening the Educational Reform and Improve Quality-Oriented Education in an All-Round Way* (1999), the *Action Plan for Invigorating Education 2003 to 2007,* the revision of the *Compulsory Education Law* (The President of PR China 2006) and the *Outline of China's National Plan for Medium and Long-term Education Reform and Development (2010–2020).* Teacher's professional development is now also linked with professional exchanges with educators from around the world (Prabhakar 2007).

Performance appraisal

Since the economic reforms, the teacher evaluation system has gone through two different stages (Liu and Teddlie 2005). Prior to 2001, teacher evaluation aimed at distinguishing between good and poor performers and the result was linked with reward or punishment. Teacher performance evaluation was usually conducted by school leaders and the voices of peers, students and parents were silent. The evaluation was based on abstract criteria and relied on student test results. The criteria included four parts: morality (political criteria: 10 per cent), diligence (attendance: 5 per cent), job related ability (workload, lesson preparation, classroom teaching, marking and research: 45 per cent) and students' test results (40 per cent) (Liu and Teddlie 2005). This system stressed numeric indicators regardless of whether the criteria were able to be quantified (Liu and Teddlie 2005). Evaluation results were not related to professional development. The heavy reliance on the test results of students led to a teaching-to-the-test phenomenon and the neglect of students' overall development.

The year 2001 served as a watershed with the introduction of a new curriculum that moved away from the overemphasis on knowledge delivery and passive learning. The curriculum reform aimed at prompting students' skills in creativity, problem-solving and independent inquiry (Forrester *et al.* 2006; Zhong 2006). To facilitate this change, a new teacher's evaluation system was required. Subsequently, laws and regulations were issued to create and build a sound teacher performance appraisal system, for example, the *Decision on Elementary Education Reform and Development* (State Council 2001) and the *Suggestions on the Employment System in Public Organizations* (State Council 2002). These regulations proposed that teacher evaluations should focus on professional development, based on the daily performance of teachers, including multiple evaluators and a combination of both qualitative and quantitative indicators (Liu and Teddlie 2005). Yet, the issues of how the teacher evaluation approach is related to teacher professional development, what is included in the assessment of a teacher's daily performance, who are included in the group of multiple evaluators and what are the qualitative and quantitative indicators for teacher's performance, have seldom been empirically explored.

Reward management

To carry out the goals of the Four Modernisations programme, China required a large number of qualified teachers; however, it was faced with a critical teacher shortage after the Cultural Revolution. In order to overcome this shortage and to make teaching an admirable and respected profession, the Chinese government decided to increase teacher's social and political status. Teacher's Day (10th September) was introduced in 1985 and the titles of teachers were changed to show social respect. For example, rather than 'feudal thinkers, degenerates, stinking scholars, enemies, freaks, smelly No. 9, and monsters' as they were called during the Cultural Revolution, teachers are now known as 'engineers of the human soul, master sculptor of the new people of the future, and people's hero and patriot' (Buley-Meissner 1991: 48).

Being granted glorious titles, nevertheless, did not alter the profession's attractiveness in the 1980s and early 1990s. The pay system of the prior reform period remained for quite a long time. For instance, teacher's pay had remained virtually static since the 1950s, while incomes of employees in other professions started to experience an exponential increase in the 1980s (Buley-Meissner 1991). Even though teacher's pay had increased from 1986, the increases were quite low compared to other occupations. Moreover, due to the low government investment in education teacher's working conditions remained harsh. Because of these factors, the teaching profession continued to be the least sought after job option and teachers were still stigmatised as failures. As one saying went: 'one is better off raising two pigs a year than being a teacher' (Lewin and Hui 1989: 15).

To change this situation, the Chinese government issued a number of documents regarding teacher's pay and improvement of working conditions, for instance, the *Outline of Education Reform and Development* (1993) and the Education Law (1995). In 2008, performance-related pay was introduced following the release of the *Guidelines on the Implementation of Performance-related Pay in Elementary Education* (State Council 2008). This document together with the *Outline of China's National Plan for Medium and Long-term Education Reform and Development (2010–2020)* regulated that teacher's income (including pay and fringe benefits) should be equivalent to or higher than that of the public servants who enjoyed high pay and social status (Ministry of Education 2010).

Impact of educational and teacher management systems

Since the commencement of the economic and educational reforms, a more effective education system has been established. Nine-year compulsory education has been nationally established and the illiteracy rate has reduced significantly. The expansion of the higher education system and the development of vocational schools have provided professionals and skilled workers to meet the needs of the economic reforms. The supply of an educated workforce has helped boost the national economy and achieved unprecedented economic success. The training system, as well as the teacher's qualification system, has transformed the largely unqualified teaching force to competent teaching professionals. Students work extremely hard to pass exams and the testing ability of the Chinese students is among the best globally. For example, in the Programme for International Student Assessment (PISA) organised by the Organisation for Economic Cooperation and Development (OECD) every 3 years, Chinese students from Shanghai achieved the best results in mathematics, science and reading in 2009 (Sharma 2011). Similar results were achieved in 2012 (OECD 2013). Nevertheless, the educational system has focused on students' test results that require students to memorise, regurgitate information and follow instructions. This system has resulted in a lack of creativity, problem-solving ability and absence of free thought (Zhong 2006). This deficiency has hindered the country from further sustainable development aiming at building a moderately prosperous society in all respects through sound human resources. Furthermore, the top-down approach of teacher management and the introduction of industry practices in teacher management are also accused of demotivating teachers and worsening teacher's physical and psychological health (Su and Zhang 2009).

Conclusion

To understand better the role of contextual factors in shaping HRM policies and practices in the Chinese school system, this chapter provided an historical account of the societal changes as well as the evolutions of the current educational systems and HRM. The chapter revealed that since the First Opium War in the 1840s when China was forced to open its doors to Western countries, the Chinese people have been endeavouring to build an independent, strong and prosperous country. Education has been regarded as one of the most significant means to achieve this goal. As such, substantial changes have taken place in education and teacher management, starting from imitating and adopting Western models to exploring more localised models. The next chapter will examine the role of contextual factors in shaping current HRM policies and practices. It begins by providing a theoretical basis for this discussion.

Note

1 Westernisation Movement: self-strengthening movement that strived to build a prosperous China through learning science and technology from the West and developing modern industries such as arms and machines (Zhou 1996).

3 Contextual factors influencing human resource management in the Chinese school sector

Introduction

In China, the significance of contextual factors in HRM has been well documented and it has led to the term 'HRM with Chinese characteristics' (Warner 1993, 2008). The institutional environment has an important influence on employee behaviour and organisational and managerial decisions in a radical transition period (Benson and Zhu 1999; Tsui *et al.* 2004; Zhu *et al.* 2007). Similarly, the traditional Chinese culture and values continue to exert important influences on contemporary people management approaches (Warner 2010). Thus, Chinese management is said to be 'context-specific' or 'context-bounded' (Child 2009: 58). Echoing these emphases, it is argued that investigating contextual factors is a 'must' when exploring the nature of HRM (Zhu *et al.* 2012: 3966).

To understand the contextual factors that shaped the HRM policies and practices in the Chinese school system, this chapter will adopt an institutional approach as it will allow the complex process of social changes in which different institutions 'interact with, influence and are influenced by the overall process of change' to be revealed (Warner *et al.* 2005: 6). These institutions include formal laws and rules and informal social patterns such as codes, norms, professional standards, roles and symbols (North 1990; Lang and Steger 2002). As such, the use of institutional theory offers a framework to understand radical changes and explain the contextual dynamics for organisational adaptations (Greenwood and Hinings 1996). It also accounts for what, why and how with regard to organisational responses to institutional factors (Scott 2004). The adoption of institutional theory importantly answers the call from Warner for 'more sophisticated analytical tools to fully understand specifically how and precisely why it [HRM] has evolved to the particular forms we find it in today' (Warner 2009: 2183).

This chapter starts by outlining institutional theory. Guided by this theoretical perspective, the second section analyses the impacts of contextual factors on the evolution of the current HRM policies and practices in Chinese schools. By adopting this approach, chapter 3 addresses the first research question: *How have contextual factors shaped HRM policies and practices?*

Institutional theory

Institutional theory has multiple roots and is utilised by a variety of disciplines such as economics, politics and sociology (Scott 2005). Each of the disciplines has different views and perspectives on institutions (Scott 2010). This study adopts a sociological view that has emerged primarily within the subfield of organisational theory (Hall and Taylor 1996). The coverage of sociological institutionalism is broad and it comprises not only formal rules, procedures or norms, which are the focus of political and economic institutionalism but also symbolic systems, cognitive scripts and moral templates (Hall and Taylor 1996). This research adopted Scott's view that defined institutions as being 'comprised of regulative, normative and cultural-cognitive elements that, together with associated activities and resources, provide stability and meaning to social life' (Scott 2008b: 48).

Acting as a powerful mechanism to drive changes and to determine the nature of change, institutionalism itself has also experienced change over time (Dacin *et al.* 2002). Institutional theory has undergone three key stages: old institutionalism, new institutionalism and neo-institutionalism. Old institutionalism suggests that an organisation adopts changes in the course of struggles with different values and interests, while new institutionalism stresses the significant role of an organisation's resistance to change (Greenwood and Hinings 1996). Combining the old and new versions of institutionalism, neo-institutionalism explains an individual organisation's responses to outside pressure as a function of that organisation's internal dynamics (Greenwood and Hinings 1996). Consequently, in accounting for how institutions evolve and how they are maintained, neo-institutionalism also considers the issue of how institutions undergo change (Scott 2008a).

This study analyses the transformation of HRM in Chinese schools by adopting three institutional frameworks: institutional isomorphism (DiMaggio and Powell 1983), three institutional settings (North 1990, 1994) and three institutional pillars (Scott 2008b). Institutional isomorphism is adopted because it is more relevant to public sector organisations (Greenwood and Hinings 1996; Scott 2010). North's (1990, 1994) three institutional settings explain incremental institutional change stressing interactions among formal and informal constraints as well as the enforcement of these two constraints. The concept of interactions among contextual factors is relevant to the formation of HRM policies and practices in the Chinese school system. Derived from neo-institutionalism, Scott (2008b) proposed a three-pillar framework to explain the 'how' and 'why' of the commonality and diversity, the past and present of institutions. Consequently, this framework is particularly useful in exploring the 'how' and 'why' issues of the formation of HRM policies and practices in the Chinese schools. The following section will elaborate on these three institutional frameworks.

Institutional isomorphism

In the early development of institutional theory, explaining similarities across organisations was emphasised. This focus led to institutional isomorphism that assumes uniformity within institutional environments and highlights similarities across organisations (Hall and Taylor 1996). It proposes a monolithic framework that imposes homogenous requirements on passive organisations (Scott 2008a). Isomorphism advocates that organisational homogenisation is the only thing that rational organisations would adopt under institutional pressure. It suggests that the more organisations make changes, the more they become alike. Such institutional homogenisation is also regarded as isomorphic structural effects.

Three mechanisms of institutional isomorphism have been proposed: institutional coercive, mimetic and normative isomorphism (DiMaggio and Powell 1983). Coercive isomorphism traces its origin from legitimacy and formal pressures, for example, government organisations, trade unions, works councils and employment legislative frameworks (DiMaggio and Powell 1983). It may also result from informal pressures from cultural expectations, for example, norms of behaviour and conventions. These pressures make public organisations, for example, schools, different from industry organisations (DiMaggio and Powell 1983). For schools, coercive isomorphism is exerted by the government through a regulatory framework, as well as formal and informal pressure to serve the public and to meet the expectations of the government and the public (DiMaggio and Powell 1983).

Mimetic isomorphism stems from standard responses to uncertainty (DiMaggio and Powell 1983). When encountering uncertain circumstances, organisations tend to learn from other organisations and they are likely to model themselves on successful organisations in their field to be more legitimate or successful (DiMaggio and Powell 1983). The mimetic function is obvious in the course of the modernisation of China. For example, empirical studies have shown that during the transition to the market-oriented economy, many Chinese firms have modelled and implemented Western HRM practices (Rowley and Benson 2002; Zhu *et al.* 2007, 2012).

Normative isomorphism is related to professionalisation. DiMaggio and Powell (1983: 152) interpreted professionalisation as the collective efforts of members of the same occupation to 'define the conditions and methods of their work, to control the production of producers, and to establish a cognitive base and legitimation for their occupational autonomy'. They identified two aspects of professionalisation as significant sources of isomorphism: formal education and training and professional networks.

Institutional isomorphism, however, has been criticised as overstating unity, coherence and independence of organisational frameworks (Scott 2008a). The overemphasis on isomorphism meant an inability to interpret intra-organisational dynamics (Greenwood and Hinings 1996). Over time, institutional scholars realised that many organisations in the same field are not monolithic, but often tend to be fragmented or conflicted, consisting of competing requirements and prescriptions (Scott 2008b). As a result, there is a need to attend not only to consensus and conformity but also to conflict and change in organisations (Scott 2005).

Three institutional settings

Aware of this pitfall, researchers shifted their focus from analysing institutional similarities to differences. North (1990, 1994) identified three institutional settings that account for institutional changes: formal institutions, informal institutions and the characteristics of enforcement. Formal institutions are structures of codified and explicit rules and their standard forms include laws, regulations, policies and formal agreements (North 1994). Formal constraints facilitate order and stability through offering authoritative behavioural guidelines (Scott 2008a). Once established, formal institutions are relatively stable. However, they are greatly influenced by cognitive understandings and the acceptance of individuals (Holmes *et al.* 2013).

Despite their importance, formal institutions are thought to constitute only a small proportion of constraints that shape change (North 1990). By contrast, informal institutions overwhelmingly define the governing structures and interactions of daily life (North 1990). Although not codified by documented rules and standards, informal institutions are enduring systems of shared meanings and understandings that form cohesion and coordination among personal interactions in a society (Scott 2005). They comprise codes of conduct, norms of behaviour and conventions that stem from socially transmitted information (North 1990). Culture represents a key component in informal institutions as it reflects and influences beliefs, values, norms and priorities as well as assumptions shared in a society (Holmes *et al.* 2013).

The third setting concerns the types and characteristics of enforcement. Enforcement refers to approaches that organisations adopt to advance collective interests and they can be codified as informal practices, formal rules or both (North 1990). The effectiveness of formal or informal rules largely depends on the efficiency of monitoring and the harshness of punishment resulting from breaking these rules (North 1990, 1994). However, as enforcement is adopted by organisations that utilise their own functions to affect outcomes, it can never be completely effective (North 1990).

A mixture of these three settings shape organisational changes and economic performance (North 1990). Focusing on only one setting can 'give rise to an inadequate and frequently misleading notion' (North 1990: 53) as formal and informal institutions, although separate, are interdependent. Formal institutions can supplement and enhance the effectiveness of informal rules (North 1990). Conversely, informal institutions help to shape formal institutions in terms of formal regulatory, political and economic constraints (Holmes *et al.* 2013).

Three institutional pillars

Based on institutional isomorphism and three institutions settings, Scott (2008b) proposes a three-pillar framework to analyse institutional changes. This framework comprises regulative, normative and cultural-cognitive pillars. The regulative pillar relates to rational choice and design, for example, governmental regulations that are important in forming organisational structure and fostering changes (Hall and Taylor 1996; Scott 2010). The regulative pillar focuses on rule-setting, monitoring and sanctioning activities that are enforced by a higher authority (Scott 2008b). It is formal, explicit and easily planned and strategically manipulated (Scott 2010). Nevertheless, it can be superficial and fleeting unless it is consistent with other elements, norms and cultural beliefs (Scott 2008b, 2010). It is subject to interpretation, manipulation, revision and elaboration (Scott 2008b). For China, it has been argued that not all key institutional changes have been the result of government regulations (Zhu 2007). If this is the case then the role of the regulative pillar in organisational change might give way to normative and culture-cognitive elements.

The normative pillar highlights the role of social beliefs, norms and values that relate to jobs or professions in a certain industry (Scott 2004, 2010). Performing the role of enforcement (North 1990, 1994), the normative pillar not only identifies goals or objectives but also delegates suitable approaches to achieve them (Scott 2008b). These approaches include conferring rights as well as responsibilities, privileges as well as duties and licenses as well as mandates (Scott 2008a). The conformity to or violation of norms largely depends on the measure of self-evaluation, remorse and/or self-respect that provide dominant inducements to comply with prevailing norms (Scott 2008b).

A consideration of cultural-cognitive elements is the most recent contribution to the institutional discourse (Scott 2010). The cultural-cognitive pillar refers to the 'shared conceptions that constitute the nature of social reality and the frames through which meaning is made' (Scott 2008b: 57). It provides a basis for normative prescriptions and regulative controls, and at the same time, it offers a framework for order (Scott 2010). The critical role of Chinese culture in shaping HRM models and practices has been noted in the literature, for example, Warner (2009), Cooke (2009) and Zhu *et al.* (2012). It is expected that the cultural-cognitive pillar will also significantly shape people management change in the Chinese education sector.

These three diverse pillars, according to Scott (2008b), are distinctive (see Table 3.1). The regulatory pillar focuses on conformity to rules, while the normative pillar highlights a deeper and moral base for assessing legitimacy. As the normative pillar tends to be internalised, both intrinsic and extrinsic rewards are important in conformity incentives (Scott 2008b). The legitimacy of a cultural-cognitive perspective strives for a compliance of a common definition of the situation, reference frame or a recognisable role or structural template (Scott 2008b). Resting on preconscious, taken-for-granted understandings, the cultural-cognitive pillar represents the deepest level for assessing legitimacy (Scott 2008b).

Despite their distinctiveness, the three pillars are interdependent. They are mostly collectively adopted in varying combinations to depict a more complete

Table 3.1 Differences between the three pillars of institutions

	Regulative	*Normative*	*Cultural-cognitive*
Basis of compliance	Expedience	Social obligation	Taken-for-grantedness Shared understanding
Basis of order	Regulative rules	Binding expectations	Constitutive schema
Mechanisms	Coercive	Normative	Mimetic
Logic	Instrumentality	Appropriateness	Orthodoxy
Indicators	Rules, laws, sanctions	Certification Accreditation	Common beliefs, shared logics of action, isomorphism
Effect	Fear guilt/innocence	Shame/honour	Certainty/confusion
Basis of legitimacy	Legally sanctioned	Morally governed	Comprehensible Recognisable Culturally supported

Source: Scott (2008b: 51)

picture of organisational change (Scott 2010). The cultural-cognitive pillar is critically significant in interpreting diffusion while regulative and normative elements are valuable at explaining adoption (Murphy and Garavan 2009). Consequently, the combination of the three elements is required when accounting for change. In most institutional settings, however, these three pillars do not equally impact on shaping change (Scott 2008b). Quite often, varying degrees of influence from each of the three pillars is observed and one element might dominate the others at a particular point in time (Scott 2008b). Moreover, it is proposed that institutionalisation is a continuous phenomenon that facilitates change (Newman 2000; Scott 2008b; Phillips *et al.* 2009). In turn, institutionalisation could be influenced by a range of multilevel interactions such as regional, national and international differences (Fujita and Krugman 2004; Phillips *et al.* 2009).

Transformation of HRM in Chinese schools

Utilising the three modes of institutional theories, the established literature, Chinese government documents and two rounds of interviews conducted in 2011 and 2012, this section explores the contextual factors that shape HRM policies and practices in the Chinese school system. The key contextual factors shaping HRM are identified in Figure 3.1. As shown in the figure, contextual issues (political, economic, sociocultural and legal contexts) influence management reforms in terms of structure, finance, people and professions, which subsequently impact on HRM in the Chinese education sector, namely, recruitment and selection, training and development, performance appraisal and reward management. While the contextual issues are mainly explored at the macro level, the management reforms are examined at both macro and micro levels.

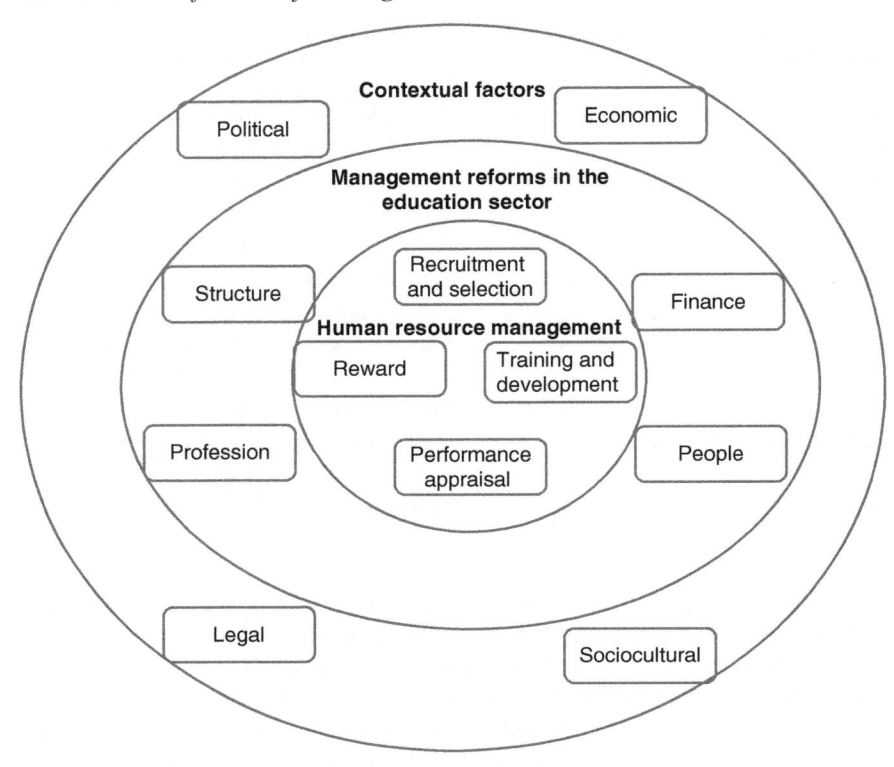

Figure 3.1 Teacher management system under the influence of contextual factors
Source: Scott (2008b), government documents and interview data (2011, 2012)

Contextual factors

Building on the work of Scott (2008) and the two rounds of interview data, the contextual factors that form the basis of the management reforms in the Chinese school systems are the political, economic, sociocultural and legal contexts (see Figure 3.2). These contextual factors are interrelated and it is difficult to separate their effects. However, for the sake of clarity, this section is divided into three parts: the interactions among political, economic and legal contexts; the inter-actions among economic, legal and sociocultural contexts; and the interactions between economic and legal contexts. These contexts and their interactions result in the strategies adopted by the Chinese government in prioritising education development and building a highly effective, strong teaching workforce.

Interaction among political, economic and legal contexts

In China, as in other communist societies, ideological issues form the basis of economic reforms (Hasan *et al.* 2009; Zhu *et al.* 2010). The past 30 years have witnessed radical changes in China in terms of political, economic, legal and

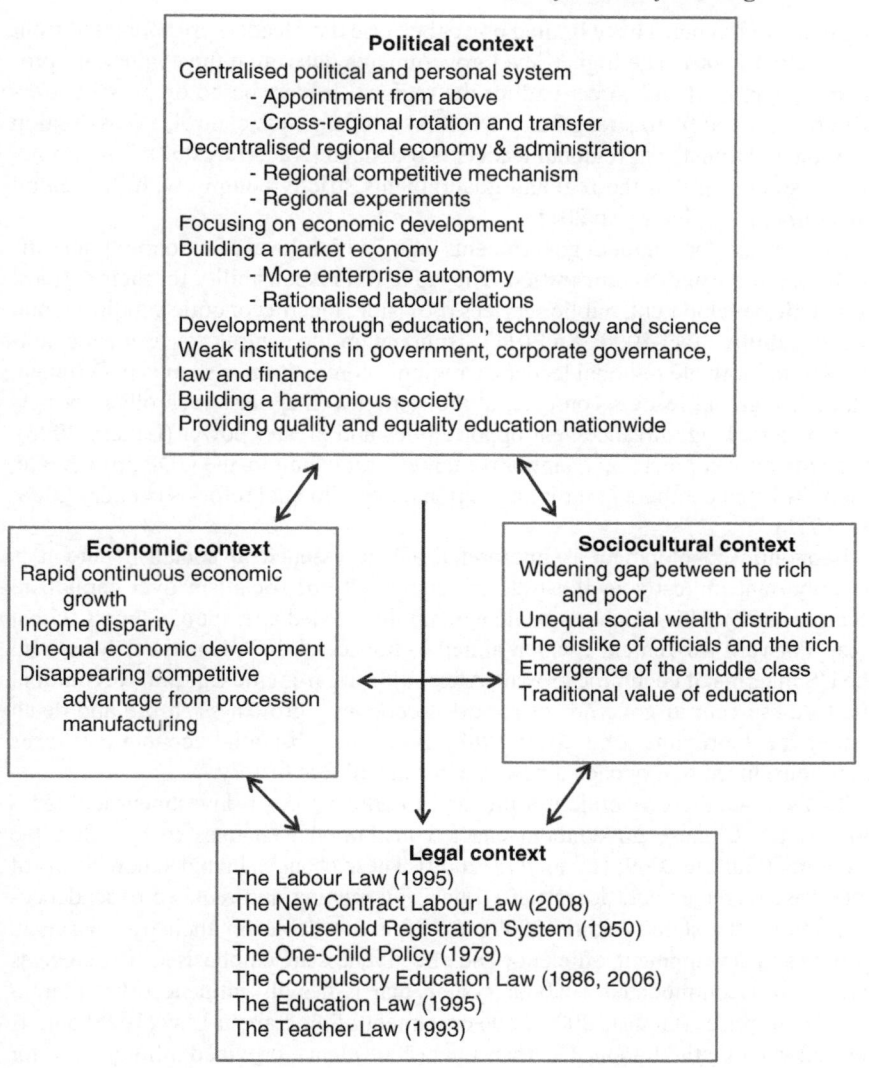

Figure 3.2 Key contexts and their interactions

Sources: Guthrie (2009), Gu (2010), Zhu *et al.* (2010), Xu (2011), government documents and interview data (2011, 2012)

sociocultural institutions. Based on an extensive literature review, Xu (2011) argued that these radical changes mainly result from the 'regionally decentralised authoritarian regime' (Xu 2011: 1078). This regime is characterised by a combination of political control and economic decentralisation (Zhang 2006; Xu 2011). The highly political and personal centralisation is achieved by the control of the Chinese Communist Party over ideology, the regional governments' personnel management, key economic sectors and the mass media (Chubanshe 2009). The regional governments have limited power because their leaders are appointed from above (Wei 2000). The higher-level governments determine the evaluation, promotion, dismissal and career path of the regional leaders based on preset targets (Chubanshe 2009). To strengthen the central government's control, a cross-region rotation and transfer of regional leaders is practiced (Xu *et al*. 2007). These practices also ensure that the regional governments strictly comply with the central government's policies (Xu 2011).

By contrast, the regional governments enjoy a high level of autonomy in terms of the economy and administration. They take full responsibility for their regions' economic development, public services provision, macroeconomic conditions and social stability (Wei 2000; Xu 2011). To maintain the central government's control and to motivate regional leaders, a regional competition system is undertaken. Chinese regional leaders compete, at the same level, against each other for performance ranking, advancement opportunities and greater power (Landry 2008). They not only compete on quantitative targets, for example, the GDP growth rate, but quite often compete in initiating regional experimental reforms (Landry 2008; Xu 2011).

Economic development is interpreted as the essence of socialism and it is an important indicator to illustrate the superiority of socialism over capitalism (Kornai 1992). This emphasis could explain the hurried attempt of China's 'Great Leap Forward Movement', which aimed to transcend the UK and catch up with the US in terms of economic growth. After suffering from the Cultural Revolution, the Chinese central government regarded economic growth as 'a life and death matter for the regime' (Xu 2011: 1088). As such, substantial economic reforms were introduced that opened a new chapter in Chinese history.

To facilitate the economic reforms and to attract foreign investment and technology, the Chinese government enacted institutional changes to liberalise the economy (Guthrie 2009; Hasan *et al*. 2009). These changes included new forms of enterprise management, decentralised decision making and reduced dependences of firms on the state (Guthrie 2009). As firms are liable for their own survival, growth and development, efficiency and effectiveness are emphasised. The changes have also accommodated a labour system that is heavily influenced by international enterprises (Guthrie 2009). The enactment of the Labour Law (1995) and its revised version, the Labour Contract Law (2008), have provided a framework for the conduct of employment relations and support for grievance procedures (Zhu *et al*. 2010). Individuals are now granted more protection and organisations are more democratically oriented (Hasan *et al*. 2009). Employees' participation in decision-making and their commitment to improved organisational performance are increasingly noted (Guthrie 2009). To accommodate the economic reforms and to improve human quality for the construction of Chinese socialism, the Chinese government enacted the Compulsory Education Law (1986), which mandates a 9-year compulsory education scheme nationwide (The President of PR China 1986).

Although China has experienced a dramatic improvement in legal institutions and the decentralisation of political institutions (Guthrie 2009), the desire of the CCP to retain a monopoly on political power hinders the full development of these institutions (Hasan *et al.* 2009). Today, China remains a country with underdeveloped institutions in government, corporate governance, law and finance (Yao and Yueh 2009). The weak institutions have fostered official corruption that has resulted in substantial costs and raised strong opposition from the public. Moreover, fierce competition among regional governments under the decentralised economic system has led to regional protection. Regional governments tend to focus on more measurable or short-term tasks, for example, the economic growth rate, while ignoring the less measurable tasks that are long-term oriented (Xu 2011). Winning competitions quite often means career advancement, whereas losing competitions risks the loss of position. As such, regional leaders are forced to participate in a 'race to the bottom', which might benefit them but will damage most other citizens (Xu 2011: 1129). Furthermore, while the socialist market economic system is developing, the Chinese government is facing the challenge of the inability of its existing public sector to facilitate economic and social development (Zhu *et al.* 2010). The education sector, in particular, has been a target of criticism for being unable to meet people's needs.

Interaction among economic, legal and sociocultural contexts

The economic reforms in China have resulted in unequal and unbalanced regional development (Wei 2000; Keng 2006; Fleisher *et al.* 2010). This situation has further deteriorated with the practice of the Household Registration System, which confines people's movement and controls their behaviour, as well as creating unequal treatment between rural and urban citizens (Wei 2000; Zhu *et al.* 2010). Because of the Household Registration System, migrant workers cannot enjoy the social benefits of the cities where they work (Han 2008). They are often badly paid and subject to poor and unsafe working conditions (Han 2008), while their children are often excluded from the local public school system (Liang and Chen 2007).

The economic reforms have also led to a widening gap between rich and poor (Han 2008). The widening gap and the uneven and unfair distribution of wealth, together with the corruption of officials, have led to the phenomenon of 'the dislike of officers and the rich'. These problems, if not dealt with appropriately and quickly, could lead to social unrest and turmoil (Han 2008; The World Bank 2013). Consequently, the Chinese government proposes to build a harmonious society with the approval of the CCP Party Central Committee's *Resolution on Major Issues of Building a Socialist Harmonious Society* in 2006 (Central Committee of the Chinese Communist Party 2006). To build a harmonious society, equality has been a focal point (Han 2008). As such, the education sector reforms highlight efficiency and effectiveness as well as openness, transparency, fairness and justice. Providing quality and equitable education around the country is also regarded as one of the most effective ways to build a harmonious society. Correspondingly, a revised version of the Compulsory Education Law (2006) was enacted that aims to provide quality and equitable 9-year compulsory education across the country (The President of PR China 2006). Since then, the Chinese government has substantially increased the investment in education.

Traditionally, Chinese people have been highly appreciative of the role of education in their development (Xu and Mei 2009). This tradition was strengthened by the introduction of the One-Child Policy that took effect in the late 1970s. Parents usually have huge expectations for their only child and are often willing to sacrifice whatever they can afford to give their child the best opportunities and educational success (Romanowski 2006). Educational expenses thus comprise an extensively increasing proportion of income expenditure for households (Zhu *et al.* 2010). For example, parents in most cities spent at least one-third of their household income on their children's education, and, in some cities, the proportion could account for half of the household income (Mok *et al.* 2009). In addition, economic reforms have led to the development of a middle class who are willing to pay extra for quality education (Yuan *et al.* 2012). Being exposed to the technology, knowledge and culture of developed countries, the emerging middle class increasingly calls for quality education for their own children.

Interaction between economic and legal contexts

The focus on economic development, together with the political centralised and economic decentralised system, has led to a boost in China's economy (Xu 2011; Zhang 2006). Nevertheless, faced with the increasingly competitive global market, the Chinese government has come to realise that relying on its previous 'world factory' development model could not maintain sustainable development (Gu 2010). Consequently, the Chinese government proposes to build a prosperous society based on education, technology and science (Zhou and Reed 2005; Xu and Mei 2009). This strategy, coupled with the goal to build a harmonious society to tackle social problems, makes developing education critically important. Therefore, prioritising education development has been a key task for various levels of government.

To consolidate the strategic priority of education, the Education Law was enacted in 1995. For the first time in China's history, this law provides the rights and responsibilities of providers and users of education (Zhou and Reed 2005; Xu and Mei 2009). It regulates the responsibilities of various levels of governments in educational development. The strategic role of teachers in further educational reforms and development had, as mentioned in chapter 1, been stressed by the issue of the *Outline of Education Reform and Development in China* (Central Committee of the Chinese Communist Party and State Council 1993). The Teacher Law, enacted in 1993 underpinned this philosophy and legally confirmed the strategic and significant role of teachers in the course of socialist economic construction. With the release of the *Action Plan for Invigorating Education 2003 to 2007*, further reform and development of education became a strategic priority of the country (Xu and Mei 2009). The role of education in the country's sustainable development has been further strengthened with the release of the *Outline of China's National Plan for Medium and Long-term Education Reform and Development (2010–2020)*, which aims to transform China into a leading country in terms of talent and innovation through developing a learning society (Gu 2010).

In summary, China has experienced substantial changes since the commencement of economic reforms. The need to build an economy based on sustainable development and the desire to build a harmonious society to tackle a series of political, economic, social and legal problems have made prioritising educational development and building a strong, effective teaching workforce critically important.

Management reforms in the Chinese school system

These political, economic, sociocultural and legal contexts have exerted considerable impact on management reforms in the Chinese education sector. The key areas of management reforms include structure, finance, people and the profession (see Figure 3.3). These areas were identified through a detailed literature review, examination of government documents and two rounds of interviews with key

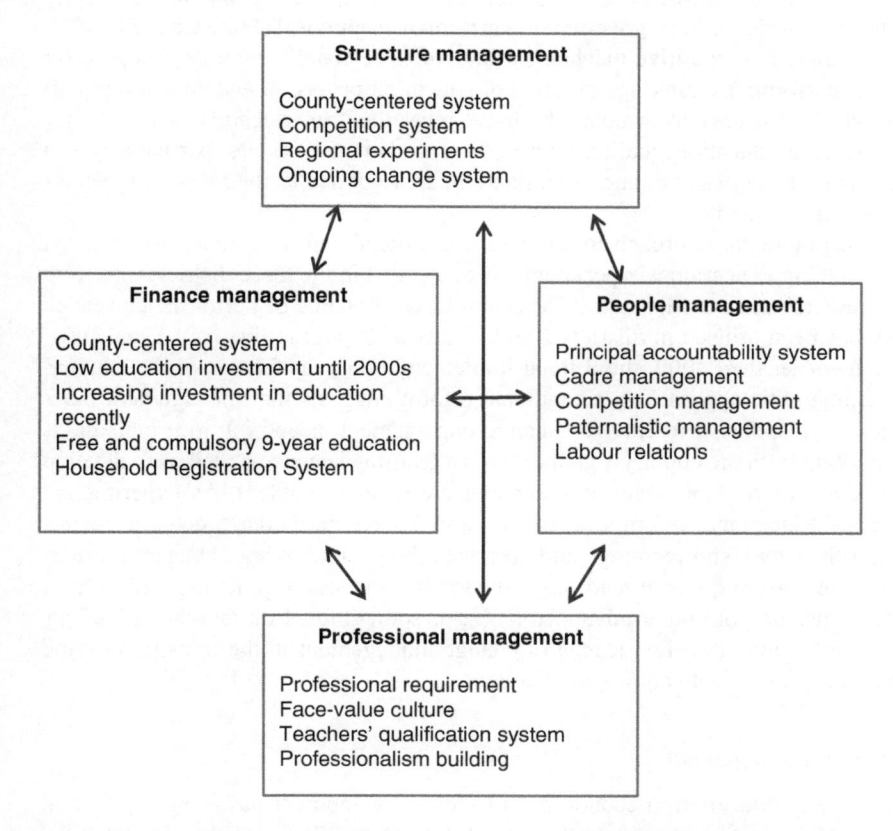

Figure 3.3 Management reforms and their interactions in the Chinese education sector

Sources: Tsang (2000), Zhou and Reed 2005, Mok *et al.* (2009), Zhu *et al.* (2010), government documents and interview data (2011, 2012)

educational administrators. Structure management is concerned with a county-centred system, a competition system, regional experiments and an on-going change programme. Financial management deals with educational funding issues. People management addresses the ways to manage teachers while professional management tackles the issues concerning the teaching profession and professionalism among teachers.

Structure management

Consistent with decentralised economic and administrative management, the provision of education is built on different levels of local government following the issue of the Compulsory Education Law in 1986 (Tsang 1996). At the same time, a county-centred system is practiced. The county-level government, as a basic unit, has the majority responsibility for education provision within its own boundary (State Council 2005). Correspondingly, a county-centred localised evaluation system has been established and investment in education has become one of the significant criteria for local government performance appraisal (State Council 2005). The regional competitive mechanism motivates regional leaders to compete for better performance rankings in terms of education provision and education quality. While it is easy to evaluate the fiscal investment in education, it is not easy to measure education quality. Quite often, student test results, particularly test results in the college entrance examination, are regarded as the relevant indicator of education quality.

The pragmatic approach to Chinese educational reforms, addressed through undertaking educational experiments, is evidenced in the three districts that were the research sites in this study. For example, the practice of performance-related pay has been utilised in districts 2 and 3 since 2002 and in district 1 since 2004, much earlier than 2009, the official implementation year for the whole country. The pragmatic approach to educational reform suggests that management practices are responsive to change. Change management, according to principals, is consistent with the country's goal to build a learning society as well as to develop an education system taking into account the Chinese context. As experimental sites of educational reforms, districts 2 and 3 were particularly quick at identifying their own shortcomings and correspondingly in making changes. Furthermore, they were quick at learning and adopting successful practices, either from each other or from other advanced areas, or sometimes, from abroad. District 1 also highlighted the significance of change management in the transition period due to the intensively competitive system.

Finance management

The role of education in economic and social development has been highlighted by the Chinese government. In the early 1980s, Deng Xiao-ping proposed that the Chinese government would commit 4 per cent of GDP to education (Mok *et al.* 2009). Echoing this, the *Outline of Educational Reform and Development in China* officially declared a goal of 4 per cent GDP educational investment (Central Committee of the Chinese Communist Party and State Council 1993). However, the Chinese government has long been criticised for its inadequate investment in education. It was not until 2012 that this 4 per cent goal was achieved (see Table 3.2).

The under-investment in education resulted in difficulties in operating schools (Tsang 1996). To address this problem, the central government at that time encouraged schools to generate funds by school-run enterprises or rental of school premises (Tsang 2000). The interview data suggests that almost every school at that time had to earn income by their own means to keep the school running. Some rural schools even resorted to raising poultry within their school premises to earn extra income. To support school expenditure, schools often imposed *ad hoc* charges. Individual schools were entitled to use their school-generated money to purchase school equipment and provide welfare benefits for staff. While these approaches mitigated, to some extent, the effects of the inadequate government investment in education, the decentralised economic and administrative management made it extremely difficult for the disadvantaged areas. These disadvantaged areas had a weak tax base to sustain compulsory education, which was

Table 3.2 Public education expenditure as a percentage of GDP (billion Yuan)

Year	GDP	Government appropriation for education	Percentage (%)
1992	2,664	73	2.74
1995	5,848	141	2.47
1999	8,207	229	2.79
2000	8,947	256	2.86
2001	9,732	306	3.14
2002	10,517	349	3.32
2003	11,739	385	3.32
2004	15,988	447	2.79
2005	183,217	5,161	2.82
2006	211,924	6,348	3.00
2007	257,306	8,280	3.22
2008	300,670	10,450	3.48
2009	340,507	12,231	3.59
2010	401,918	14,670	3.65
2011	472,882	18,586	3.93
2012	519,322	22,236	4.28
2013	568,845	24,488	4.30

Sources: Mok *et al.* (2009: 506); Ministry of Education, National Bureau of Statistics and Ministry of Finance (2014); National Statistics Bureau of China (2014). GDP, gross domestic product

based on free tuition and had no charges for textbooks and some other expenses (Tsang 1996). As such, it was difficult for parents in these areas to afford education for their children and the dropout rate was high (Zhu *et al.* 2010). This situation was in sharp contrast to the country's resolution to build a developed economy through education, technology and science.

Echoing the proposal to build a harmonious society and the Compulsory Education Law (2006), the Chinese government substantially increased education investment (see Table 5.1). The continuously increasing investment in education demonstrates the Chinese government's determination to prioritise educational development. To tackle the problem of educational inequality, the central government has borne more responsibilities and it has increased its investment in less developed areas (State Council 2005). For example, in western China, the central government pays 80 per cent of funding for education, while the local government is responsible for 20 per cent. In central China, the central government invests 60 per cent, while the local government is responsible for 40 per cent. By comparison, the local governments in most developed areas pay a higher share (State Council 2005). Located in the most developed areas in China, the governments of districts 1, 2 and 3 pay 80 per cent of costs and the central government only subsidises 20 per cent. With the increasing investment in education, the Chinese government has made considerable efforts to standardise schools' financial management. To ensure the provision of free compulsory education for every child, schools are now prohibited to collect any *ad hoc* fees and to generate their own income following the enactment of the *Suggestion on Further Strengthening Financial Management in Primary and Middle Schools* by the Finance and Education Ministry in 2008. However, as the sayings go, 'regulations from above and manoeuvres from below' (*shang you zhengce, xiayou duice*) and 'the mountains are high and the Emperor is far away' (*shangao huangdi yuan*) (Zhu 2007: 1510). Schools, particularly in some rural areas, still charge students some *ad hoc* fees.

Notwithstanding the above, over the past 3 decades, the Chinese government has made significant improvements in education. By 2011, compulsory education is available almost throughout the whole country (State Council 2012). A compulsory 'Education Funding Guarantee Mechanism' has been established and this mechanism is backed by law through specifying the responsibilities of governments at different levels. Schools now can concentrate on teaching activities without worrying about making money to keep the school operating smoothly. Moreover, a new school financial management system has been developing that specifies ways to manage and use the educational funding (Ministry of Finance and Ministry of Education 2006).

Nevertheless, the Chinese government is still faced with challenges in providing quality and equitable education nationwide. Education quality has developed unevenly with a big gap between cities and rural areas (State Council 2012). The gap has been a target of criticism and opposition from the public. Education development has become further uneven with the practices of the decentralised economic system and the household registration system. Because of these two systems, students are entitled to enjoy free compulsory education only in their own household registration area. Students who want to attend schools beyond their household registration area will have to pay large sums of extra money for the services provided, namely, the school selection fee. For example, the typical school-selection fee for ordinary schools in districts 1, 2 and 3 in 2011 and 2012 ranged from RMB 20,000 to 35,000 per student depending on the school's location and reputation. Moreover, students are required to have a good personal network (*guanxi*). Even though objecting to this system, parents usually try every means to have their children enter a better school. However, due to the limited capability of good schools, not many people succeed, even though they could afford the school selection fee. This situation is even worse in the case of migrant workers who cannot afford the fees and have no other social network to support them. As a result, their children often have to stay in their hometown with their grandparents. The issue of 'left-behind children' has raised considerable concerns from the public and the government (State Council 2006). More recently, some private schools were established to accept migrant worker's children. However, in these schools, students have to pay full fees and the teaching quality was quite poor compared to the local public schools. Even though the new experimental project of 'accumulating points for schooling' provides possibilities for non-resident students to enter local public schools, the criteria for this kind of schooling are stringent and only a lucky few are eligible. Clearly, a quality and equitable education in China is still some time off.

Reforming school management systems

During the planned economy, the party/state has absolute control over education (see chapter 2). The local party committee or the school party secretary was the person in charge of the school (Niu 2009). This approach resulted in the phenomenon of 'non-professionals leading professionals' and the education quality suffered. Following the trend of the separation between the party and school management, the principal accountability system (*xiaozhang fuzezhi*) has been practiced after the implementation of the Compulsory Education Law (1986). Principals are granted decision-making power in managing schools, appointment of teachers and school finance (The President of PR China 1986). Like the management of regional leaders, the appointment of principals is from above but under increasingly strict, competitive and transparent procedures. To fight against corruption, 'being clean' (*lianjie*) has become one of the critical criteria for a principal's performance appraisal and further appointment. The cross-school rotation and transferring system is practiced and principals can stay with the same schools for up to two rounds of tenure (8 years). Principals are encouraged to conduct innovative experiments to build 'characteristic schools', which can reflect their unique strengths. Under the new management system, principals are granted more autonomy in and responsibility for managing their schools. For example, in town 1, district 3, principals were recently allowed the right to form and lead their own management team (*xiaozhang zuge*). If proven successful, this practice would be widely promoted to other areas.

Echoing the competitive mechanism of the regional leaders (see chapter 5), competition in the education sector has been a powerful means in encouraging principals and teachers to work hard and achieve improved student performance. This phenomenon has been highlighted by numerous principals, for example, 'competition is a norm in the education sector' (principals of D1V1, D1T1P1, D1T2P1, D2S2, D3V1 and D3T2P1).There are numerous competitions at various levels, such as the school, town, county, municipal, provincial and country levels. Because the leaders of the regional government mainly care about students' test results, the test results have become critical competitive indicators. In order to reflect the fairness of the competition, all the final exam papers are created by the relevant education bureaus and schools cannot get access to exam papers until the exam day. The exams are marked by other teachers in the same school who are not involved in teaching that particular class. After the exam, the education bureau will often release the ranking and result of individual schools. By performing well in such competitions, particularly competitions at higher levels, principals and teachers are more likely to be promoted and better rewarded. Losing competitions, particularly significant competitions, makes their career progression chances remote. For example, D2S1 (a key senior middle school) was awarded RMB 2 million in 2013 by the district government for their outstanding result in the college entrance exam (director in district 2). In contrast, principals of senior middle schools in district 3 were summoned by government officials to analyse reasons and work out action plans because they failed to meet their targets in the college entrance exam in 2013 (HR manager in district 3).

Like many other sectors, some elements of paternalistic practices are still common in the school management system. Paternalistic management is a traditional Chinese management model derived from Confucius values with three key components: benevolence, morality and authoritarianism (Zhu *et al*. 2012). Benevolence refers to the care of leaders for subordinates' personal and family wellbeing (Chen *et al*. 2014). Morality is regarded as a leader's model role by demonstrating superior moral characteristics and integrity while authoritarianism is concerned about leader's strong authority and control over subordinates (Chen *et al*. 2014).

Principals show considerable benevolence towards their staff and usually treat them as their extended family members. Schools often hold birthday parties for teachers. Around half of the schools principals in the present study (23 schools) paid visits to teachers during the Spring Festival with gifts to show their caring for teachers. The majority of principals (32) knew the family situations of teachers and all principals indicated that they would provide support for teachers' families whenever needed. Some schools (12) invited teachers' family members to their weekly sports day and provided dinner for them in the school canteen. These practices also help build a spirit of teamwork, a cooperative culture and a sense of belonging that is critically important in the school context. The principal accountability system, which grants the rights for principals to address teachers' personnel issues, enhances the traditional leadership authoritarianism approach. At the same time, a more advanced labour relation is practiced. The

Teacher Law grants teachers the right to participate in managing their schools (The President of PR China 1993).

Professional management

Teaching, as a profession, has characteristics that are different from professional work in other sectors, such as manufacturing or the profit-oriented service sector. Teachers need to be prepared to teach in a wide variety of settings, to use specific pedagogical strategies with diverse learners and to be ready for standards-based reforms (Berry 2004). They are required to undertake continuous training to acquire new skills to meet the changing needs of a more diverse society (OECD 2005b). As a result, the teaching profession is sophisticated, requires complex skills and demands a considerable degree of preparation, support and professionalisation (Cochran-Smith and Fries 2001; Berry 2004). In addition, the teaching profession is a 'conscience project' (Director of the Education Bureau in district 2) and has high requirements for professional morality (HR manager of D3T2). Teachers are expected to act as role models for students (HR manager of D1T1), and thus, are assumed to have high ethical behavioural standards (Principal of D1T2S1). People's expectations of the teaching profession are also high. For example, teaching is now regarded as the most brilliant career and teachers are always compared to burning candles that give light to others at the expense of their own lives. They are considered to be the engineer of the human soul and bear responsibility for knowledge inheritance and intelligence development.

Teachers highly value 'face' (*mianzi*) and care about their reputations. Losing face, particular in public, can be disastrous for them. Being confined to a relatively small community, teachers who lose face find it more difficult to gain respect from their colleagues, students and students' parents. This may subsequently have a negative impact on their job performance. According to the principal of D1T1J1, 'if teachers lose face, they lose almost everything in the community'. At the same time, teachers treasure intrinsic rewards and hope for recognition from the education bureaus, their schools, colleagues, students, parents and the community where they are serving.

Teachers belong to the state cadres who occupy around 5 per cent of the total workforce engaging in prestigious managerial and professional jobs (Brodsgaard 2012). A personnel planning approach is based on a quota system (*bianzhi*) that refers to 'the sanctioned number of employees in an organisation based on the budget' (Brodsgaard 2012: 76). Teachers, as cadres, are usually offered more career development opportunities (Bian 2002) and have high job security. According to the interviewed participants, teacher dismissal seldom occurs.

Recognising the important role of teachers, the Teacher Law identifies teaching as a profession that requires standardised criteria and special training (Xu and Mei 2009). Correspondingly, the teacher certification system is introduced in the same law. A teacher qualification certificate is a precondition for teachers to enter the profession (Xu and Mei 2009). To obtain a certificate, a candidate should have relevant 'educational credential, pass the national teacher certification exam and demonstrate teaching competence' (Zhou and Reed 2005: 206).

Aiming to build a strong and effective professional teaching force, the Teacher Law also specifies a number of teacher management issues. It introduces a contract system that defines the rights, obligations and responsibilities of both schools and teachers (Xu and Mei 2009). It proposes public and transparent hiring approaches (Xu and Mei 2009). Teachers have the right to take refresher courses and pursue further education, and at the same time, they have the obligation to improve professional competence through continuous training (Xu and Mei 2009). It also suggests setting up a performance evaluation system for teachers (Zhou and Reed 2005). Additionally, the law stresses teachers' economic status by specifying that teachers' income should be no less than that of the local public servants and their medical insurances should be equivalent to that of the local public servants (Zhou and Reed 2005; Xu and Mei 2009).

In summary, the political, economic, sociocultural and legal contexts exert substantial influences on management reforms in Chinese schools in terms of schools' systems, finance, people and professions. The pragmatic approach and competitive mechanism as well as the traditional paternalistic management approach has played a significant role in the transformation of HRM in Chinese schools.

Conclusion

Based on an historical analysis of the social and educational evolution, this chapter examined the contextual factors shaping HRM policies and practices in the Chinese school system. The findings show that the strategies of prioritising education development, providing quality and equitable education nationwide and cultivating a highly competent teaching workforce are the products of the interactions of political, economic, sociocultural and legal contexts. These strategies reflect the Chinese government's determination to build a strong, sound, prosperous and harmonious society through education, science and technology. These contextual factors, subsequently, influenced management reforms. Together they formed the basis for the transformation of people management in the Chinese school sector. The following chapter will explore, in detail, the transition of human resource management in that sector.

4 The transition of human resource management in the Chinese school sector

Introduction

The past 30 years have witnessed the rise of China from a backward and isolated country into a rapidly expanding industrial power where poverty has been reduced 'at a scale unparalleled in world history' (Xu 2011: 1077). The economic gains have been 'the long march of Chinese history' (Warner 2009: 177). Running parallel to the economic reforms, China has also experienced substantial social changes (Zhu *et al*. 2010). The changes have been unprecedented and have 'turned the world of the average Chinese worker upside-down' (Warner 2009: 2169). The rapid economic growth and the accompanying social changes makes China 'an exciting context for understanding the transformation of organisations along with its associated management challenges in an emerging market economy' (Tsui *et al*. 2004: 134).

In response to this changing environment, HRM practices have undergone critical changes from a centrally planned personnel system characterised by lifetime employment (the 'iron rice bowl') to a basic HRM approach and then to the adoption of a strategic HRM paradigm under the market-oriented economy (Akhtar *et al*. 2008; Warner 2009; Kim *et al*. 2010). Attempting to capture the nature and transition of HRM, research has identified various transitional models of HRM in China. These models showed a convergence and divergence between traditional and Western HRM models. For example, various research studies have presented different models, such as the transitional convergent model moving from personnel management to Western HRM as in Ding *et al*. (2001) and a mixture of soft and hard HRM in Cooke (2004). Further examples are a blend of convergent and divergent models in Benson and Zhu (1999), Goodall and Warner (1997) and Rowley and Benson (2002), a hybrid model in Zhu *et al*. (2007), a more convergent European model in Björkman *et al*. (2008), a hybrid Confucian model in Warner (2010) and a continuous transitional model from paternalistic to transactional management in Zhu *et al*. (2012). These studies have substantially contributed to the knowledge of transitional HRM systems within the Chinese context and they have important implications for HRM theories and practices.

The majority of studies exploring the transitional HRM models in China have been almost exclusively conducted in the manufacturing industry and have neglected the public sector, such as education (for studies examining HRM models in China, please refer to appendix 1). There are substantial differences between the education sector and industry in terms of organisational structure and employee motivation. The education sector is more bureaucratic. Quite often, employees in the education sector are less materialistic and more intrinsically motivated compared to their counterparts in industry. They are less profit-driven but more service-oriented. As such, the research findings of the people management models derived from industry might not be equally applicable to the education sector. To address this deficiency, this chapter explores the transitional management models in the Chinese school sector. By doing so, this chapter addresses the second research question namely '*How can the current HRM system in Chinese schools be best characterised*'.

This chapter begins with a literature review on the transition of people management systems in general and the adoption of different HRM practices in China in particular (Qiao *et al.* 2009). The focus of this chapter is on HRM practices and how they are integrated with local Chinese approaches of humanised, paternalistic and pragmatic management. It is followed by an exploration of the current HRM practices in the Chinese school system, which could be identified as a pragmatic integrated transitional management model.

The transition of people management systems

Globalisation, increasing competition, continuous changes in markets and developments in technology and knowledge have led to substantial and strategic shifts in people management approaches. During this transitional course, three key concepts have evolved, namely, personnel management (PM), human resource management and strategic human resource management (SHRM). This section outlines the general developmental process and models of people management.

Personnel management model

PM stemmed from Taylorism and Fordism, which argued that a firm's success relied on its ability to meet management production targets with greater speed and larger quantities (Kravetz 1988). PM was originally adopted in high-profile manufacturing plants where the pace of work was usually controlled by machinery programs to maximise productivity (Bach 2000).

To meet the goal of mass production with standardisation and cost minimisation (Storey and Sisson 1993), PM had the following characteristics. Managing people was regarded as an enforcement of rules (Ulrich 1997) with cumbersome bureaucratic procedures (Caldwell and Storey 2007). PM ensured that employees understood and executed orders 'as diligently and obediently as possible' (Aktour 1992: 410). The key role of the personnel department was to provide welfare, monitor consistency and fairness, perform record keeping and file maintenance, as well as other largely clerical administrative duties (Legge 2007; Mello 2010). Correspondingly, personnel managers were considered to be organisational police (Legge 2007) who enforced rules and policies, prioritised process-following and pushed people for compliance and other bureaucratic reasons (Torrington 1989). They also acted as an intermediary between line managers and workers (Storey 2007b) and guaranteed a supply of appropriate, reliable and inexpensive labour in the workplace to keep the organisation functioning smoothly (Torrington 1989). Employees were regarded as a cost, a burden and a source of annoyance to the organisation (Becker *et al.* 1997). As such, employees' engagement with work was low (Storey and Sisson 1993). Overall, PM was 'overly diversified and overly centralised' thus unable to meet the increasing consumer expectations (Legge 2007: 41).

Human resource management model

The advent of HRM was a response to the changing business environment. Quite different from most people's perception that HRM was a purely Western concept, HRM was actually a combination of both East and West notions (Benson and Debroux 1997; Zhu *et al.* 2007). In the 1970s and early 1980s, due to increasing environmental costs, profit margins from the mass production model in Western countries declined (Aktour 1992). At the same time, Japan and some other Pacific Rim countries made significant gains, thus causing Western countries to lose their competitiveness in the increasingly intensified global market (Hendry and Pettigrew 1990). The previously prevailing successful models of Taylorism and Fordism, which focused on making products faster and faster at a lowest cost, failed to meet the new challenges. Furthermore, the development of technology and the decline in the manufacturing industry, as well as the development of the service industry, resulted in a diversified workforce that required a different mode of management (Brockbank 1999). Education also nurtured highly qualified employees who wanted a higher level of discretion in their jobs and thus a distinctive management model was needed (Kravetz 1988). Meanwhile, the development of management, strategy and organisation theories underlined the notion that employees are one of the most vital assets of an organisation and employees play an increasingly significant role in creating a competitive advantage (Armstrong 2011; Becker *et al.* 1997). Under such circumstances, the prevailing PM model, which regarded employees as a cost, was no longer appropriate.

HRM has been regarded as a concept with two distinct models: 'hard' and 'soft'. Traced back to Taylorism, hard HRM, also termed the 'instrumental approach' (Storey 2007a: 11), focuses on the resource aspect and conceptualises employees as another asset or commodity under the control of management (Roan *et al.* 2001). Employees are considered a tool to be utilised by the organisation and a passive factor of production or expense (Storey 2007a). The cost of labour is to be minimised and labour should be as flexible as possible through such mechanisms as outsourcing, subcontracting and franchising (Druker *et al.* 1996: 406).

Soft HRM, also known as 'developmental humanist', suggests that organisational performance can be achieved by developing staff and by winning employees' commitment (Legge 2005). This approach can trace it roots to the human relations approach with its emphasis on communication, training and development, motivation, culture, values and involvement (Storey 2007a). While hard HRM provides limited training, benefits and wages, soft HRM offers more extensive, general skills training as well as additional extensive benefits and relatively high wages (Arthur 1992).

These two dimensions, however, are seldom implemented in their pure form (Truss *et al.* 1997). In times of pressure, for efficiency and pragmatism, firms are more likely to turn to hard HRM (Legge 2005). Quite often, the soft HRM tends to be a rhetorical cloak for the practices of hard HRM to cover work identification under the appearance of job enrichment and multiskilling (Roan *et al.* 2001). Interestingly, even though the concepts of hard and soft HRM can be traced to US academics (soft HRM associated with the Harvard School and hard HRM associated with the Michigan School), they have rarely been used in the US context (Truss *et al.* 1997). While acknowledging the distinctions between the concepts and assumptions of hard and soft models of HRM, both Guest (1987) and Storey (1992) abandoned the differences but incorporated both hard and soft concepts into their HRM theory or models.

HRM thus became a distinctive people management approach striving to contribute to organisational competitive advantage by the strategic development of a highly committed and capable workforce (Storey 1995). Instead of regarding employees as a cost, HRM believes a competitive advantage is provided by human resources (Storey 2007a). Employees are thus considered an asset and as an investment in achieving the organisation's goals (Becker *et al.* 1997). People management had thus shifted from ensuring compliance with rules and regulation to striving for commitment and engagement from employees (Legge 2007). To support the organisation's strategic goals, the functions of the HR department focus on developing a competent, flexible and committed workforce that produces ideas, seeks out continual improvements and responds spontaneously to ever-changing customer requirements (Storey and Sisson 1993). However, people management at this stage focuses on individual performance (Becker and Huselid 2006). HR functions were essentially isolated from each other (Wright *et al.* 2001) and were implemented in a 'pick and mix' way in which it was assumed that HRM functions were not mutually dependent upon each other (Storey and Sisson 1993: 23).

Strategic human resource management model

Since the 1990s, organisations have experienced unprecedented changes with the issues of downsizing, workplace re-engineering, skill shortages, demographic changes, workforce diversity and increasing global competition (Mello 2010). These changes have diminished many traditional sources of competitive advantage such as patents and economies of scale (Becker and Huselid 2006). With more applications of strategic management theory into the field of HRM, especially the resource-based view of the firm, it was argued that competitive advantage could be attained from aligning HRM policies and practices with overall organisational strategic goals (Wright and McMahan 2011). By doing so, HR policies and practices could themselves contribute to the creation of competitive advantage of an organisation (Armstrong 2011). SHRM was thus defined as 'an approach to the development and implementation of HR strategies that are integrated with business strategies and enable the organization to achieve its goals' (Armstrong 2011: 1).

The most significant distinction between HRM and SHRM lies in the HRM alignment to achieve horizontal and vertical fit to support and shape business objectives (Delery and Doty 1996; Delery 1998; Posthuma *et al*. 2013). Horizontal fit means internal consistency of HR policies and practices, while vertical fit refers to congruence of the HR system with organisational strategy (Delery and Doty 1996; Delery 1998). Drawn from the best practice or the universalistic perspective, horizontal fit advocates that individual practices cannot be effectively implemented in isolation. On the contrary, it is crucial to combine them into complementary, coordinated and coherent bundles to enhance organisational effectiveness (Armstrong 2011). Horizontal fit is regarded as instrumental for efficiently managing human resources (Wright and Snell 1998). The vertical alignment adopts the best-fit or contingency perspective to ensure an explicit link between internal people management and the external business strategy (Delery and Doty 1996). Through successful linking with organisational strategies, people management can enhance organisational performance (Posthuma *et al*. 2013).

These two alignments are not an 'either/or story' (Becker and Huselid 2006: 903). According to configuration theory, an organisation must develop a HR system that can realise both horizontal and vertical integration to effectively achieve organisational strategic goals (Delery and Doty 1996). As a result, adopting either the horizontal integration (best practices approach) or vertical integration (best-fit approach) is unlikely to achieve the intended SHRM goals (Delery and Doty 1996).

In the contemporary strategic HRM field, HPWS are horizontally integrated (alignment among HR practices) and they can also be vertically consistent (integration with organisational goals) (Evans and Davis 2005; Subramony 2009; Buller and McEvoy 2012; Kehoe and Wright 2013; Posthuma *et al*. 2013). They comprise the elements of best practice, for instance, selective staffing, individual and group incentives, a range of employee benefits, intensive training and development, comprehensive performance appraisal, team-based work, employee involvement, work-life balance programs and information sharing (Way 2002). HPWS aims to enhance organisational performance and achieve a competitive advantage by improving employee motivation, participation, involvement and commitment (Jiang *et al*. 2012; Aryee *et al*. 2013; Posthuma *et al*. 2013). The term is now generally regarded as a synonym for 'high-commitment work systems', 'high-involvement work systems', 'high commitment management', 'high involvement management' and 'progressive human resource management' (Beltrán-Martín *et al*. 2008: 1012; Jiang *et al*. 2012: 1264).

By linking HRM policies and practices into organisational strategic decision-making, SHRM is a viable approach to change in the environment to gain a competitive advantage (Storey 2007b). Compared to operational HRM, SHRM has the following key distinctions. SHRM can shape organisational strategies by acting as a strategic partner and change agent (Mello 2010; Ulrich 1997). It emphasises human capital contributions, strategic capabilities and organisational performance (Becker and Huselid 2006). Due to the fast and ever-changing business environment, organisations might have different strategies at any one particular time (Storey 2007b) or different sets of HR practices for different employees at the same time (Mello 2010). The chief executive and senior management teams are required to be involved in HRM strategy development and line managers are critical to the effective delivery of HRM policies (Storey 2007b). Besides the competencies of HRM functional expertise, HR managers are also required to have knowledge of business and change management and be good at organisational design and intervention methods (Becker *et al*. 1997). To facilitate changes, they also need to have analytical and interpersonal skills (Beer 1997).

In summary, the concepts of PM, HRM and SHRM are interrelated and belong to different developmental stages of people management. Each developmental stage, from the administration of personnel activities to the integration with the overall organisational strategy, signifies a more advanced paradigm.

Local management approaches in the Chinese context

Based on path dependency theory, the past will have enduring influence on current institutions (Boas 2007). China's culture has been highly influenced by Confucianism and Confucianism has shaped the management approaches of humanised management and paternalistic management in the Chinese context. More recently, pragmatic management, which stresses constant improvements, has been playing a significant role in the Chinese economy (Xu 2011). The following will elaborate on these three management styles that are relevant to the public sector.

Humanised management and its influence in China

Developed mainly from the mid-twentieth century in Western countries, the concept of humanistic management traces its root to human motivations to counteract the dominant scientific management of Taylor that stresses productivity and efficiency while giving little attention to the needs of workers (Mele 2003). Humanistic management is defined as a management approach that 'emphasizes the human condition and is oriented to the development of human virtue, in all its forms, to its fullest extent' (Mele 2003: 79). This concept highlights 'the unconditional human dignity' of individuals within an economic context (Spitzeck 2011: 51). As such, to foster unconditional human dignity has been a clear direction for humanistic management (Spitzeck 2011). This management approach is assumed to lead to employees changing from job compliance to job commitment by meeting their job-related personal needs and treating them with respect (McGuire *et al*. 2005). Consequently, humanistic management is desired to 'build tomorrow's business and for effective ways to deal with an ailing economy' (Acevedo 2012: 199).

Humanism is deeply influenced by philosophies, religions, ethics (Tsui and Jia 2013) and cultures (Mele 2003). In China, the phrase 'humanised management' first came into popular use in major Chinese human resources and management websites around 2005 to 2006 (Choi and Peng 2015). However, its essence is arguably parallel to the Chinese concepts of *renwen* and *rendao,* terms that have their origins in one of the most ancient Chinese classics in around 1050 BC: *Classic of Changes* (*yijing*) (Wang 1995). *Renwen* means cultures in the relationship between the natural phenomena and cultural phenomena while *rendao* indicates the ethical norms that are acceptable under such a relationship (Wang 1995). As such, humanised management suggests a harmonious relationship between ethical norms and natural phenomena. With the societal changes, the concept of humanised management in China is a hybrid norm reflecting the impact of Western ideologies and Chinese Confucianism and communist symbolism (Choi and Peng 2015). The concept stresses showing respect and courtesy for individuals' dignity (Tsui and Jia 2013).

Paternalistic management and its influence in China

Traditionally, China has been deeply impacted by Confucian ideology that stresses paternalistic management (Cooke 2009). Paternalistic management is defined as a management style that 'combines strong discipline and authority with fatherly benevolence and moral integrity couched in a personalistic atmosphere' (Farh and Cheng 2000: 94). It is suggested that paternalistic management is prevalent in people management in the Chinese context (Farh and Cheng 2000). Echoing this view, Warner also indicates that Chinese firms, no matter what kinds of ownership, 'still have more or less paternalistic people-management regimes' (Warner 2009: 780). Even though both paternalistic management and humanised management trace their origins from the Chinese culture, they belong to two different concepts. Paternalistic management focuses on 'father-like leadership style in which clear and strong authority is combined with concern and considerateness and elements of moral leadership' (Farh and Cheng 2000: 85) while humanised management emphasises 'respect for the dignity of human and justice in decisions regarding the allocation of resources, opportunities, and rewards' (Tsui and Jia 2013: 1). Consequently, paternalistic management emphasises control under the umbrella of kindness and righteousness of a leader, whereas humanised management focuses on showing respect for employees' dignity.

Paternalistic management initiates and sustains a familial employment relationship through ways of fatherly benevolence, moral guidance and authority (Farh and Cheng 2000). By doing so, it is hoped that organisations and their employees can be involved in an open-ended reciprocal exchange relationship on a moral bounded basis (Zhu *et al.* 2012). Based on an extensive literature review, Farh and Cheng (2000) identified three key components of paternalistic management: fatherly benevolent, moral integrity and authoritarianism. The benevolent approach concerns individuals' personal and family wellbeing while moral integrity requires superior personal virtues or qualities to act as role models for subordinates (Farh and Cheng 2000). Authoritarianism refers to approaches that maintain 'absolute authority and control over subordinates and demand unquestionable obedience from subordinates' (Farh and Cheng 2000: 94).

This approach is grounded in the norms of reciprocity that aims to generate employees' gratitude, trust, loyalty and commitment by demonstrating kindness, consideration and granting favours (Cheng *et al.* 2004). The roots of benevolence originate from Confucianism, which proposed kind, gentle, righteous and benevolent superiors (*ren*); which, in turn, gain respect and loyalty from inferiors (*bao*) (Farh and Cheng 2000). Based on Confucianism, the ideal societal relations are 'benevolent ruler with loyal minister', 'kind father with filial son', 'righteous husband with submissive wife', 'gentle elder brother with obedient younger brother' and 'kind elder with deferent junior' (Farh and Cheng 2000: 104). These ideal relationships expect that leaders should show benevolence to their subordinates. The common benevolent approach comprises treating employees as family members, providing job security, assisting during personal crises, showing holistic concerns and protecting subordinates even when they make grave errors (Farh and Cheng 2000).

Morality and integrity is embedded in the Confucian philosophy of governance (Farh and Cheng 2000). Confucius suggested that the foundation of society is the cultivation of individual virtues (Farh and Cheng 2000). In terms of governance, Confucius stressed the adoption of moral principles and examples (Farh and Cheng 2000). At the highest level, the emperors were regarded as the son of Heaven, and therefore, they should rule the country by virtue in order to enjoy absolute and sustainable powers. At the lower level, imperial officials had to prove moral rectitude prior to their appointment (Farh and Cheng 2000). Morality and integrity has two facets: one is the proper and virtuous behaviour of the leader to act as a role model; another is the decision of the leader based on the wellbeing of all concerned rather than their own interests (Westwood 1997). As a result, the leader should not be selfish and should act as a role model for his/her subordinates.

Authoritarianism is rooted in the 3,000 years of imperial rule of politicised Confucianism (Farh and Cheng 2000). In Confucianism, there were three bonds: sons submissive to the will of fathers, ministers submissive to the will of emperors and wives submissive to the will of husbands (Farh and Cheng 2000). These dependent relationships emphasised the subordinates' duty to obey and strengthen legitimate acts of power (Hamilton 1990). Thus, the relationships justified the belief that all individuals were responsible for conforming to their roles for a harmonious society (Hamilton 1990). The major ways of authoritarian comprise affirming authority and control, undervaluing subordinates' competence, creating power distance and behaving in a didactic style (Farh and Cheng 2000). Having elaborated on the role of authoritarianism in paternalistic management, it is worth noting that authoritarianism tended to be rejected by contemporary Chinese employees given the deterioration of the traditional value of submission to authority (Farh and Cheng 2000). As such, the practice of authoritarianism might be transformed to suit the modern context and future research to explore the transformation of authoritarianism is required (Farh and Cheng 2000).

Pragmatic management and its influence in China

Pragmatic management refers to a practical but realistic approach that constantly experiments, assesses, adjusts, adapts, reforms and improves (Xu 2011). To some extent, it is like a cautious trial and error model but with gradual refinement and improvement. Pragmatic management is a common Chinese mode of development, known as 'crossing the river by touching the stones'. This approach reduces the uncertainty and risks of reforms and it increases success rate while moving forward (Head 2010).

China's mode of development, arguably, does not have a sound theoretical base (Warner 2008, 2009). Rather, it adopts a pragmatic approach. Due to the uncertainties of reforms, new ideas are first tested on a small-scale pilot basis and, if proved successful, are then promoted to other places. This approach reduces resistance to reforms, avoids risks and increases success rates (Xu 2011). Regional governments are encouraged to conduct experiments without official endorsement (Qian *et al.* 2007). Regional governments are good at learning from each other and from Western countries (Dong *et al.* 2010). The centralised personal system and decentralised economic system motivate local leaders to be entrepreneurs (Landry 2008). This practice helps explain why China enjoyed unprecedented success from experiments while other socialist countries, for example, the former Soviet Union and central-eastern European countries, failed (Xu 2011).

The transition of HRM in the Chinese school system

Based on the data from two-rounds of interviews with educational officers and principals, a pragmatic, integrated transitional HRM model was identified in the Chinese school system (Figure 4.1). This model comprised

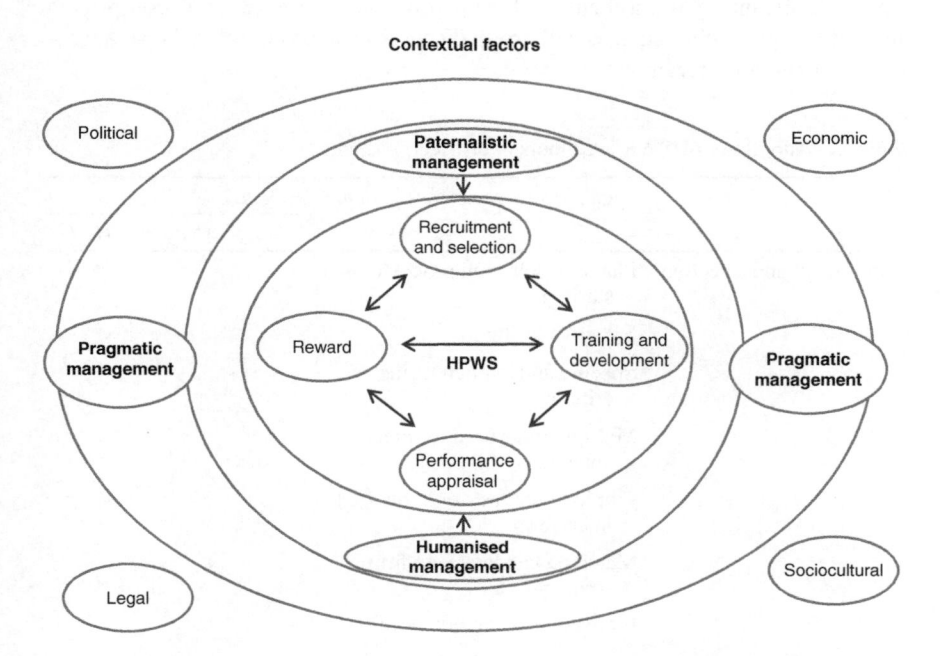

Figure 4.1 Pragmatic integrated transitional human resource management model

four management approaches: high performance work systems, paternalistic management, humanised management and pragmatic management. As illustrated in Figure 4.1, the Western generated HPWS model is an essential, although an insufficient approach, and dominates the new teacher management system. This management approach is facilitated and enhanced by traditional paternalistic and humanised management. The integrated model attempts to combine the essence of both Western and Chinese elements to achieve improved performance. Underpinning this integrated transitional management model is pragmatic management that suggests that this current approach is not an endpoint. Figure 4.1 also indicates that this new management model has evolved and developed under the interactive and interrelated influences of the institutional contexts and management reforms (see chapter 3).

High performance work system

Benchmarked by the HPWS model based on the criteria identified by Posthuma *et al.* (2013) and based on data from two rounds of interviews (for details of HRM practices in the Chinese school system, please refer to chapter 5), the overall degree of adoption of HPWS in the three districts is significant (see Table 4.1). Recruitment and selection is selective and competitive with strict, specific and explicit hiring criteria being employed. Multiple tools are used to screen applicants. Comprehensive hiring procedures are adopted comprising innovative approaches such as cell group discussion, a psychological test, a written exam and an interview.

Table 4.1 Adoption of HPWS in schools in districts 1, 2, and 3

	High performance work systems	*Degree*		
		Low	*Medium*	*High*
Recruitment and selection	Planning selection processes and staffing			✓
	Selective hiring			✓
	Specific and explicit hiring criteria			✓
	Multiple tools used to screen applicants			✓
	Employment tests or structured interviews			✓
	Matching candidates to firm strategy		✓	
	Innovative hiring practices			✓

(Continued)

Table 4.1 (Continued)

	High performance work systems	Degree		
		Low	Medium	High
Training and development	Training extensiveness			✓
	Use of training to improve performance			✓
	Training for job or firm specific skills			✓
	Training for career development		✓	
	Evaluation of training		✓	
	Cross-function or multiskill training	✓		
	New employee training and orientation			✓
	Promotion from within			✓
	Merit-based promotion			✓
	Career planning	✓		
	Promotion opportunities		✓	
	Career paths and job ladders			✓
Performance appraisal	Objective appraisal criteria			✓
	Appraisals for development/potential		✓	
	Frequent performance appraisal meetings		✓	
	Written performance plan with defined objectives			✓
	Multisource feedback and peer appraisal			✓
	Appraisal based on strategic or team goals			✓
Reward	Pay for performance			✓
	Formal appraisal for pay			✓
	External pay equity/competitiveness			✓
	Incentive compensation			✓
	Comprehensive benefits		✓	
	Pay for skills/knowledge			✓
	Equitable pay processes		✓	
	Public recognition/non-financial rewards			✓
	Group-based pay	✓		

Criteria of high performance work systems adopted from Posthuma *et al.* (2013: 1192–3)

Extensive training programs aimed at improving performance are provided. Before being granted tenure, new employees are required to attend intensive orientation training courses and to pass all the relevant exams and appraisals. Leaders are promoted from within, largely on a merit basis even though personal connection or relationships (*guanxi*) are still important. Performance appraisal in the Chinese school system has comprehensive, objective appraisal criteria, which needs the approval of over 60 per cent of teachers. A 360-degree performance appraisal approach is adopted. Performance-related pay is widely utilised coupled with formal appraisal. Skills and knowledge form a significant component of the reward management approach. Teachers are largely paid for skills/knowledge, with both public recognition and non-financial rewards offered to motivate teachers.

Despite different levels of implementation, key elements of the HPWS model were found to be dominant in Chinese schools. The four key HR functions have been strategically combined into complementary, coordinated and coherent bundles of practices to build a strong, effective teaching workforce. Teacher recruitment and selection has been linked to teacher training and reward management. Training has been correlated with recruitment and selection, development, performance appraisal and reward management. Performance appraisal has been central to training, development and reward systems. Rewards, in turn, have been linked with recruitment and selection, training, development and performance appraisal. As such, the horizontal fit of strategic HRM in terms of HPWS was achieved. Overall, HRM practice in Chinese schools can be characterised by HPWS, although with various degrees of compliance.

Paternalistic management

The second element of the transitional HRM model is the maintenance of the traditional paternalistic management comprising benevolence, morality and authoritarianism. School leaders, in general, show a high level of benevolence in their attempts to cultivate a family-like, cooperative, supportive and harmonious working environment. Schools often held birthday parties for teachers. Around half of the schools principals in the present study (23 schools) visited teachers during the Spring Festival with gifts to show their caring nature and recognition of teachers' efforts. The majority of principals (32 principals) knew the family situations of teachers and all principals indicated that they would provide support for teachers' families whenever needed. These principals also provided home-visits to teachers in the event of marriage, sickness and family bereavement. Social harmony is of critical importance in Chinese societies (Farh and Cheng 2000). In some boarding schools, teachers took turns to have a weekly sports day. Some schools (18) had a weekly sports day for teachers to build friendship. Some schools (12) invited teachers' family members to their weekly sports day and provided dinner for them in the school canteen. In addition, principals also indicated that they held different activities to help teachers to work cooperatively, for example, a basketball competition between different disciplines. These practices, according to the principals, helped build a spirit of teamwork, a cooperative culture, a sense of belonging and organisational commitment, which are critically important in the school context. As suggested by the principal of D2T1J1:

> Most of [the] teachers in our schools seldom change their jobs and seldom change schools. We want to create a good community for them. That is why we also invite their family to the sports day. We want to build teachers' sense of belonging and friendships. We want [the] teacher to experience the warmth from our big family. Within the school, we are a family.

Similarly, morality underpins the selection of principals in that substantial efforts are made to appoint candidates that are morally sound. The interviewed principals indicated that acting as a role model for teachers is a basic requirement for quality management. This notion is consistent with the Chinese traditional value, Daoism, which stresses a governance of non-action (*wuwei*) focusing on morality building (Warner *et al*. 2005). This explains why morality is the first and basic performance evaluation criterion in the Chinese context. In the educational sector, high level of morality is required and teachers' behaviours are expected to be the representative of morality. As leaders of teachers, principals are required to display even higher levels of morality as they are presumed to be the role models of teachers. As commented by the HR director of D1:

> The whole society has high expectations for morality demonstration of teachers, demonstrated by a saying: a teacher should be a master of profound knowledge and a role model of integrity (*xuegao weishi, shenzhengweifan*). Being elites among teachers, principals should first display high levels of righteousness and integrity. In terms of morality requirements, they are 'the higher of the higher'. Actually, possessing integrity is our paramount criterion for selecting principals.

At the same time, the principal accountability system (*xiaozhang fuzezhi*) consolidates authoritarian management. This system grants principles' the rights to determine teachers' appointment, training and development opportunities, promotions, appraising performance and rewards. To some extent, teachers' futures are in the hands of the principal. As such, principals have considerable authority over teachers. There is a popular saying in China: 'there is one fundamental rule in surviving in the organisation: the decisions and orders made by leaders are always right (*lingdao de hua yongyuan shi duide*)'. Teachers in China are used to obeying leaders' decisions, even though the decisions might not be favoured by them, to avoid direct confrontations or potential difficult situations resulting from disobedience. This kind of wisdom reflects the traditional Confucian value: be submissive to the will of superiors (Hamilton 1990). With the deepening of the reforms, principals in district 3 (an educational experimental site) were even allowed the right to form and lead their own management team (*xiaozhang zuge*). If proven successful, this practice would be widely promoted to other areas. It can be foreseen that in the future, principals might be granted more power in managing their schools under the principal accountability system.

However, consistent with the observation of Farh and Cheng (2000), adoption of authoritarianism in contemporary Chinese organisations has decreased. The Teacher Law grants teachers the right to participate in managing their schools (The President of PR China 1993). This law limits principals' power over teachers. Principals' authority is further constrained by the performance appraisal system that regulates that principals must gain over 60 per cent of approval by teachers in order to secure their positions. This system encourages principals to care for and value teachers to gain teachers' recognition and support, sometimes at the expense of their authority. In addition, the competitive mechanism also inspires principals to lessen control, thereby improving performance by gaining commitment and support from teachers.

Humanised management

The third element of the transitional management model is humanised management (*renxinghua guanli*), which stresses empathy, recognition, appreciation and face-saving. This management style can be traced to Confucianism and Daoism, which proposes harmonisation in order to maintain a stable and sustained relationship (Warner *et al.* 2005). Principals referred to this approach as 'attracting commitment project' because 'gentlemen die for those who appreciate them'. For example, 10 schools held a celebration meeting at a restaurant at the end of each semester to express the school's appreciation, acknowledgment and recognition for the teachers' contribution. During this meeting, principals or relevant leaders would only mention teachers' strong points and they would provide some suggestions for their future development. As explained by the principal of D3T2J2:

> I usually have private meetings to discuss problems with teachers. In public, I will say positive things about their achievement. Every teacher has strong points and I praise teachers publicly. Once teachers feel they are understood, respected, and recognised, they will work hard for the good of the school.

Principals seldom criticise teachers in the public. When problems occurred, principals or relevant leaders would usually conduct private one-to-one conversations aimed at identifying problems and solutions. For instance, principals would invite teachers to have a heart-to-heart conversation individually at morning tea or dinner. Special care is usually taken not to damage teachers' self-respect. At the very beginning of the meeting, principals usually stress the constraints upon the school to gain teachers' trust before tackling problems. Good communication skills are also required in this process as demonstrated by the comments of the principal of D1T2J3:

> I would invite those [low performing] teachers to my office to have a cup of tea. I try to create a pleasant atmosphere by starting with some positive things about the teachers, both job- and family-related issues. I also stress that insufficient

support provided by our school to teachers. Then I ask them what kind of support they are expecting from our school and from me, as a principal. Only by this time, we begin to talk about the problems and try to work out solutions.

Some schools (10) build teachers' sense of achievement, sense of recognition, self-efficacy and self-esteem by holding a teachers' showcase. This activity provides a platform for teachers to reveal their interests and expertise. For example, a music teacher gave a presentation on how to appreciate the ancient music instrument of Chinese zither (*guzheng*); after the presentation, the teacher played *guzheng* to other colleagues. Combining the activities of reading books, schools (D1V2, D1T1J3, D1T2P1, D2T2P1, D2T1J1, D3V1, D3T2P1 and D3T1P1) also hold a book-sharing forum for teachers. Teachers go to the showcase to tell their colleagues about their reflections and assessment of books. Teachers' showcases also provide a good opportunity for teachers to get to know each other better. These schools have teachers' showcases once a semester usually before summer or winter holidays.

Pragmatic management

Underpinning all these management techniques, the pragmatic approach is apparent. Educational bureaus and schools are encouraged, under the supervision of a higher-level department, to conduct their own experiments. The experimental practices, if proven successful, will be promoted more widely. During the implementation process, the education bureaus and schools are quick at learning, identifying problems and making corresponding changes. The Chinese school system is continually seeking ways to improve the efficiency and effectiveness of teaching and is willing and able to implement changes quite quickly. For example, in the 18 months between the first and second round of interviews, some important changes that aimed to address problems were implemented. The following will elaborate on some significant changes that occurred in this period.

Being aware of the pitfalls derived from the recruitment and selection practices (see chapter 4), prompt actions were taken. The centralised hiring approach was quickly changed to the semi-centralised practice in districts 2 and 3. Under the supervision of the recruitment committee, senior middle schools and vocational schools could go to key universities to recruit top graduates. In 2012, some relatively remote areas in district 2 were granted the right to hire teachers ahead of schedule. District 3 held a recruitment fair specifically for local candidates in 2013 in order to address the problem of exclusion of local candidates. This pragmatic approach manifests the Chinese government's resolution to find the most suitable ways to recruit teachers.

A more formal leadership advancement system has also evolved. Districts 2 and 3 conducted a new round of competition for principals in 2012. The new approach introduced a principal-exit mechanism that encouraged principals who were nearing retirement to step down from their posts by ensuring their pay and benefits continued. By doing so, it created vacancies and provided pathways for high performing, although less experienced candidates. In addition, the element of personal connection (*guanxi*) was less obvious. For example, the principal who criticised the leadership advancement system at the first round of interviews admitted that even though *guanxi* still played a significant role, it has become less manifest and competency now plays a more critical role in teacher advancement.

A dynamic management approach is adopted in performance appraisal planning and the scheme is subject to changes every year, mainly in response to teachers' suggestions. Even though it is generally passed by getting approval from the majority of teachers, problems and conflicts often arise in the implementation process. Under these circumstances, the current scheme is still in operation until the next academic year. A new round of drafting following the same eight-step procedure is undertaken the next year. As explained by the principal of D1T1J2:

> Nothing is perfect and it is impossible to design a PA plan that can meet every individual's needs. When the scheme gets the OK from most teachers, I always tell teachers that since we have tried our best to do this scheme and no better solution is provided, we must stick to this plan until next year. After over 3 years' practice, teachers seem to have accepted this norm.

The competitive mechanism pushes leaders (education bureaus and schools) and teachers to undertake constant innovative activities to improve their performance and competitiveness. As such, even standardised management approaches, such as HPWS, are undergoing continuous changes to enhance performance. Change management, according to the principals, is consistent with the country's goal to build a learning society as well as to develop an education system taking into account the Chinese context.

Conclusion

Drawing on the literature and data from two rounds of interviews, this chapter identified a transitional HRM model in the Chinese school system: a pragmatic, integrated transitional management model. Four key elements were demonstrated in this model: high performance work systems, paternalistic management, humanised management and pragmatic management. Among these four elements, the HPWS is most prevalent, underpinned by the other three approaches. This integrated model shows that a new management approach has evolved that has the merits of the East and West approaches. The pragmatic element of this model highlights ongoing refinement and improvement, reflecting the Chinese government's resolution to build a prosperous country in a holistic way. This identified model might provide a glimpse of reasons behind China's rapid economic growth.

5 Human resource management practices and systems in Chinese schools

Introduction

This chapter investigates the central theme of the transformation of HRM in the Chinese school sector. Based on two rounds of interview data (2011 and 2012) with 51 educational officers and principals of various types of schools, this chapter addresses the third research question: *'How is HRM conducted in terms of recruitment and selection, training and development, performance appraisal and reward management?'* The chapter begins with an examination of teacher recruitment and selection. This is followed by a consideration of teacher training and development strategies and practices. The chapter concludes with an examination of teacher performance appraisal and reward management. In undertaking these tasks, much of the contextual background provided in chapters 3 and 4 will underpin the discussion.

Recruitment and selection

Open recruitment

The central job allocation system and the subsequent principal accountability system for hiring teachers, as discussed earlier, have been criticised for their secrecy, nepotism and favouritism (Robinson and Yi 2008; Niu 2009). To address these concerns and to facilitate further economic reforms, the 'Open Recruitment' (*gongkai zhaopin*) system was officially introduced to public institutions in 2006 with the issue of the *Temporary Guideline for Open Recruitment by the Personnel Ministry* (Ministry of Personnel 2005). The Guideline stresses openness, fairness, justice and transparency (*gongkai, gongping, gongzheng, touming*) in all areas of recruitment and selection, namely recruitment information, selection procedures and appointment results.

According to officers of the education bureaus, the Open Recruitment practice in public institutions addresses the following issues. First, it answers the call to build a market economy by deepening HR reforms in public institutions. Second, it meets the needs to build a harmonious society by ensuring employment fairness, which is considered the most direct way to obtain social equality and stability. Third, it fulfils the aim of providing quality education and building a highly competent teaching workforce through inviting all candidates to compete for the positions. Fourth, it helps in the fight against secrecy, nepotism, favouritism and corruption at the school and district education-bureau levels as Open Recruitment is under the supervision of government organisations and the public.

The Open Recruitment practice aims to hire talented teachers by introducing a competitive mechanism, broadening recruitment to the whole country, encouraging a systematic planning procedure, increasing the entry standard and criteria and having a rigorous selection process. The following sections explore how Open Recruitment is conducted in terms of planning, effectiveness and selection criteria and procedures.

Planning

The quota system plays a significant role in managing the number of teachers. In the Chinese education sector, the quota system is based on a teacher–student ratio. This ratio is stated in the guideline document *Suggestion on Compiling Quota for Teaching and Administrative Staff* (Central Quota Office, Ministry of Education and Ministry of Finance 2001). As shown in Table 5.1, the quota is subject to the school type (primary, junior middle, senior middle and vocational schools) and the school location (municipal, county and village).

The teacher–student ratio in the research districts is provided in Table 5.2. Despite the teacher–student ratio regulation issued in 2001, not all the requirements were met. As the centre of an important city in Guangdong province, district 1 complied with all the rules. Nevertheless, the ratios in primary and junior middle schools in district 2 and primary schools in district 3 were higher than the regulated criteria, indicating violation of the rule. The violation, according to the officers in the education bureaus, was mainly due to financial constraints, suggesting that the ratio is also responsive to local social and economic situations. Several

Table 5.1 Quotas: teacher–student ratios in the Chinese school system

Schools	Locations	Teacher–student ratio
Senior middle schools and vocational schools	Municipal level	1:12.5
	County level	1:13
	Village level	1:13.5
Junior middle schools	Municipal level	1:13.5
	County level	1:16
	Village level	1:18
Primary schools	Municipal level	1:19
	County level	1:21
	Village level	1:23

Source: Central Quota Office, Ministry of Education and Ministry of Finance (2001)

Table 5.2 Teacher–student ratios in the investigated districts

Level of schools	District 1	District 2	District 3
Vocational schools	1:13	1:13	1:12.2
Senior middle schools	1:13	1:14	1:13
Junior middle schools	1:14	**1:17**	1:14
Primary schools	1:19	**1:24**	**1:22**

Source: Interview data (2011, 2012). Figures in bold suggested a failure to meet the official requirements

principals had expressed their concerns to the education bureaus for several years and commented that education quality suffered because of a shortage of teachers. With the increasing investment from governments, the HR manager in district 3 suggested that this situation would change within the next 2 years. The director in district 2 also indicated that their teacher–student ratio would meet the municipal criteria within 5 years.

The quota system has been criticised for its excessive control by the government and a lack of flexibility. Whilst regulating the number of teachers, it fails to balance the needs of different subjects. This approach has resulted in an imbalance of discipline teachers. For example, a school may have surplus of Chinese teachers but a shortage of English teachers, even though the overall number of teachers at that school met the quota requirement. Theoretically, the internal transfer system might solve this problem. Practically, this system does not always work, as quite often, the whole region is short of particular subject teachers or the surplus subject teachers refuse to transfer to a less favoured school or the transferred teachers are rejected by schools due to their poor performance records. One school principal (D2T2J3) complained that they failed to get new teachers for 7 years as the region had reached the quota requirement, even though this school was approved to have more teachers based on the quota system. In these circumstances, schools were forced to employ temporary teachers at their own expense. In response to this issue, the officers from the education bureaus suggested that this situation would be improved in the near future with the implementation of a flexible and looser quota standard to facilitate sabbatical leave for famous teachers (a detailed discussion on sabbatical leave is provided later in this chapter). Famous teachers refers to those leading teachers who have outstanding performance in both teaching and research in teaching practices. They act as role models for others and take the responsibility of conducting research and training teachers in addition to their daily teaching activities.

At the beginning of the school year (around September), the education bureau conducts an employment survey. Schools are required to submit a report on the number of students for the current and following year. They also need to provide detailed personal and job-related information on teachers. Based on the teacher–student ratio, if schools are in need of teachers, they would submit applications to their education bureau for approval. The education bureau then transfers teachers to these schools. After the transfer, the education bureau develops a recruitment plan and conducts the hiring activities.

Selection criteria

Strict selection criteria have been set in order to hire teachers with 'ability and moral integrity' (*decai jianbei*). These criteria include academic achievement, qualification certificates, relevant work experience and teaching awards for non-graduates, age, ethics and health. In order to pass the initial screening test, applicants need to meet all of the first four criteria. Ethics and health are assessed in the later selection stages. However, unlike Western practices, resumes and references are not valued in the staffing process. The principals suggested that the resumes and references were too subjective and they preferred evidence that is more objective. This practice suggests that, despite the reforms, a sound personal credibility system has not been fully established in China.

Educational credentials and degrees are highlighted. Applicants should have a degree from one of the '211 Project Universities' that are the top 100 universities in China. This criterion guarantees a highly regarded teaching workforce considering there were 2,442 higher education institutions in China by 2012 (Ministry of Education 2013a). Candidates who apply for key senior middle schools are required to hold a master's degree and both their bachelor and master's degrees should be awarded by the '211 Project Universities'. In addition, it is preferred that candidates have leadership experience or academic achievement within the top 20 per cent of their universities, or hold a first- or second-grade merit-based scholarship.

Consistent with the requirement of the certificate system, all applicants should possess qualification certificates. Graduates from non-normal (non-educational) universities that do not provide teaching courses or experienced applicants applying for vocational schools should obtain the certificate during their probation period. Experienced candidates outside the education system are not considered, with the exception of vocational schools that focus on cultivating students' practical skills and preparing students for the job market. These candidates should have at least 2 years relevant work experience and relevant technical qualification certificates. Practicing teachers should have teaching-related awards from the district education bureaus.

Even though the Chinese culture respects the wisdom of mature aged people, the preference for young, talented candidates is prevalent in recruiting teachers. Applicants who apply for primary schools and middle schools should be less than 35 and 40 years old respectively. The age requirement for applicants with outstanding teaching records may be extended to 40 years old for primary schools and 45 years old for middle schools. Having acknowledged the contributions of experienced teachers, the majority of principals and HR managers still considered the age criteria reasonable. They suggested that more experienced teachers were usually embedded in their previous work culture and thus were less adaptable to a new environment and students. More importantly, principals indicated that the increasing generation gap between the experienced teachers and students could be a hurdle in effectively communicating with students and thus make it more difficult in achieving good teaching results.

Given the high pressure and characteristics of the teaching profession, health conditions (both psychological and physical) are critical when selecting teachers. People with infectious diseases are forbidden to take up teaching jobs. Acting as role models to students, teachers are expected to be positive, optimistic, upright and have a good attitude towards life and the world. Thus, good ethics and good attitudes are highlighted. Several interviewees commented that the professional nature of teaching required that applicants must have a keen interest in the teaching profession, be a virtue model for others, be disciplined, obey laws and take pleasure in giving (principals of D1V2, D1T1P1, D1T2J2 and D3V2). All three districts included psychological tests either in the interview or in the written exam.

A local applicant protection policy of using less stringent recruitment criteria was adopted to encourage more local candidates. This approach was warmly welcomed by the schools. The typical reasons given were 'local teachers are more effective in communicating with students and their parents' (HR manager in D1); 'we are local schools and need to support our local communities and cultivate the local culture' (director in D2); and 'local teachers are in a better position to establish good relationships with local official organisations' (HR management in D3). However, even though they may be accepted in the selection procedure, local candidates are often not competitive in the written exam, which is the most important component in the hiring procedure. As a result, local applicants are usually not successful under the Open Recruitment system. Given the significant role of local people and the over-representation of non-local teachers in districts 1, 2 and 3, the failure to hire local candidates has raised some concerns.

Hiring procedure

The hiring procedure is rigorous, strict and competitive. It comprises recruitment information advertisement, initial screening and qualification assessment, a written exam, an interview, a psychological test, a teaching plan design demonstration and/or teaching demonstration, public notification, health checks and contract signing. The entire hiring process is lengthy, starting in September and typically running to May of the following year.

To achieve the goal of openness, fairness and justice, the process is under the supervision of a recruitment committee that comprises officers of the education bureau as well as officers from local government, the personnel bureau, the human resource management centre and the discipline inspection bureau. This procedure is strict and if anyone attempts to circumvent the process, they would be held fully accountable and their position would be in jeopardy. The impact of such an approach was highlighted by one principal (D3T2J3):

> Last year I was asked by a good friend to help his son get a teaching job. He offered me RMB 300,000 [around 50,000 US dollars] and I refused to do it. I dare not risk my future and my career.

To ensure openness, fairness and justice, the initial screening process, based on a set of written criteria, is conducted by the hiring panels at either the school level or town bureau level and then reassessed by the district education bureau. A written exam is critical in the selection procedure as it is deemed fair. In addition, the design and marking of exams are conducted confidentially. The teachers or principals who design exams are required to sign contracts with the district education bureau that links the leakage of the exams with dismissals. The process is confidential and systematic as demonstrated by the experience of the principal of D2V1:

> Marking the exam is something like working for the Central Intelligence Office of the United States. I was told to attend a meeting in the district education bureau at 7 o'clock in the morning and I was required to arrive within half an hour. I even didn't have time to tell my colleagues and hurried to the bureau. Only when I arrived did I know that my task was to mark the exam. Handing over all my communication tools, I was confined to a separate office which had a built-in toilet. I saw that five people were already there. We were kept in the office until we finished all the work. The lunch and dinner were sent into the office. We didn't have any chance to communicate with people outside.

The objective of openness, fairness and justice is also guaranteed by the practice of public notification. All the recruitment information is required to be posted on the website of the education bureaus and a website that specialises in teacher recruitment. Passing the initial screening test, the names of candidates are published on the website of the education bureau. After the lengthy and competitive hiring procedure, the names of the final candidates are released on the website of the education bureau for 1 week for public comment. If no objection is received during this period, the final candidates are accepted. According to the interviewees, this approach weeds out fake applications and reinforces the goal of openness, fairness, transparency and justice.

Two different approaches, namely, centralised and semi-centralised, were identified in the three districts. Whatever the approach, the procedure is complex and competitive. In the centralised approach, the district education bureau takes full responsibility and the involvement of lower level education bureaus and individual schools is low. District 1 adopted this approach (see Figure 5.1). A written exam that tests knowledge on pedagogy, psychology and education regulations is the first hurdle for the candidates. The final candidates are allocated to individual schools by the district education bureau. At the beginning, all three districts implemented this approach. However, as this approach was borrowed from the experience of hiring public servants, it was deemed inappropriate for the teaching profession by most principals.

Disappointed in the centralised approach, districts 2 and 3 developed a semi-centralised practice (see Figure 5.1). In this approach, the town education bureaus (on behalf of schools at the compulsory stage) and vocational and senior middle

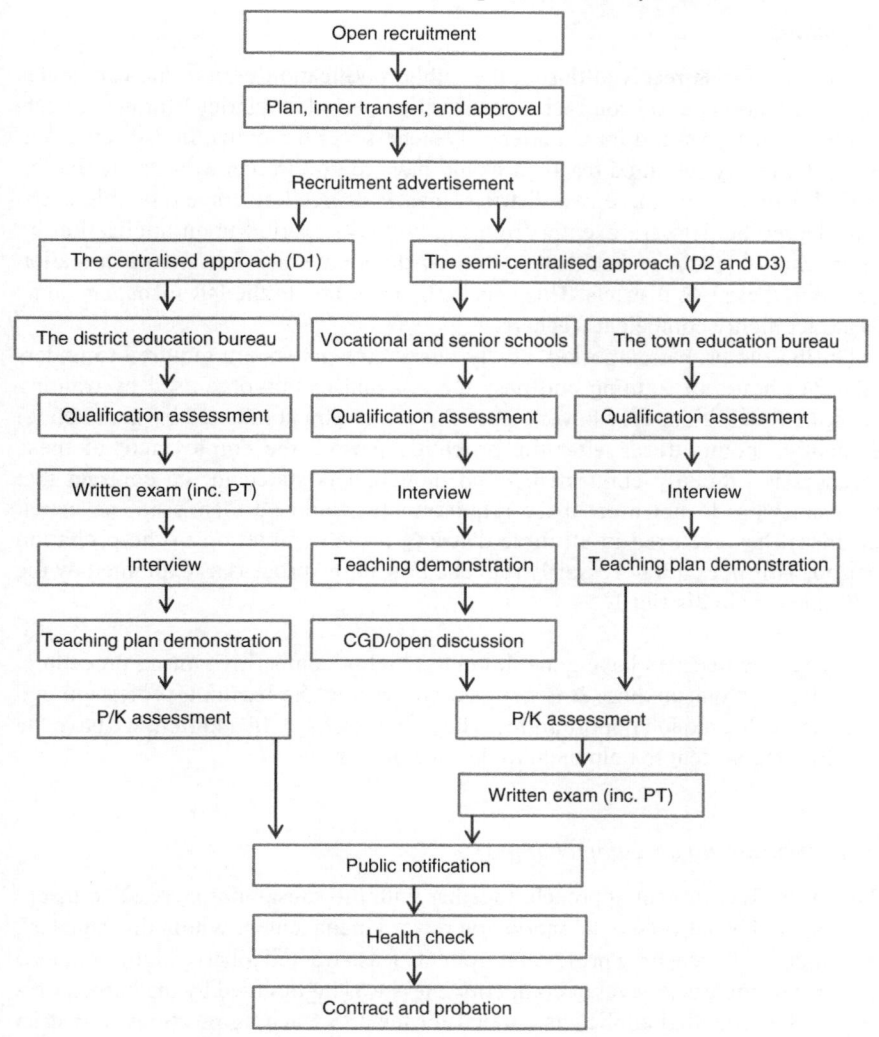

Figure 5.1 Hiring procedure

Source: interview data (2011, 2012). D1, district 1; D2, district 2; D3, district 3; PT, psychological test; P/K, professional knowledge; CGD, cell group discussion

schools are granted the right to conduct initial screening tests and interviews as well as the teaching plan demonstration and professional knowledge assessment, while the district education bureau undertakes the written exam, psychological test, health check and public notifications. The interview, which is considered more appropriate, is conducted before the written exam. As shown in Figure 5.1, this approach is more rigorous than the centralised one, but it can be subject to more local influences and thus could diminish the degree of openness.

Probation

If no objection is received during the public notification period, the candidates sign a probation period contract. The probation period in district 1 for new undergraduates is 1-year and for experienced teachers it is 6 months. In districts 2 and 3, all the newly recruited teachers would have to go through a 1-year probation period. However, in these two districts, master degree holders and double bachelor degree holders are exempt from the probation period upon application by their schools. 'Famous teachers' or 'key teachers'[1] are also free from a probation period in these two districts. This approach, according to the HR managers, aims to attract highly competent teachers.

During the probation period, newly recruited teachers are required to undertake 240 hours of training and pass the relevant exams organised by training schools. In addition, they have to pass the evaluation conducted by their school evaluation committees. After the probation period, the employment of these teachers is officially confirmed. Even though it is stated in the contract that teachers who do not meet these requirements would be dismissed, no actual dismissal has occurred in all three districts at the completion of the probation period. This does not necessarily reflect a flaw in the process as explained by the HR manager in district 1:

> The new teachers have gone through a highly competitive hiring procedure. They are outstanding. It is not easy to get into the teaching profession and they value the job opportunities. They all work hard. In addition, we have the training system to help them to develop and grow.

Effectiveness and on-going changes

The Open Recruitment approach, together with the substantial increase in teachers' pay and benefits (see the section on reward management within this chapter), has changed the teaching profession from the least-wanted job to a highly-pursued career. The increased level of competitiveness was highlighted by the bureau officers: 4,829 qualified applicants applied for the 125 teaching positions in district 1 in 2011, a ratio of over 38:1. The ratio of the qualified applicants to vacancies in districts 2 and 3 was 40:1 and 35:1 respectively. In some popular subjects, for example, Chinese and English, the ratio of the qualified applicants to vacancies reached 70:1 in districts 2 and 3.

The Open Recruitment system in the Chinese education sector has generally achieved its goal of openness, fairness and justice. The stringent selection criteria and procedures have ensured a quality work force as the successful candidates had to 'force five passes and slay six captains' (*guowuguan, zhanliujiang*)[2] (HR manager in district 3). Principals, in general, suggested that the Open Recruitment practice helped build a harmonious society by addressing the call from the public for fairness and transparency. Principals also indicated that this approach was good for them as they were free from the tedious nature of recruiting teachers and being suspected of corruption and accepting bribes.

Nevertheless, the centralised approach, even though strict, complex and competitive, is not always considered the best way to recruit teachers. Some principals argued that this approach was 'just like a father looking for a wife for his son and whether his son loves her or not, he has to take her' (principals in D3S1 and D1S2; HR manager in district 3). They maintained that a written exam should not be the first step in eliminating candidates, as 'people who are good at exams are not always good at teaching' (principals of D2T2J2, D3V1 and D1S2). This practice produced a considerable number of candidates who were 'with high marks but low competencies' (principals of D2T1J3, D3T2J2 and D1T1J2). The over-emphasis on written exam in the hiring procedure has added to the gender imbalance that already exists in the education sector, as women often did better in exams than their male counterparts. Moreover, the over-emphasis on the exam also excludes many local candidates. As such, principals expressed their concerns about the centralised approach with comments such as 'we cannot highlight openness, fairness, and justice at the expense of children's overall development' (HR manager in district 1; principals of D1S1, D1V2, D2S1, D2S3, D3S1 and D3S2) and 'hiring a bad teacher will ruin countless students for 30 years' (principals of D1T1P1, D1T1J2 and D2T2J3).

In contrast, the semi-centralised approach appears to be well accepted and a feasible compromise. While ensuring the principle of openness, fairness, transparency and justice, this approach highlights teaching professional characteristics by stressing interviews and practical skills. The increased involvement of individual schools and the decreased involvement of the education bureaus improved the teacher-school fit, which, according to Liu and Johnson (2006), would benefit school effectiveness. This pragmatic approach manifests the Chinese government's resolution to find the most suitable ways to recruit teachers. As the experimental sites, districts 2 and 3, have continued to explore practices that are deemed suitable for the Chinese context. They are quick at identifying problems and solutions as well as implementing changes. For example, in addition to Open Recruitment, senior middle schools and vocational schools could go to key universities to recruit excellent graduates under the supervision of the recruitment committee. Some relatively remote areas in district 2 were granted the right to hire teachers ahead of schedule in 2012. To address the problem of the exclusion of local candidates, district 3 held a recruitment fair in 2013 specifically for local candidates.

The changes so far, according to principals in districts 2 and 3, have made improvements to the teacher hiring system. Principals also suggested that the hiring practices have become enlightened and more humane. Around half of the principals (15 or 54 per cent) in these two districts suggested that 'this is the best approach so far'. Overall, principals felt that the Chinese government has taken considerable strides in attracting highly qualified candidates for the teaching profession.

Training and development

The teaching profession is universally expected to undertake continuous training to acquire new knowledge and skills if they are to meet the changing needs of the society (OECD 2005b). In China, the need for training was acute after the destruction of the education system during the Cultural Revolution. With the establishment of the strategy of development through education, science and technology, the government regards teacher training and development as a focal point and it has made substantial efforts to make it a priority. Since the beginning of the economic reforms, dozens of policies and regulations regarding training have been published. To guarantee sufficient funds for teacher in-service training, an accountability system for the local government, particularly the county-level government, has been implemented (State Council 2005). Strict regulations regarding training provisions and training requirements have been adopted (Ministry of Education, National Development and Reform Commission and Ministry of Finance 2012).

Echoing the government's emphasis, all HR managers and principals acknowledged the significance of in-service training. They maintained that due to the rapidly changing society, students were different year by year. As such, 'past successful experience sometimes can be a stumbling block [in teaching]' (principal of D2T2J2). Similarly, the principal of D1T1V2 also suggested that the common expression of 'in order to give students a cup of water, teachers should have a bucket of water' is no longer suitable; rather, this phrase has been replaced by 'in order to give students a cup of water, teachers should be at least a rushing river'. To be a 'rushing river', according to the principals, teachers should undertake life-long learning.

Over the past 30 years, a systematic in-service training and development model for teachers has evolved in China. This model includes dedicated training budgets, training needs analysis and specified training requirements; substantial and comprehensive training programs; varieties of training contents; an evolving training auditing practice; and career development and advancement.

Training planning

Training budget

With the establishment of the strategy of prioritising educational development, large sums of money have been invested in in-service training. The finance bureaus in districts 1, 2 and 3 are responsible for allocating the training funds, which represents 2 per cent of the teacher's payroll (interviews with education bureau officers). The officers also indicated that training funds would be increased to 3 per cent within 5 years. This investment in training is similar to the US, where training generally represented an investment of 1 to 3 per cent of the payroll (Bersin 2004).

At the school level, the 2006 *Temporary Policy on Managing the Administration Fund in Primary and Middle Schools* (Ministry of Finance and Ministry of Education 2006) requires that 5 per cent of the administrative fund of a school should be used for teacher training. To ensure strict adherence to this rule, the *Guideline on Deepening the Training Model Reforms and Increasing the Overall Training Quality* (Ministry of Education 2013b) requires that the implementation of the training fund is an important performance appraisal indicator for local governments, education bureaus and schools. The majority of schools (32) indicated that they allocated 5 per cent of the administrative fund to teacher training. The other 10 schools (D1S1, D1S2, D1T2J3, D2S1, D2S2, D2T2P1, D2T1J2, D3S1, D3S2 and D3T1J1) claimed that they invested around 10 per cent of their administrative funds on such activities.

Senior middle schools generally have more training funds as they have income from tuition fees and school-selection fees. In addition, as the test results of the college entrance exam are considered a fundamental indicator of education quality (see chapter 3), senior middle schools usually receive more money from the government in the hope of improved student performance. Consequently, in 2011, the senior middle schools had around RMB 3,500 per teacher while other schools had only around RMB 800 to 1,000. A slight increase was reported in 2012, for example, RMB 3,650 for senior middle schools and RMB 900 to 1,100 for the other schools. The relatively high investment in senior middle schools makes large-scale, off-the-job training possible.

In addition to the standard administrative fund, local governments that prioritised training and development could also contribute extra money towards schools. However, this is not a common occurrence. Out of the six town education bureaus, only two (D2T2 and D3T1) provided extra funds. In these two towns in 2011, schools with more than 1,000 students received RMB 100,000 and schools with less students received RMB 80,000. In 2012, the training fund was doubled in D2T2. With sufficient funds, these schools could afford to outsource training programmes to specialised training organisations that are generally considered more effective.

Although all the principals claimed that they followed the training funding rule, some principals suggested that this was not always the case. As the training fund is at the discretion of individual principals, the principals' priorities decide the actual usage of the money. Some schools appeared not to spend the requested amount of money on teacher training. This was often due to the test result-oriented culture as demonstrated by the following comment by the principal of D1S1:

> The training effects cannot be obvious in a short time or immediately after the training course. Some principals think that the exam results do not change much after teacher training, thus they tend to think teacher training is a waste of resources, time, and money.

Training needs analysis

Training needs analysis in the three districts is conducted on a regular basis. The education bureaus in districts 2 and 3 conducted large-scale surveys that included at least 40 per cent of schools, while district 1 surveyed around 20 per cent. Supporting the education bureaus' statement, principals mentioned that their education bureaus conducted a training needs survey at least once a year. In addition to the education bureaus, teacher-training institutions also undertook regular training needs analysis. The principals indicated that at the beginning of each training course, training institutions would ask teachers for their training preferences concerning their most pressing training needs for the coming years.

At the school level, principals and subject team leaders, as well as leaders in different departments, usually act as trainers and decide the training content. In 2011, out of the 42 schools, slightly less than a quarter of schools (10) indicated that they asked their subordinates for their training requirements. For the other schools (32), principals mentioned that they normally designed the training courses based on their knowledge and the training requirements of the education bureaus. This situation, however, is in a state of flux. Follow-up discussions with principals 18 months later indicated that an extra 12 schools had asked for teachers' opinions on training needs and principals of another 10 schools said that they would ask teachers about their training preference in the near future. The reasons given for this change included the need for increasing engagement, commitment and motivation in training, the higher requirement for training efficiency and to keep up with the rapidly changing world.

Training time requirement

The Teacher Law regulates that training is both a teacher's right and responsibility. From the 2000s, in-service training has been increasingly emphasised with more rigorous requirements. Teachers are now required to undertake 360 training hours every 5 years (replacing the previous 240 training hours) in accordance with the *Suggestion on Reinforcing Primary and Middle School Teacher Training* (Ministry of Education 2011). Strict rules apply to the calculation of training hours. The regular on-the-job training programmes offered by schools do not normally count as training hours. Only off-the-job training, online training, degree training and conferences are regarded as training hours. Study hours in research projects are considered only if the project is approved and filed with the education bureau. Given the difficulty of teachers getting time off for training, the most common form is through online training. According to the officers in the education bureaus, the training hour requirement was strictly implemented in the three districts.

Training requirements are associated with performance appraisal, awards, pay and benefits, career advancement, further employment, the application for a teacher qualification certificate and the award of professional titles as outlined in the document *Suggestion on Reinforcing Primary and Middle School Teacher Training* (Ministry of Education 2011). These rules, according to the HR managers and principals, were strictly applied in the three districts. To ensure in-service training goes smoothly, a special committee, the 'Teacher Continuous Education Committee', has been established, although principals take full responsibility for in-service training implementation.

Training programmes

Teachers' typical training programmes comprise on-the-job training (school-based training), off-the-job training and online training (see Table 5.3).

On-the-job training

On-the-job or school-based training is a fundamental and traditional form of teacher training in China as in many other countries. As mentioned previously, a fixed amount of money is allocated (5 per cent of the administrative fees) to ensure adequate training can be undertaken. School-based training aims to meet individual schools' unique training needs. The typical school-based training programmes include weekly training, class teacher training, mentoring programmes, orientation, inviting experts to deliver a course, subject team study, competitions, lesson-preparation study groups and experience sharing. These programmes are conducted on a frequent basis by all the schools in this study, although the degree of involvement varies (see Table 5.3). Generally speaking, senior middle schools and model schools in urban areas appear more serious and effective in undertaking such training.

More recently, training by conducting research projects, teacher's showcasing and training outsourcing have emerged and they have become increasingly popular. Over half of the investigated schools (24) had research projects led and supervised by professors from normal universities. The professors and experts visited schools regularly to provide guidelines and feedback on the project. Teacher showcasing was adopted by 10 schools to motivate teachers by building their sense of achievement and self-efficacy through establishing a platform to demonstrate their expertise. Under the training outsourcing approach, schools have tailored and developed extensive training programmes. However, as this kind of training requires substantial investment, only six schools in D2T2 and D3T1, which had received extra training fund from the local government, could afford to outsource training. Schools usually sign a contract with training institutions and experts from these institutions delivered training on a regular basis. For example, D2T2P1 had implemented an 18-month project called 'Teachers' Professional Development' in cooperation with Beijing Normal University. At the beginning of the project, professors attended teachers' classes and talked with teachers. Then the professors and each teacher met to design a tailored development plan. The professors visited the school on a monthly basis to attend teachers' classes and give feedback. At the end of the project, the professors evaluated each teacher's progress and provided overall feedback as well as future directions. This kind of training is deemed effective and welcomed by quite a number of principals (principals of D1V2, D1S2, D1SJ1, D2T2J2, D2V2, D2T1J1, D2S1, D2S2, D3S1, D3T2P1 and D3T1P2).

However, the competitive mechanisms can lead to regional protection[3] (Xu 2011). As competition has become a norm in the education sector, it has been a common phenomenon in the three districts. To tackle the problem of a teacher's

Table 5.3 Teacher training programmes

Training programme	Methods	Training provider	Trainees	Training frequency
On-the-job training	Weekly training	Principal	All teachers	Once a week
	Subject team training	Team leader	Teachers in the same subject	Once a week
	Teaching demonstration	Team leader	Same as above	Once a semester
	Lesson-preparing study group	Grade team leader	Teachers in the same subject/grade	Once a week
	Class teacher training	Principal and moral department leader	Class teachers	Once a week/2 weeks
	Orientation	Principal and department leaders	New teachers	Once a year
	Mentorship	Mentor	New teachers or teachers in need	Daily activities
	Teachers' competition	Relevant school leaders	All teachers or teachers involved	Once a semester
	Experts training	Experts from outside	All teachers	At least once a semester
	Experience sharing	Models teachers	All teachers	Once a semester/year
	Research project	Experts from outside	Teachers involved	Variable
	Training outsourcing	Experts from outside	All teachers	Variable
	Teachers' showcase	All teachers	All teachers	Once a semester/year
Off-the-job training	Overseas training	Overseas training institutions	English teachers	3–6 months
			Principals and key leaders	6 weeks to 3 months
	Domestic training	Domestic teacher training institutions	Principals, famous and new teachers	Regular and systematic
	Visiting benchmark schools	Outward-bounded benchmark schools	Principals and key leaders	4–6 weeks
		Local benchmark schools	Ordinary teachers	Once a semester
Online training	Various programmes	Online training platform	All teachers	Any time

Source: interview data (2011, 2012)

self-protection in terms of teaching activities, a lesson-preparing study group has been established for teachers in the same subject and in the same grade to do lesson-preparation together on a weekly basis. The training emphasises cooperation and teamwork. This approach is particularly prevalent in senior and junior middle schools that face high pressure from exams. The key goals of the training, according to the principals, are to 'make sure that students of different classes under different teachers have a unified teaching pace, unified teaching requirements, and unified exercise materials' (principal of D3S1). In addition, they are to 'balance teaching quality' (principal of D1T2J2) and to 'balance students' exam results under different classes and different teachers in the same discipline in the same grade' (principal of D2S2). This approach reflects the test result-oriented culture in the Chinese education sector.

Off-the-job training

Off-the-job training is usually provided for principals, midlevel leaders and famous teachers so that they can play a leading role in educational reforms and can effectively conduct training of other teachers. The most common off-the-job training programmes comprise overseas training, training delivered by domestic training organisations and training by visiting benchmark schools.

Overseas training involves large sums of money as well as considerable planning. English teachers are the main recipients of overseas training. District 3 has been conducting overseas training for English teachers for more than 10 years. This district has trained 500 teachers during this period and plans to have all of its 1,700 English teachers undertake this type of training in the future. Even though overseas training requires extensive investment, the HR manager suggested it was worth the money and effort as 'the students' English test result in the college entrance exam has been No.1 for 7 years after implementing this type of training in our province' and 'our English teachers do exceptionally well in various competitions' (HR manager in district 3). Following in the footsteps of district 3, districts 1 and 2 also have English teacher overseas training, although on a less systematic basis. More recently, the three districts also organised some overseas training for principals and famous teachers. Principals highly value overseas training and regarded this opportunity as the highest honour. For example, the principal of D2T2J2 stated:

> In 2009, I got the chance to go to the UK for training. This was my first time to go abroad. I felt extremely excited about it. It was my great honour as this had been the first and only time that principals went abroad to undertake training so far. Only a few outstanding principals could go. I also felt a sense of recognition and achievement. My family felt happy for me as well.

Domestic training for administrative leaders and famous teachers is organised on a regular and systematic basis by education bureaus. Districts 2 and 3 have their own teacher training schools and all of the off-the-job training is organised or delivered by these schools. Off-the-job training activities in district 1 are organised by the education bureaus in cooperation with training institutions. New teacher training is conducted by the training schools or the education bureaus locally. Leaders and excellent teacher training is conducted either locally or in places with an advanced educational system, for example, Shanghai, Beijing, Changzhou, Suzhou, Zhejiang, Guangzhou and Hangzhou. Long-term cooperative relationships have been established between the three education bureaus and training institutions. Some key senior middle schools, which have received extra training funds, also organise regular off-the-job training. Schools highly valued off-the-job training as 'this helps nurture teacher's teamwork spirits and teacher's sense of happiness and sense of belonging to the school' (principals of D1S1, D1S2 and D3S1).

Training by visiting benchmark schools is conducted both externally and locally. The external training is usually designed for principals and midlevel leaders to benchmark schools by observing and participating in key activities (*yidi guazhi*) ranging from 1 to 6 weeks. It is a mode of 'learning by doing' in which trainees participate and experience all the activities of school management. Focusing on practical management issues and participating in all-around school management is viewed as effective and it is welcomed and regarded as recognition and an honour by the trainees. Training by visiting local benchmark schools is designed for ordinary teachers to learn good practices. This training is common and all the principals mentioned that every teacher attended this type of training at least once a semester. Even though the training time is short, it is viewed as necessary and effective as 'other schools' successful experiences are important' (HR manager in district 1).

Online training

Online training is a cost-effective way to deliver training to the entire teaching population and to increase teacher overall quality, especially with a limited budget. Guangdong province has an online training system with a variety of tailored online training courses for different disciplines and different levels, for example, principals, midlevel leaders, grade leaders, discipline leaders, class teachers and teachers. Each online course has a discussion board for learners to discuss issues and engage with other participants. The online training system also has online mentors. The online mentors are the highest-ranked famous teachers and experts in Guangdong province. This method is favoured by the principals because 'there are lots of experts online and we can discuss with experts and teachers from the whole province' (principal of D2V1) and 'the training model is convenient, interactive and resourceful' (principal of D1S3). Each teacher in the three districts is provided with a laptop for online training and lesson preparation. However, teachers cannot get time off to undertake online training. As such, the conflict between working hours and training hours is a hurdle for these teachers and threatens the effectiveness of such training.

Training content

Training content covers a range of areas including ideological and political education, teacher's moral cultivation, education legislation and regulations, professional knowledge expansion and update, teaching theories and practices and modern education and technology. In addition, elements of paternalistic management are demonstrated as courses concerning physical and mental health are also provided. For example, six schools conducted Yoga training for teachers (D2T2P1, D3T2P1, D3S1, D2S3, D1S2 and D2T1J2). Nine schools invited experts to deliver courses regarding teacher's mental health (D1T1P1, D1V1, D1T1J1, D1T2J3, D2S2, D2T1J1, D3V1, C3T1J1 and D3T1J3). Other schools delivered courses on how to deal with stress (D1V1, D1T2J3, D2V1, D2S2, D2T2P1, D2T1J1, D3V1, D1S3 and D3T1P1). Some schools also included programmes on how to be a happy teacher and enjoy a happy life (D1V2, D2V1, D2T2J2, D3T3J2 and D3T1P1).

Stressing efficiency and effectiveness, industry management theory and practice courses are also provided in some schools and education bureaus, although on an ad hoc basis. For example, in 2009, district 2 organised principals to visit local industries to learn about their management approaches and practices. In addition, management-training courses outside of the teaching sphere are also provided to principals. All three districts had their famous principals undertake training conducted by the Hong Kong Vocational Training Council with other high-ranked leaders from local industry. These programmes were welcomed by principals as they gained 'wisdom, energy, and implications from industry management' (director of district 2) and 'the training opens a new management horizon to principals' (HR manager in D3T2).

Some schools (D3S2, D1T1J3, D2S2, D1S1 and D3V1) implemented their own industrial management theory and practice training programmes. For example, D1T1J3 adopted result-oriented approaches and each teacher was equipped with the books entitled '*Please Give me the Results*' and '*There are Always More Solutions than Problems*'. The principal of this school delivered training concerning these books at weekly staff meetings. A key senior middle school's slogan was 'to effectively work for 8 hours a day'. As such, this school aimed to train teachers and students to be more effective in their work. The training courses were conducted regularly and assiduously as demonstrated by the following example from the principal of D3S2:

> Our teachers took turns to go to Zhongshan to undertake 4-day training delivered by experts from Hong Kong. After that, our school held a fortnightly meeting to study and discuss the training implications for our daily practices. We also held experience sharing and problems-solving salons. At the end of the year, we rewarded the outstanding teachers.

Training evaluation

Most of the off-the-job training programmes were evaluated. Training institutions usually conduct surveys immediately after the training courses whilst training programmes by school-based research projects are assessed at the end of each semester. On-the-job training is one of the criteria for the principals' annual job performance appraisal. Education bureaus focused the evaluation on whether a school had detailed training plans and whether the training plan was carried out. The inspection method, however, focused on the preparations of training materials. As such, this practice made some schools only work on the preparation of the paperwork and led to a rather superficial assessment.

Similarly, the evaluation of the online training programmes focused on how many teachers completed the courses rather than on whether the training courses were effective. According to the HR officer in the Department of Education in Guangdong province, the main reason for the lack of effective assessment was that government officers were reluctant to know the outcome as a negative comment could mean trouble for them. The majority of principals (25) also expressed concerns. They indicated that many teachers logged onto the system and then minimised the screen, doing other things instead. As long as teachers clicked on the link, they passed the training courses. Principals recommended that the supervision of online training should be strengthened to enhance training quality and avoid wasting resources.

Career development

Career development comprises administrative leadership advancement and professional advancement. All the bureaus have official development policies in order to motivate, nurture and retain highly effective teachers. An appointment committee is normally established to ensure the process of teacher promotion is fair, transparent and just.

The appointment of administrative leaders, particularly principals and deputy principals, is made from above to ensure the government's control over education. A competitive mechanism has been practiced under formally written criteria and procedures following the *Regulation of Cadres' Employment of the Party's Cadres* (Ministry of Personnel 2000). The revised regulations strengthened the emphasis on political and moral quality as well as competence (*decai jianbei*), relevant leadership experience, educational qualifications, health, age, relevant professional qualifications and job performance. The ability to resist corruption is also included in the selection criteria, even though it is difficult to measure.

Since becoming an established and desirable profession, a structured career development ladder for teachers has been developed. Advancement includes five progressive ranks, namely, 'third-grade teacher', 'second-grade teacher', 'first-grade teacher', 'senior teacher' and 'special-grade teacher'. This official career system involves the applicants submitting materials for assessment. Such a professional qualification approach is life-long and it has become important for pay, fringe benefits and further advancement. At the moment, however, there is a large gap between 'senior teacher' and 'first-grade teacher' in terms of pay and benefits (see the section on reward management). As the percentage of 'senior teachers' is confined to 30 per cent of the total teachers in a school, then the career ladder development system overvalues seniority and thus may not be sufficient to motivate teachers.

To motivate teachers and improve performance, a new professional development system has been evolving. This system provides a new outlet for teachers who are good at teaching but not suitable as management leaders. District 1 had the 'Three Famous Project', which included famous principals, famous teachers and famous class teachers at different levels. Similarly, districts 2 and 3 also had a hierarchical system of professional development for teachers (key teachers/principals, senior key teachers/principals and benchmark teachers/principals at different levels). Like the administrative leadership advancement system, this new system is dynamic and one round of training usually lasts for 4 years. This approach, according to HR managers, helps to motivate teachers to work hard to keep up their good performance and to motivate other competent teachers to compete for this advancement. According to the HR manager in district 3, 'it gives a signal to teachers that nowadays as long as you work hard and have outstanding job performance, you have chances'. Famous teachers, senior famous teachers and benchmark famous teachers receive the same treatment and welfare benefits equivalent to deputy directors, directors and deputy principals respectively. Famous teachers also receive extra money for the responsibility of supporting, helping and leading other teachers in their respective areas.

On-going changes

The Chinese government is continually seeking ways to improve efficiency and effectiveness of teaching and it is willing and able to implement changes quite quickly. In the 18 months between the first and second round of interviews, some important changes were identified. The majority of the online training courses were theory-based and deemed broad and empty. As some of the compulsory courses provided limited practical implications for teachers' daily teaching skills, teachers regarded online training as a waste of time and a burden (principals of D3S1, D2V2, D2V1, D1T1J2 and D2T2J3). Being aware of these criticisms the *Guideline on Deepening the Teacher Training Model Reforms of Middle and Primary Schools and Increasing the Overall Training Quality by the Ministry of Education* was issued in 2013 (Ministry of Education 2013b). This guideline emphasises the needs for more practical training content and programmes (practical programmes should be more than 50 per cent of the overall programmes). It encourages autonomy in determining training content and programmes to meet different training needs.

To cultivate a performance culture and motivate famous teachers, the famous teachers at district level are entitled to have an office as their workstation, which is similar to that of the principal. Famous teachers use the office as a base for conducting research and training of other teachers. Another shift is the promotion of sabbatical leave for famous teachers. Famous teachers at the district level or above are granted a 6-month sabbatical leave. This approach serves as the highest honour and recognition for famous teachers and thus motivates teachers to work hard for their goals (director in D2).

In 2012, a teacher professional development-planning scheme was also introduced. Teachers are now required to have a 3-year career development plan that outlines their goals and the proposed approaches to achieve these goals. Teachers are also required to state the training needed to achieve these goals. According to the participants, this approach helps teachers to have a clear understanding of their future and make realistic goals for themselves. The professional development plan also helps to design appropriate training courses that can meet the needs of teachers.

Performance appraisal

Performance appraisal (PA) is difficult as highlighted in Berman *et al.*: 'if anyone can solve the performance evaluation problem, he should be entitled to the Nobel, the Pulitzer, and the Heisman in the same year' (Berman *et al.* 2006: 245). This task is even more complicated in the education system as teachers' input and output is hard to evaluate and it is not easy to identify the most productive teachers (Fryer 2011). The majority of principals suggested that teacher PA was 'a kind of headache'. The teaching job is 'long-term, implicit and cooperative' that makes explicit appraisal criteria almost impossible (HR managers of districts 1 and 3, principals of D1S1, D2V1 and D3S1). Despite these difficulties, all the principals indicated that PA was critically necessary; otherwise, teachers would become 'wily old birds' (principals of D1T1J2 and D2T1P1).

According to the HR managers and principals, PA in the Chinese education sector aims to build a strong teaching workforce, to cultivate a performance-oriented culture and to motivate teachers. It serves as a solid foundation for the allocation of performance-related pay and benefits, registration for teacher qualification certificates, position employment, career advancement and training and development. To facilitate the successful implementation of performance-related pay, the *Guidelines on Teacher Performance Appraisal of Compulsory Education Schools* was issued (Ministry of Education 2008). To achieve the principle of fairness, justness, openness and transparency, an appraisal committee, which consists of five to 13 members (depending on the size of schools), has been established in each school. With teachers' representatives accounting for no less than one-third of the total membership, the appraisal committee organises, guides and conducts a series of appraisal activities. The PA system, which includes careful planning, detailed criteria, inclusive approaches and rigorous procedures will now be explored.

Planning

Based on the guidelines of the education bureau, individual schools are required to design their own schemes, which should be approved by over 60 per cent of teachers through public voting. Schools are also requested to submit their PA schemes to the education bureaus for approval and filing. These schemes usually comprise detailed information on job descriptions, which serve as the basis for evaluation. To get support from over 60 per cent of teachers, the drafting procedure is strict and often needs several drafts before the final one is accepted and put into effect. A typical drafting procedure comprises eight steps and it is shown in Figure 5.2. Once it receives approval, the PA scheme is active for one academic year.

In the drafting process, positive labour relations are encouraged as teacher's active participation is the key for a widely accepted PA scheme. As PA is directly related to rewards and career advancement, it is of concern to every teacher. Relying only on principals and the appraisal committee, without teacher's active participation in drafting the PA scheme, is unlikely to work well and may well have negative outcomes despite its good intention. Such an approach was common in schools where principals are less experienced. For example, the PA schemes

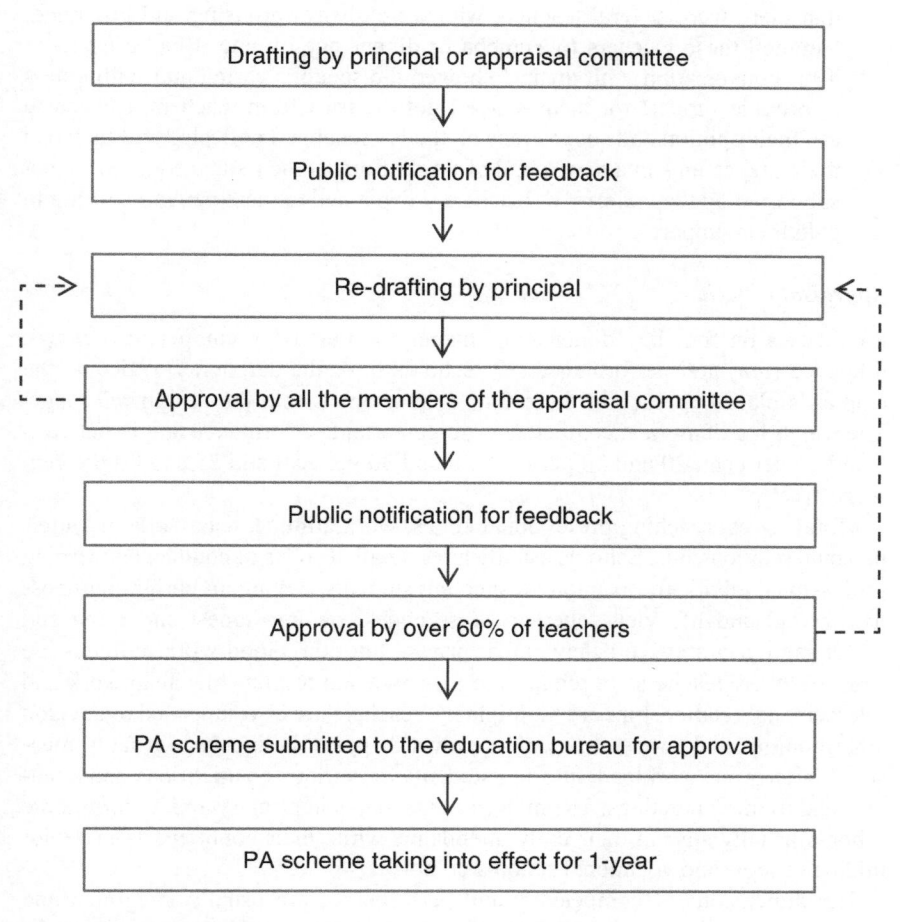

Figure 5.2 Drafting procedure for performance appraisal
Source: interview data (2011, 2012). PA, performance appraisal

produced numerous conflicts and discontent in D2T1J3, D2T2J4 and D3T2J2 – all schools where principals were relatively inexperienced.

As such, principals' experience and competence as well as their management style are critical. Most principals suggested that whatever efforts had been made, the PA scheme would have some defects and there were always some teachers that were not easy to please. These particular teachers, if not managed well, could have unpredictable negative impacts. As such, the way to manage these particular teachers determines whether a PA scheme is successful. Principals indicated that a paternalistic management style is needed. The most common approach is private one-to-one conversation. The following is a typical example from the principal of D1T1J3:

> During the drafting procedure of the PA scheme, the midlevel leaders told me that there were several teachers who were always grousing and gossiping. I invited these teachers to Yumcha or dinner one by one. I had a heart-to-heart conversation with them. I showed the school's caring and willingness to provide support for them. Once I got the trust from teachers, I began to ask their opinion and suggestions on the PA scheme. I collected and included their suggestions in a new round of PA drafting. If their suggestions were not supported by the majority of teachers, I explained to them patiently, trying to gain their support.

Appraisal criteria

PA focuses on four key dimensions, namely, morals (*de*), competency (*neng*), diligence (*qin*) and performance (*ji*). Schools have the autonomy to decide the emphasis placed on each of these four dimensions within the designated range. The weighting of morale, competency, diligence and performance ranges between 8 and 15 per cent, 20 and 30 per cent, 20 and 30 per cent and 25 and 40 per cent respectively.

Morals stress teaching professional ethics, work attitude, teamwork and inter-personal relationships. Schools usually have detailed codes of conduct concerning professional ethics, for example, respecting students, having an upright and positive world and life view, obeying dress codes, staying honest and clean and not engaging in abusive behaviour or private tutoring. Good work attitudes are stressed where teachers are required to be active and responsible. Teamwork and interpersonal relationships are highlighted. Teachers are also supposed to develop a harmonious and cooperative attitude towards peers. Diligence is usually measured in terms of workload, tutoring students for various competitions and attendance at training meetings. The majority of teachers in primary and junior middle schools usually sign in their daily attendance while their counterparts in senior middle schools and vocational schools do not.

The dimensions of competency and performance are usually integrated and evaluated in two stages, namely, process management and outcome management. Process management focuses on daily working activities while outcome management emphasises teaching-related outcomes. The common criteria for process management includes lesson preparation, teaching quality, homework marking, class management, the quality of teaching demonstration, training courses and student cultivation and development. Outcome management often evaluates teachers in terms of student test results, teacher competition results, student competition results and teacher awards.

Even though there are four dimensions, teaching outcomes, particularly student test results, is a critical factor in teacher evaluation. In order to survive under the competitive mechanisms, teachers have to work hard to improve test results. However, this may, to a large extent, lead to the neglect of the overall development of students. As one principal commented 'we cannot survive today if we focus on student's overall development; however, we cannot survive tomorrow because we focus on student test results today' (principal of D2T2J2). Despite teachers, principals and even government officials being well aware of this pitfall, the short-term goal (test results) is still often stressed at the expense of the long-term goal of student's overall development. In order to get higher test results, teamwork is highlighted as individual teacher's self-protection and conservatism usually undermines the overall performance of a school. As such, whenever possible, teachers are evaluated and rewarded on a group basis in terms of test results.

Appraisal methods

Evaluation is conducted on a semester basis following a relatively stringent procedure. All the schools adopted a 360-degree appraisal approach that is shown in Figure 5.3. The most common approaches included evaluation by divisions, subject leaders, grade leaders, teacher themselves, students and their parents and the school appraisal committee.

Leaders' appraisal evaluates teachers on the four key criteria on a regular basis according to the three key divisions of logistic, moral and teaching. The logistic division evaluates teachers in terms of diligence. The moral division assesses teachers regarding morality and the teaching division focuses on competence and performance. The subject leader's evaluation highlights competence and performance while the grade leader's evaluation emphasises diligence and morality. Students' evaluation was conducted in all the schools investigated. Most primary schools used the results only for reference and feedback to teachers and were not included in the final calculation of the performance grade. The most quoted reason for this approach was that students in primary schools, especially in the lower levels, are not mature enough to give accurate comments. Student evaluation in other schools, however, was significant, ranging from 15 to 20 per cent of the final score. Most schools had a tailored student appraisal form that evaluates teachers in terms of teaching attitudes, teaching atmosphere, lesson preparation, teaching guiding methods, teaching activities, homework marking, active learning encouragement, timely feedback, teachers' care and overall teaching ability. Around half the schools (22) conducted student evaluation once per semester while four senior middle schools conducted them on a weekly basis. The most extreme case was a

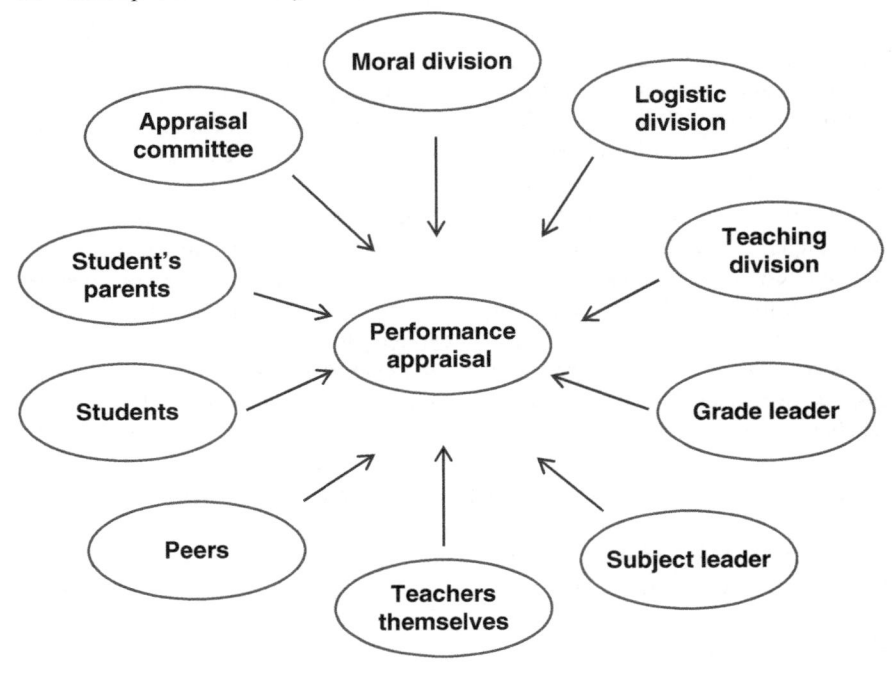

Figure 5.3 360-degree performance appraisal
Source: interview data (2011, 2012)

national model junior middle school (D1T2J3) in district 1 that conducted student evaluations at every lesson of every day, facilitated by a software system. Parent evaluation was usually conducted on a semester or yearly basis. The result only served as supporting evidence to supplement the overall process.

Evaluation procedure

A typical overall evaluation procedure at the end of each semester consists of the following eight steps that are outlined in Figure 5.4. Based on the accumulated evaluation information from students, parents, division leaders, subject leaders and grade leaders, an evaluation meeting is held. During this meeting, teachers give a small presentation regarding their performance and contribution. Most schools (31) requested teachers to write a performance report (around 300 words) before the presentation. Immediately after the presentations, peers assessments, subject leader evaluations, grade leader evaluations and appraisal committee evaluations were conducted.

After all the evaluations are finished, the appraisal committee calculates and decides the final grade based on a pre-determined weighting. For example, student's evaluation (15 to 20 per cent), teacher's self-evaluation (10 per cent), peer evaluation (15 to 30 per cent), subject leader evaluation (15 to 20 per cent), grade leader evaluation (15 to 20 per cent) and school appraisal committee (15 to 20 per cent). The final evaluation result is listed for public notification for five working days. Upon request from teachers, the appraisal committee can do a recheck and review. If no further queries are received during the five notification days, teachers are requested to sign the evaluation form, which will be later sent to the relevant education bureau for filing purposes. By signing the evaluation forms, teachers formally agree with, and accept, the evaluation results.

Even though the entire procedure seemed to be complicated and complex, most of the principals (33) suggested the evaluation procedure (evaluation by individual, peers, subject leaders, division leaders and the evaluation committee) was usually completed within 3 hours. The principal of D1T2J3 where student evaluation was conducted on a daily basis suggested that teacher evaluation in his school usually lasted about 1-hour. Two key reasons for this efficiency were highlighted by principals. The first was a detailed PA scheme with a comprehensive job description and evaluation criteria. The second reason was a sound record and file management system for the evaluation process. Principals suggested that,

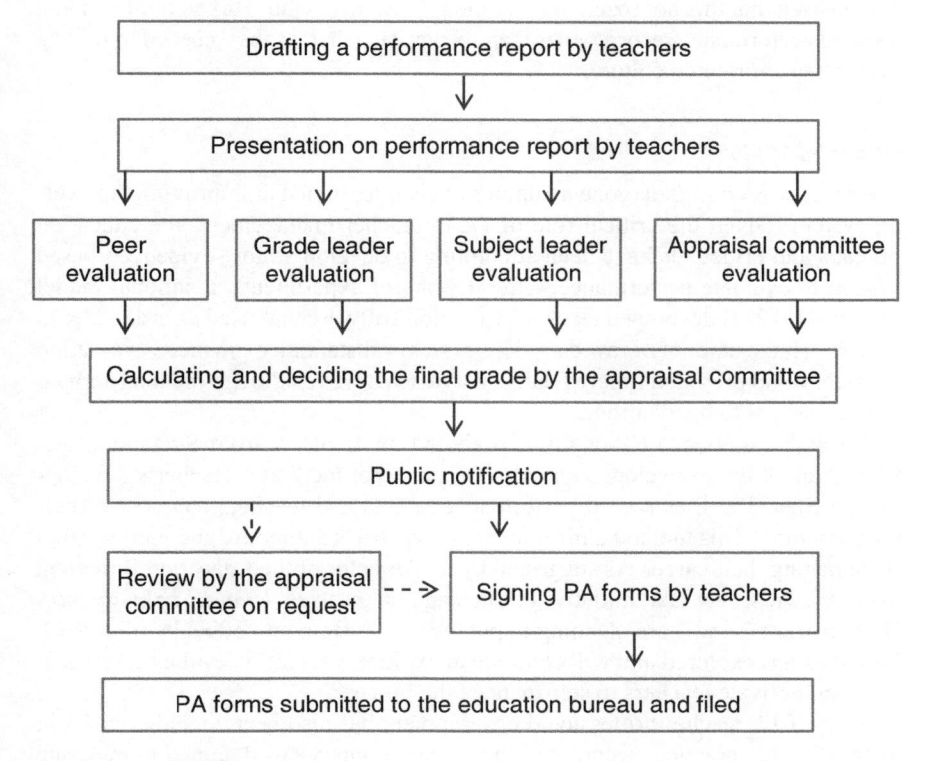

Figure 5.4 Appraisal procedure
Source: interview data (2011, 2012). PA, performance appraisal

based on the PA scheme and the record of their performance, teachers themselves could calculate their own grade even before the evaluation meeting. This approach is to 'let the facts speak for themselves' and contributes to the theme of objective, open, just, transparent and accurate (principals of D1S2, D1T2J3, D2V1 and D3T1J2).

The PA process and report serves as the basis of pay, awards, training, career advancement and further employment. There are four levels of ratings: outstanding, qualified, barely qualified and unqualified. The number of outstanding teachers should be no more than 30 per cent of teachers in a school. As being awarded 'outstanding' is a basic requirement for advancement while 'unqualified' suggests possible dismissal, teachers usually work hard to compete against each other for better performance rankings. To balance teachers' needs for career advancement, for example, by applying for professional titles, the majority of schools (36) adopted a paternalistic approach. Principals of these schools suggested that teachers at similar performance levels would take turns to receive the 'outstanding' award. Special favour is given to teachers who are applying for professional titles. This approach, according to the principals, helps build a cooperative, supportive and harmonious working environment. However, these principals also emphasised that this approach only applied to teachers who worked hard and had a sound performance record rather than to every teacher, as they needed to build a performance-oriented culture.

On-going changes

The teacher PA has undergone a number of changes aimed at improving the overall system. Given the critical role of PA in teacher management, the education bureaus and principals have been attempting to develop a more evidenced-based system to evaluate performance. After 3 years of experiments, a national model school (D1T2J3) developed teacher evaluation software that used a card reader to process a huge amount of raw data. This system substantially enhanced evaluation efficiency and provided timely feedback to teachers, even though the long-termed impact has yet to be identified.

Through experience nationally and abroad, particularly from Singapore, districts 2 and 3 have developed an online system that facilitates teacher's developmental files. The files record performance results and teachers can access their files any time. This method aims to increase teacher's autonomy and participation in managing their career. As suggested by the Director of the Education Bureau in district 2, 'teachers take initiatives to manage themselves' (*jiaoshi zizhu guanli*). Both districts 2 and 3 are planning to put the new system into effect by mid-2013. District 1 has explored and will continue to explore, a scientific evaluation system that can motivate teachers to self-manage the process.

From 2012, teacher professional development has also been included in PA in district 2. This practice, according to those being interviewed, aimed to motivate teachers to conduct on-going and life-long learning. The HR managers in districts 1 and 3 suggested that the inclusion of professional development is value adding and they would include it in the PA and performance-related pay (PRP) system in the near future.

Reward management

Prior to 2009, the pay system typically emphasised position, professional titles and tenure but generally ignored performance. This system did little to motivate teachers as it focused on 'whether teachers did their work' rather than 'how much they did and how well they did it' (HR director in district 2). To cultivate a performance-oriented culture, a new pay system, including a PRP component, was officially introduced in the Chinese education system in 2009 with the issue of the *Guidelines on Performance-related Pay in Elementary Education* (State Council 2008). This new pay system is underpinned by the following principles: (i) openness, justice, fairness and transparency; (ii) working is different from not working; (iii) working more is different from working less; (iv) working well is different from working badly; and (v) taking on more responsibility is different from taking on less responsibility (State Council 2008). This section explores how the new pay system was implemented in terms of pay increase, pay component practices, PRP, non-monetary reward and on-going changes.

Rapid pay increases

The new pay system emphasises the principle of 'Two Equals'. This approach regulates that within the same district, teacher's income should be *equivalent to* that of public servants and the income of teachers in rural areas should be *equivalent to* that of their counterparts in urban areas (State Council 2008). This principle is expected to contribute to a strong teaching workforce as well as the provision of quality and equitable education by ensuring decent and equitable income.

The new pay system has significantly increased teacher's pay. For example, since 2009, district 3 invested RMB 10, 20 and 30 billion in 2009, 2010 and 2011 respectively in teacher's pay and benefits. In 2011, the average annual pay increased by RMB 15,245, 15,884, 12,665 and 6,804 for primary schools, junior middle schools, senior middle and vocational schools respectively. In this district, the average pay was RMB 88,905, 93,185 and 98,745 for teachers in primary schools, junior middle schools and senior middle and vocational schools respectively. A similar situation was found in districts 1 and 2. By 2011, the annual pay in district 1 was RMB 89,000, 95,000 and 100,900 in primary schools, junior middle schools and senior middle schools. In district 2, the average annual pay was RMB 85,600 in primary schools, 90,400 in junior middle schools and 105,000 in senior middle and vocational schools. The increase in pay in the three districts reached around 20 per cent during 2010 and 2011. Since these pay increases, teacher's income is considerably higher than the average pay in the same area. As indicated in Table 5.4, average teacher's pay was at least double the average annual pay of the public sector in the three districts. Pay, together with benefits, make the teaching profession an attractive job option.

Table 5.4 Teacher's average pay and comparison in 2011 (RMB/year)

	District 1			District 2			District 3		
	PS	*JMS*	*SMVS*	*PS*	*JMS*	*SMVS*	*PS*	*JMS*	*SMVS*
Teacher	89,000	95,000	100,900	85,600	90,400	105,000	88,905	*93,185*	*98,745*
Others	42,663			41,066			41,209		

Source: interview data (2011). PS, primary school; JMS, junior middle school; SMVS, senior middle and vocational school; teacher: annual average pay; others: average annual pay of employees in the public sector

The substantial increase in pay has achieved the goal of attracting and retaining highly competent teachers. The pay increases also reflects the Chinese Government's determination to prioritise education development.

Pay components and practice

Teacher's pay under the new pay system comprises basic pay, PRP and benefits (see Table 5.5). The basic pay is sponsored by the central government. It includes post salary, qualification pay or scale salary, teaching years pay and a regional subsidy. The salary scale is based on professional titles and it accounts for the largest proportion of the basic pay. There are five scales for teachers in primary and middle schools (see Table 5.6). Table 5.6 also provides an example of the amount of basic pay in district 1 in 2012.

Contrary to the basic pay amount that is largely the same across the country for similar teachers, PRP is based on the economic development of a district or county. The county/district level government is responsible for the PRP funding and the implementation of PRP is one of the key criteria of the government's performance appraisal. The amount of PRP funding is formulated by the district/county's organisation department, education bureau and finance bureau based on the criteria that teachers' pay should be no less than the income of the local public servants. A government accountability system is undertaken to ensure the 'Two Equals' are being strictly implemented. PRP will be further examined later in this chapter, as it is the focus of the new pay system.

In addition to the basic pay and PRP, there are special subsidies and benefits (see Table 5.5). Special subsidies include the rural and remote subsidy and the famous teacher subsidy. The rural and remote subsidy is allocated by the central government to encourage teachers to work in less favoured places to provide quality education to all. The famous teacher subsidy is paid by the relevant government, for example, the famous teacher subsidy awarded by the town education bureau is paid by the town education bureau and the famous teacher subsidy awarded by the provincial education department is paid by the provincial education department. The higher the rank, the more money is received. For example, a famous teacher at a provincial level in district 2 in 2011 received an extra 24,000 RMB/year while one at a municipal level got 18,000 RMB/year, a district/county level 14,400 RMB/year and at a town level 12,000 RMB/year.

Table 5.5 Pay components and sponsorship

Pay components		Details	Sponsored by
1	Basic pay	Post pay Scale salary Tenure Regional subsidy	Central Government
2	Basic PRP	Position subsidies Holiday subsidies (seven holidays)	County/district government
3	Incentive PRP	Workload Attendance Daily job performance Teaching outcome (student test results and teachers' awards)	County/district government
4	Special subsidies	Rural and remote subsidies Famous teacher subsidies	Central Government Relevant local government
5	Benefits	Medical subsidy Social insurance subsidy Pension insurance subsidy Housing accumulation fund Housing subsidy Other common benefits	County/district government

Sources: interview data (2011, 2012) and State Council (2008). PRP, performance-related pay

Table 5.6 Classification of teacher salary scale and range of basic pay (RMB/year)

	Salary scale	Basic pay in 2011
1	Special grade in middle schools	33,600
2	Senior grade in middle schools Special grade in primary schools	27,600 27,600
3	First grade in middle schools Senior grade in primary schools	22,800 22,800
4	Second grade in middle schools First grade in primary schools	18,000 18,000
5	Third grade in middle schools Second grade in primary schools	15,600 15,600

Source: interview data (2012)

Benefits include an end of the year bonus, medical insurance subsidy, social insurance subsidy, pension insurance subsidy, housing accumulation fund, housing subsidy, free annual health check and other common benefits regulated by the Labour Law such as maternity leave and wedding leave. The medical insurance subsidy, social insurance subsidy, pension insurance subsidy, housing accumulation fund and housing subsidy are tax-free. An example of teacher's benefits in district 2 in 2011 and 2012 is provided in Table 5.7. There was an obvious increase in teacher's benefits from the year 2010 to 2011. A similar range of benefits was

Table 5.7 Teacher benefits in district 2 (RMB/year)

	End of the year bonus	Medical subsidy	Social insurance subsidy	Housing accumulation fund	Housing subsidy	Total
			2010			
PS	3,000	3,300	6,610	8,140	5,300	26,350
JMS	3,000	3,300	6,610	8,140	5,400	26,450
SMVS	3,000	3,300	6,610	10,700	5,400	29,010
			2011			
PS	4,500	3,300	7,150	10,320	6,100	31,370
JMS	4,500	3,300	7,150	10,320	6,200	31,470
SMVS	4,500	3,300	7,150	12,800	6,200	33,950

Source: interview data (2011, 2012). PS, primary school; JMS, junior middle school; SMVS, senior middle and vocational school

reported in districts 1 and 3 with district 1 slightly higher (around 3 per cent). Benefits, together with the pay listed earlier, and the two long paid holidays (summer holiday and winter holiday), have put the teaching profession among one of the most highly paid careers and highly sought after jobs in China.

Performance-related pay

In contrast to the widely held perception, PRP in the Chinese education sector does not relate solely to performance. It comprises two components: basic PRP and incentive PRP. Only the incentive PRP is related to performance. The basic PRP represents the larger part (70 per cent) and it is paid to teachers on a monthly basis. This suggests that every teacher received at least 70 per cent of PRP. This approach, according to the HR managers, helps the PRP concept to be accepted by teachers and aims to facilitate change to a performance-oriented culture.

The basic PRP includes position subsidies and holiday subsidies. The position subsidies under the basic PRP consist of two parts: the post subsidy of PRP and the position subsidy. Post subsidy is similar to scale salary that is based on professional titles. While the post subsidy of PRP applies to every teacher, position subsidy only refers to teachers occupying certain positions. A typical example of position pay in the three districts is provided in Table 5.8. As shown in the table, principals, who take on more responsibility, receive the highest subsidy. This approach reflects the principle of 'taking on more responsibility is different from taking on less responsibility' (HR managers in D1T1, D3 and D3T2). Principals in district 3 received the highest position pay compared to their counterparts in districts 1 and 2 in 2012. The holiday subsidies illustrate a traditional paternalistic management to show the schools' caring and recognition for teachers. Table 5.9 list the holiday subsidies in the three districts in 2010, 2011 and 2012. As shown in the table, holiday subsidies substantially increased

Table 5.8 Position pay in 2012 (RMB/year)

Position	Primary schools	JMS	SMVS
Principal	19,800–36,000	20,400–40,800	21,000–45,600
D principal	12,600–32,400	13,200–37,200	13,800–42,000
Director	10,200–30,000	10,800–34,800	11,400–39,600
D director	9,000–10,200	9,600–10,800	10,200–11,400
Grade leader	4,800–6,000	7,800–9,000	8,400–9,600
Subject leader	4,800–6,000	7,800–9,000	8,400–9,600
LP leader	N/A	2,400–3,600	2,400–3,600
Class teacher	3,600–4,800	6,000–7,200	7,800–9,000
D class teacher	1,200–4,400	N/A	N/A

Source: interview data (2011; 2012). JMS, junior middle schools; SMVS, senior middle and vocational schools; D, deputy; LP leader, lesson preparation leader

Table 5.9 Teacher's holiday subsidies (RMB/year)

	District 1			District 2			District 3		
Year	2010	2011	2012	2010	2011	2012	2010	2011	2012
NY	1,000	2,000	2,000	1,000	1,000	2,000	1,000	2,000	2,000
SF	2,000	3,000	4,000	2,000	3,000	3,000	2,000	3,000	3,000
MF	1,000	1,000	1,000	N/A	1,000	1,000	N/A	1,000	1,000
QF	1,000	1,000	1,000	N/A	1,000	1,000	N/A	1,000	1,000
TD	1,000	1,000	1,000	1,000	1,000	1,000	1,000	1,000	1,000
ND	1,000	1,000	2,000	1,000	1,000	2,000	1,000	1,000	2,000
LD	1,000	1,000	2,000	1,000	1,000	1,000	1,000	1,000	2,000
Total	8,000	11,000	14,000	6,000	10,000	12,000	6,000	11,000	13,000

Source: interview data (2011, 2012). NY, New Year; SF, Spring Festival; MF, Mid-Autumn Festival; QF, Qingming Festival; TD, Teacher's Day; ND, National Day; LD, Labour Day

from 2009 to 2012, reflecting the government's resolution to build a strong and highly effective teaching workforce. Compared with the other pay components, incentive PRP reflects more school variability as it is based on PA schemes of individual schools. The inclusion of workload aims to demonstrate the principle of 'working more is different from working less'. Teachers who do not take leave were granted the 'Full Attendance Bonus' in all the schools investigated in this study. Participants suggested that this approach was to give appreciation and recognition to teachers.

Teacher performance has the greatest weighting in the incentive PRP. Given the significance of teamwork in the education sector, a teamwork approach is highlighted. Teachers are rewarded on a group basis in terms of student test results. The majority of schools had special prizes that were granted to the outstanding subject team and outstanding grade team. By contrast, teachers who formed a 'small circle' or behaved inappropriately were penalised in some schools (13). Teachers who were deemed 'outstanding' receive an extra month's basic salary. Consistent with PA, the reward criteria is short-term and focuses on student test results. The gap between high performers and low performers is small in most primary schools and vocational schools, while in middle schools, particularly in senior middle school, it is relatively large. For example, the gap in D1S1, D2S2, D2S2, D3S1 and D3S2 reached around 16,000 RMB/year in 2012.

Perceptions of performance-related pay

The introduction of PRP aims to deepen personnel reforms highlighting effectiveness and efficiency. The majority of principals, particularly officers from the education bureaus, suggested that PRP has successfully changed the organisational culture from the 'wily old bird' to a performance-oriented style. They maintained that PRP was critically important to counteract the negative influence of the Cultural Revolution when people who worked hard tended to be despised and a lazy culture emerged (director of D2). Most principals (30) suggested that the old pay system in which 'everyone was eating within the same pot' (*chi daguofan*) was unfair to teachers who worked hard and to students who needed quality education. Even though it is impossible to have a perfect PRP scheme, PRP is considered necessary as 'we all have a scale in our mind which can tell the difference between teachers' (HR manager of D3).

Nevertheless, 14 principals and one HR manager in D1T2 were against PRP. These principals maintained that PRP harmed teamwork spirit and created conflicts among teachers. As PRP is allocated to individual schools based on the number of teachers, teachers who fail to get the average amount of money tend to think that their own money is taken by others and schools take their money to reward other teachers. Some resentful or cursing remarks from teachers have been heard, for example, 'it is fine for you to take my money, but I wish the money you take from me will be used to buy a coffin or medicine for you' (principal in D2T2P1). These principals suggested that teachers became more 'narrow-minded' and were not willing to take on responsibilities that were not rewarded. They indicated that there was some evidence to suggest that teacher's health and wellbeing deteriorated after the implementation of PRP. They tended to believe that 'teachers should not be pressed to work hard' (principals of D1T2J3 and D2T2P1) and 'if teachers are not happy, how can they cultivate happy students?' (principals of D1T1J2 and D1T2P1). They argued that 'teachers value their face more than money' and thus 'the attempt to use money to motivate teachers will surely fail' (principal of D1T2J3, D1T2P2 and D3T2P1). These principals tended to abandon PRP but turned to career development, for example, by providing outsourced training programmes and off-the-job training opportunities to motivate teachers.

Non-financial rewards

Intrinsic rewards are highlighted in the education sector. At the end of every study year, the education bureaus give various non-financial awards to teachers based on their performance, for example, the award of 'famous teachers', 'famous class teachers' and 'famous principals'. Honour certificates are accordingly provided for teachers. In addition, the education bureaus hold a variety of teachers' competitions every semester and the winners are awarded honour certificates. Every year immediately before Teacher Day, a merit commendation meeting that involves all teaching staff is held to recognise and honour high performing teachers.

At the school level, principals regard non-financial rewards as a significant way to motivate teachers. To award a model teacher who has outstanding job performance and serves as a model to others is the common way to recognise effort and good performance. A photo and examples of the model teacher's outstanding performance are usually posted on the public notice board. According to the participants, this is an effective way to signal the school's recognition for model teachers because students and their parents, as well as other teachers, know about the model teachers. Reputation is thus enhanced and this practice also motivates other teachers to learn from the model teachers.

Conclusion

Following the previous two chapters that explored the evolution of Chinese society and the education system, this chapter examined the HRM practices in the Chinese school system. Regarding education and the quality of the teaching professionals as a significant tool to develop the country, China has explored a variety of ways to hire, develop, retain and motivate highly qualified teachers. The Open Recruitment approach has turned teaching into a highly desirable profession with high entry criteria and a competitive comprehensive selection procedure manifesting the principles of openness, justice and fairness. All-inclusive and wide-ranging training programmes have been offered and on-going career development opportunities are provided. A 360-degree evaluation approach comprising students, parents, peers, leaders and the appraisal committee have been conducted following a stringent evaluation procedure. Pay is now more performance-oriented with the introduction of a performance-related pay scheme. The pay rate for teachers is competitive in the job market and extensive benefits are provided. Whether these changes have had significant impacts on teachers' job performance and students' quality of school life will be explored in the next chapter.

Notes

1 In China, teachers' career path follows a sequential ladder: new teachers – experienced teachers – key teachers – famous teachers. Key teachers are outstanding teachers while famous teachers are the elite teachers among key teachers. The process from new teachers to key teachers usually takes around 10 years, whereas the process from key

teachers to famous teachers often needs another 10 years. The famous teachers are the leading figures in their own fields of expertise.

2 The expression 'force five passes and slay six captains' means overcoming all the difficulties in the way.

3 Regional protection: because of the regional competition mechanism, leaders in a region with higher growth rates enjoy greater powers and better promotional opportunities. In order to perform better, leaders might not be willing to share resources with their counterparts in other regions and they might have some unique local policies and practices.

6 High performance work systems, teacher performance and students' quality of school life

Introduction

Chapters 4 and 5 have demonstrated that HPWS were prevalent in the Chinese school system. This chapter investigates the influence of HPWS on teachers' attitude and behaviour as well as students' quality of school life. Research has established the link between HPWS and organisational performance in terms of profitability, growth, market and financial returns, for example, Huselid (1995), Wright *et al.* (2003, 2005) and Combs *et al.* (2006). Yet, it is unclear how HRM affects non-profit organisations such as public schools. This chapter will commence with a theoretical discussion and the development of hypotheses. It then provides an overview of the research methods and the approach to data analysis. This is followed by sections outlining the findings and discussing their implications.

Contextual background

HRM and organisational performance: an ambiguous link

Research has increasingly recognised the role of HRM practices in improving organisational performance (Kehoe and Wright 2013). Empirical studies have established a significant link between HRM, in particular, HPWS and organisational financial and market outcomes (Huselid 1995; Wright *et al.* 2003, 2005; Combs *et al.* 2006). However, such a relationship has been questioned by a number of scholars (Paauwe 2009; Guest 2011; Thompson 2011). This ambiguity is compounded by the adoption of performance indicators, such as profits or sales revenue, that might be more influenced by internal and external factors that have a limited relationship with HRM practices (Paauwe 2009). As a consequence, a stronger grasp of discipline-specific performance indicators that can address the link between HRM practices and organisational performance, for example, service quality, is called for (Paauwe 2009; Richard *et al.* 2009; Guest 2011).

To address this knowledge gap, this study adopted students' quality of school life (QSL) as the indicator of organisational performance to test the HPWS-performance relationship in the Chinese school system. QSL is defined as 'a general sense of student wellbeing, determined strictly by school-related factors and educational experiences resulting from pupils' involvement in school life and their engagement in school climate' (Karatzias *et al.* 2001: 266). Analogous to service quality, QSL has been viewed as a significant indicator of teacher and school effectiveness (Leonard *et al.* 2004; Jimmieson *et al.* 2010). As teachers play a significant part in students' QSL, the relationship between HPWS and QSL is more direct and proximal than financial or market indicators. Thus, we argue that quality of school life is a better organisational performance indicator than the commonly adopted alternatives. In addition, we argue that the education sector is a better place to test the HRM–performance relationship due to the characteristics of the teaching profession, namely, a more direct and ongoing relationship between teachers and students and the complex role of teachers.

Research has shown that the HRM–performance relationship is sequential: first on employees' attitudes and behaviours, and, in turn, on organisational outcomes (Becker *et al.* 1997; Messersmith *et al.* 2011; Kehoe and Wright 2013). However, the vast majority of HRM research has focused on the impact of HRM on either employee or organisational outcomes (Lengnick-Hall *et al.* 2009). The lack of alignment of HR and organisational outcomes in HR research is 'problematic' and it has failed to explain the links between HRM and organisational performance (Jiang *et al.* 2012: 1265). This research therefore examines a comprehensive mediating model that simultaneously explores employee and organisational outcomes variables in the context of the school system. It provides a strong theoretically based understanding of HPWS impact on employees' attitudes (POS) and behaviours [in-role behaviour (IRB) and organisational citizenship behaviour (OCB)] and then subsequently on organisational performance (students' quality of school life). These relationships are illustrated in Figure 6.1.

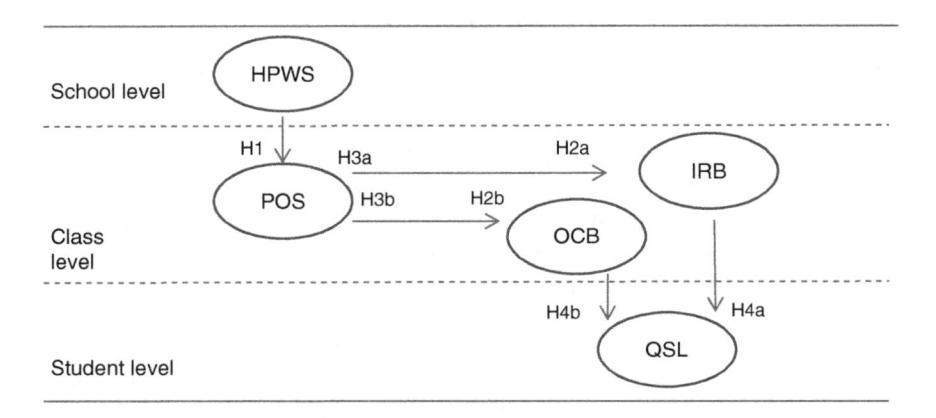

Figure 6.1 Conceptual research model

HPWS, High performance work systems; POS, perceived organisational support; IRB, in-role behaviour; OCB, organisational citizen behaviour; QSL, quality of school life

Our investigation of the HRM–performance relationship is underpinned by organisational support theory (Eisenberger *et al*. 1986; Shore and Shore 1995), social exchange theory (Blau 1964) and norms of reciprocity (Gouldner 1960). Organisational support theory suggests that employees will perceive a high level of organisational support if their organisation values their contributions, rewards increased work effort and cares about their wellbeing (Eisenberger *et al*. 1986, 2001). Perceived as a sign of support and care for employees, high performance work systems are expected to raise employees' sense of POS (Allen *et al*. 2003). The sense of support, through the mechanism of social exchange and norms of reciprocity, will obligate employees to reciprocate with increased effort that, in turn, benefits the organisation (Sun *et al*. 2007). As such, they are expected to have improved job performance, which, in turn, positively affects organisational outcomes (Liao *et al*. 2009).

We proposed a fully mediation model based on theoretical, methodological and empirical considerations. Theoretically, as noted earlier, the impact of HRM is sequential through employees' attitudes and behaviours to organisational outcomes (Becker *et al*. 1997; Nishii *et al*. 2008; Messersmith *et al*. 2011; Kehoe and Wright 2013). Methodologically, a full mediation model is more parsimonious (LeBreton *et al*. 2009). Empirically, POS has been found to be a mediator between HRM and employee performance in the service setting (Allen *et al*. 2003; Liao *et al*. 2009), whilst employee job performance, for example, OCB, has been found to be a significant mediator between employees' job attitudes and service quality (Nishii *et al*. 2008).

The uniqueness of the education sector

Compared to many other sectors, the education sector is arguably a more appropriate place to test the HRM–performance link due to the characteristics of the teaching profession, namely, a more direct relationship between teachers and students, the complex role of teachers and the blurring boundaries between IRB and OCB.

A direct relationship between teachers and students

It is argued that HRM plays a more significant role in the service sector than manufacturing organisations (Hitt *et al*. 2001). Compared to manufactured goods, services are less tangible (Chuang and Liao 2010). There are extensive direct contacts between employees and customers (Lau 2000; Bartel 2004). Experiencing mental and physical wellbeing, the service sector employees are likely to transfer their feeling to customers (Kandasamy and Ancheri 2009). A satisfied employee will tend to provide a better external service quality that, in turn, could result in increased customer satisfaction (Griffeth *et al*. 2000).

The education sector, being part of the service sector, is expected to experience a more critical impact of HRM. While products are involved in the service process in the profit-oriented service sector, no actual tangible products are included in the service procedure in the education sector. Largely, the service quality of teachers and students' learning experiences are the actual products. Quite often, students' learning experience depends on teachers' service quality as teachers represent the single largest school-related factor in the achievement of students (Cohen-Vogel 2011). For example, teaching activities rely on one main teacher in most elementary schools or on several different discipline teachers in high schools. Therefore, the more direct relationship between teachers and students makes the education sector an ideal place to investigate the relationship between HRM and organisational performance.

Complex role

A teacher's role is variable, non-routine and autonomous. It is complex and is a combination of various dimensions of teacher's ability, motivation and work situation (Rowan *et al.* 1997). Teacher's tasks include, but are not limited to, pedagogical and instructional delivery, giving feedback, classroom management, addressing the growing demands of standardised testing, handling students' disruptive behaviours, disciplining students and acting as a role model to students. In addition to the formal instructional role, teachers are expected to establish supportive and collaborative relationships with parents and professionally deal with administrators and colleagues (Jennings and Greenberg 2009).

According to contingency theory, organisation mechanisms vary in response to the nature of the work (Simpson 1985). In organisations where routine, unvarying and repetitive tasks are the key themes, high degrees of centralisation, formalisation and directive management styles are assumed to improve employees' productivity (Rowan *et al.* 1993). However, organisations that are characterised by variability, non-routine autonomous work will benefit from participative decision-making, collaborative problem solving and supportive organisational practices (Rowan *et al.* 1993). The education sector is categorised as having high professional autonomy, high emotional demands and high levels of work stress (Hoy and DiPaola 2005; Jimmieson *et al.* 2010). As HRM strives to elicit employee commitment and involvement, it is proposed that HRM can explain a large part of superior performance.

Unclear boundary of IRB and OCB

IRB and OCB are two significant aspects of employees' work behaviours (Borman and Motowidlo 1993; Christensen and Whiting 2009). They contribute to organisational effectiveness (Grant and Mayer 2009) and competitiveness (Podsakoff *et al.* 2009). IRB refers to behaviours expected of employees, largely based on job descriptions and commonly accepted norms (Wright *et al.* 2003). There is extensive organisational monitoring of IRB (Chen *et al.* 2009), which is normally assessed through formal performance appraisal (Borman and Motowidlo 1997). High IRB is formally rewarded and failure in its engagement can be penalised (Organ 1988; Borman and Motowidlo 1993). This kind of behaviour serves as a significant predictor of job performance (Ilies *et al.* 2007; Whiting *et al.* 2008).

OCB is also known as extra-role performance and prosocial organisational behaviour (Christensen and Whiting 2009). OCB refers to individual behaviour that 'is discretionary, not directly or explicitly recognised by the formal reward system' (Organ 1988: 4). OCB involves actions of being helpful and cooperative, tolerating inconveniences at work, taking on additional responsibilities and keeping up with organisational affairs (Organ *et al.* 2006). Unlike IRB, participants of OCB can choose to perform or withhold such behaviours without the concerns of sanctions or formal incentives (Organ 1990). OCB is not usually recognised by the organisations' reward system; nevertheless, it is necessary for organisations' long-term survival and growth (Moorman and Harland 2002).

Teaching tasks are considered to be ambiguous and uncertain (Jimmieson *et al.* 2010). The boundary of teaching is vague and the input-process-outcome connection is unclear (Oplatka 2006; Elstad *et al.* 2012). OCB in the education sphere is desirable because the nature of teacher's jobs cannot be systematically prescribed in job descriptions or contracts (DiPaola and Tschannen-Moran 2001; Sesen and Basim 2012). In fact, many teacher's professional activities and behaviours are beyond their work-defined roles (Somech and Bogler 2002; Oplatka 2006). For example, teachers often help students after school and continue to do their work after office hours (Hoy and DiPaola 2005). Quite often, teachers are expected to display additional attentiveness, caring and emotional comfort to students, which is often regarded as discretional and non-obligatory (Oplatke 2006). Consequently, successfully performing job tasks is necessary but is an insufficient condition for teaching effectiveness (Somech and Drach-Zahavy 2000; Bogler and Somech 2004). Instead, OCB plays a critical role in school effectiveness (Hoy and DiPaola 2005; Jimmieson *et al.* 2010; Elstad *et al.* 2012) and is a 'fundamental component' of that effectiveness (Somech and Drach-Zahavy 2000). As such, both IRB and OCB are critical for organisational effectiveness in the education sector.

Hypotheses development

HPWS and POS

As a strategic approach to HRM, HPWS aims to enhance organisational performance by improving employee motivation, participation, involvement and commitment (Aryee *et al.* 2013; Posthuma *et al.* 2013). The term, HPWS, is generally synonymous with 'high-commitment work systems', 'high-involvement work systems', 'high commitment management', 'high involvement management' and 'progressive human resource management' (Beltrán-Martín *et al.* 2008: 1012; Jiang *et al.* 2012: 1264). POS is defined as 'the global belief held by an employee that the organization values his/her contributions and cares about their wellbeing' (Eisenberger *et al.* 1986: 501). It is viewed as an assurance that the organisation will support and help employees in difficult times (Rhoades and Eisenberger 2002).

Based on organisational support theory, employees would perceive a high level of organisational support if their employer values their contributions and cares about their wellbeing (Eisenberger *et al.* 1986, 2001). HPWS are perceived as a sign of employer support and a signal of an organisation's willingness to establish a long-term exchange relationship with its employees (Allen *et al*. 2003). As a result, HPWS are expected to be positively linked to employees' POS. Similarly, if schools adopt HPWS, teachers are expected to have a high sense of POS. Hence, it is proposed that:

Hypothesis 1: HPWS are positively related to teachers' POS

Teachers' POS, IRP and OCB

As discussed earlier, employee job performance is a multidimensional construct that can be broadly divided into IRB and OCB (Borman and Motowidlo 1993). Given the complexity of work performance in schools, successfully performing job tasks is a necessity but insufficient condition for school effectiveness (Somech and Drach-Zahavy 2000; Bogler and Somech 2004). In this context, OCB also plays a critical role (Hoy and DiPaola 2005; Jimmieson *et al*. 2010; Elstad *et al*. 2012) and it is a fundamental component for school effectiveness (Somech and Drach-Zahavy 2000). As such, we included both IRB and OCB in this mediating model.

Utilising social exchange theory (Blau 1964) and the norm of reciprocity (Gouldner 1960), an organisation's positive and beneficial actions towards employees are expected to contribute to a high quality exchange relationship (Settoon *et al*. 1996). HPWS are likely to arouse employees' perception of a supportive environment by providing job security, extensive skills training, advancement opportunity, regular unbiased performance feedback and fair and attractive rewards (Kehoe and Wright 2013). Feeling supported, employees are likely to value their organisation and they are subsequently willing to engage in positive and beneficial reciprocation to the organisation (Dawley *et al*. 2010; Tremblay *et al*. 2010). This exchange relationship, in turn, will create an obligation among employees to reward an organisation with loyalty, citizenship and performance (Dawley *et al*. 2010). The positive relationship between POS and IRB, and OCB, has been demonstrated by empirical studies (Riggle *et al*. 2009; Tremblay *et al*. 2010). These results were also supported by a meta-analysis based on 20 performance studies (Rhoades and Eisenberger 2002). The same result is also expected in the school system because teachers with high POS are found to be more satisfied intrinsically and extrinsically (Bogler and Nir 2012). Consequently, it is hypothesised that:

Hypothesis 2a: teachers' POS is positively related to their IRB
Hypothesis 2b: teachers' POS is positively related to their OCB

Based on hypothesis 1 and hypothesis 2a and 2b, it is proposed that:

Hypothesis 3a: teachers' POS mediates the relationship between HPWS and their IRB
Hypothesis 3b: teachers' POS mediates the relationship between HPWS and their OCB

Teachers' IRB, OCB and students' QSL

QSL focuses on the non-intellectual impacts of schooling experience to enhance students' wellbeing and promote academic outcomes (Caprara *et al*. 2006). As schooling constitutes a major part of student life, student's QSL deserves to be extensively explored to enhance education quality and effectiveness (Thien and Razak 2013). Teachers play a critical part in students' educational attainment and QSL (Caprara *et al*. 2006). Research results generated from different countries have shown that the classroom effect is more critical than school impact in shaping students' learning outcomes (Kyriakides *et al*. 2009). Student achievement relies heavily on the quality of instruction at the class level (Thoonen *et al*. 2011). Students' quality of school life is largely determined by their classroom experiences delivered by their teachers (Jimmieson *et al*. 2010). Teachers set the tone of the classroom, create supportive and encouraging relationships with their students, design lessons aimed at enhancing student strengths and abilities, establish and implement behavioural guidelines that promote intrinsic motivation and act as a role model in exhibiting OCB (Jennings and Greenberg 2009). These teacher core-task behaviours are strong predictors of student's quality of school life (Epstein and McPartland 1976; Kong 2008). As such, it is proposed that:

> *Hypothesis 4a: teachers' IRB is positively related to their students' quality of school life*

Teachers with high OCB are much more likely to work harder to introduce new ways of learning to arouse greater intrinsic interests within students (Oplatka 2006). They are also likely to set goals that are more ambitious for themselves and focus more on students' development (Hoy and DiPaola 2005). Teachers with enthusiasm and warmth towards students help build good relationships between teachers and students that are perceived as important in promoting pupil motivation, feelings of safety and wellbeing (Tangen 2009). Furthermore, teachers with high OCB tend to be more engaged in extracurricular activities, which help promote student achievement (Tangen 2009). They are more supportive of students' learning, which, in turn, influences motivation and classroom performance of the students (Jennings and Greenberg 2009). These teachers tend to provide more emotional support to students that leads to greater student motivation, interest, enjoyment, engagement and less deviant behaviours (Brackett *et al*. 2011). Hence, it is proposed that:

> *Hypothesis 4b: teachers' OCB is positively related to students' quality of school life*

Method

Sample and procedure

We collected data from 63 schools (six primary schools, 30 junior middle schools, 19 senior middle schools and eight vocational schools) in the districts 1, 2, and 3 of Guangdong province in the period from November 2012 to January 2013. Endorsement letters with permission to involve schools and teachers in the study were obtained from the district education bureaus. To minimise common method variance, we collected data from three different sources, namely, class teachers, their immediate supervisors and their students. Class teachers (*banzhuren*) spend more time and have more responsibilities for their students and they are expected to have more influence on their students' learning experience and their QSL. Consequently, they were chosen to be the research respondents. In middle and vocational schools, class teachers of Grades 1 and 2 were included whilst their counterparts in Grade 3 were excluded, as they were busy preparing for exams (middle schools) or job searches (vocational schools). In primary schools, class teachers of years five and six were invited to participate, as their students were between 11 and 12 years old and were regarded as old enough to independently complete questionnaires concerning their QSL. A form of stratified random sampling was conducted with the student participants. In China, all students are assigned a class number and those with the number of 5, 15, 25, 35 and 45 of each of the participating class teachers were selected for this research. Class teachers provided information on HPWS practices and POS while their supervisors answered questions regarding the teachers' IRB and OCB. Students completed questionnaires concerning their QSL.

One-week prior to the survey, the class teachers and their immediate supervisors received a letter from the HRM manager of the local Education Bureau. This letter explained the significance and purposes of the research and asked for their voluntary participation. To maximise the response rate and to enhance data quality, the first author gave a briefing and answered teachers' questions and concerns during weekly school meetings. After the briefing, each respondent class teacher received a package including the three sets of questionnaires: one for themselves, one for their immediate supervisors and five questionnaires for the selected students. The respondents then forwarded the relevant questionnaire to their immediate supervisors and selected students. Each questionnaire was marked with a code for identification and data analysis purposes.

Participants were requested to put the completed questionnaire in a locked collection box placed at the exit of the school building. Due to the strong support received from the education authorities and school principals, as well as approval for participants to use school time to complete the survey, the response rate was high. Out of the 1,230 distributed sets of questionnaires, 1,186 were completed by class teachers, 1,165 from their supervisors and 5,839 from their students. This represented a 96.4 per cent, 94.7 per cent and 94.9 per cent response rate for class teachers, supervisors and students respectively. As such, non-response bias was not a major issue in our study. After excluding the missing data and unmatched questionnaires, 1,051 completed and usable sets of questionnaires were adopted for data analysis. Among the class teachers, 143, 333, 496 and 79 were from vocational schools, senior middle schools, junior middle schools and primary schools respectively. Most respondents were female (63 per cent) and married (74.9 per cent). The majority was from primary and junior middle schools (54.7 per cent), had a bachelor degree (89.3 per cent), were under 40 years of age (82 per cent) and had worked for less than 2 decades (56.3 per cent).

Measures

We adopted previously published and validated measures for our study. The questionnaires were originally designed in English and then were translated into Chinese by the first author who is bilingual in Chinese and English and who has had teaching experience in China. Back-translation was conducted by two academics who were also bilingual and had overseas experience working at a major Chinese university. Following this procedure, both the Chinese and English versions were checked by an academic who has education and management experience within an Australian university. A pilot study, comprising 20 teachers, their immediate supervisors and their students, was undertaken prior to the survey. These participants were from a primary, a junior, a senior middle and a vocational school in China. They were requested to evaluate the questionnaires on issues such as relevance, clear instructions and wording. The pilot study confirmed that the questionnaires were suitable, although minor changes to wording and expression were needed to fit the Chinese school system. Seven-point Likert scales ranging from 'strongly disagree (value of 1) to 'strongly agree' (value of 7) were employed.

Independent variable

A 17-item scale from Sun *et al.* (2007), which was developed in the Chinese context, was used to measure HPWS. This scale represented the key goals of the strategic HPWS approach and included the most popular HR practices, such as selection and recruitment, training and development, job description, performance appraisal and reward (Boselie *et al.* 2005; Paauwe 2009). A sample item for recruitment and selection was 'great effort is taken to select the right person'. For training and development: 'Extensive training programmes are provided for teachers'. For job description: 'The duties in this job are clearly defined'. For performance appraisal: 'Performance is more often measured with objective quantifiable results'. For reward management: 'Teachers' reward in this school is competitive in the job market'.

HPWS was conceptualised as a second-order construct in this study, as confirmed by Takeuchi *et al.* (2007), Beltrán-Martín *et al.* (2008), Wu and Chaturvedi (2009), Aryee *et al.* (2013) and Hartog *et al.* (2013). The confirmatory factor analysis showed acceptable fit: χ^2 (115)=743.07, p<0.001, CFI=0.91, TLI=0.90, RMSEA=0.07 and SRMR=0.07. These parameters met the commonly accepted cut-off value for CFI and TLI (0.90) as well as SRMR and RMSEA (0.08) (Hu and Bentler 1999). The Cronbach's alpha for the four factors were 0.81, 0.88, 0.73 and 0.77 respectively. The overall Cronbach's alpha value was 0.91.

Mediating variables

POS was measured by seven items adopted from Eisenberger *et al.* (1986). The word 'organisation' was changed to 'school' to suit the teaching profession. Sample items included 'my school strongly considers my goals and values' and 'my school cares about my opinions'. The results indicated a good fit: $\chi^2(14)=56.128$, p<0.001, CFI=0.99, TLI=0.98, RMSEA=0.05 and SRMR=0.02. The value of the Cronbach's alpha was 0.91.

IRB was measured by a six-item scale developed by Williams and Anderson (1991). In order to suit the educational context, the wording 'the employee' was changed to 'the class teacher'. Sample items included 'the class teacher adequately completes assigned duties' and 'the class teacher fulfils responsibilities specified in job description'. The result indicated a good fit: $\chi^2(9)=52.43$, p<0.001, CFI=0.97, TLI=0.96, RMSEA=0.07 and SRMR=0.03.The value of the Cronbach's alpha was 0.85.

Teachers' OCB was measured by the scale developed by Jimmieson *et al.* (2010) specifically for teachers. This research focused on student-related activities (seven items) that are considered a critical component of OCB in the education context (Somech and Drach-Zahavy 2000; DiPaola and Tschannen-Moran 2001). The student-directed behaviour is similar to the concept of customer-directed OCB and includes both factors of conscientiousness and pro-activity (Jimmieson *et al.* 2010). Sample items included 'the class teacher spends free time planning interactive learning activities' and 'the class teacher stays back at lunch time to assist students'. The fit was good: $\chi^2(14)=80$, p<0.001, CFI=0.96, TLI=0.94, RMSEA=0.07 and SRMR=0.03. The value of Cronbach's alpha was 0.84.

Dependent variables

Students' QSL was measured by the scale developed by Kong (2008) that was validated in Hong Kong with 19,477 students. This measure was based on a Chinese version of the original Australian scale. This scale includes five dimensions: teacher–student relationship, sense of achievement, social integration, adventurous experience and general satisfaction. A sample item for the teacher–student relationship dimension was 'my teacher guides me patiently'. For the sense of achievement dimension: 'I achieve a satisfactory standard in my work'. For the social integration dimension: 'I get on well with the other students in my class'. For the adventurous experience dimension: 'The work we do is interesting' and for the general satisfaction dimension: 'I get enjoyment from being there'. The fit was exceptionally good: $\chi^2(424)=2,154.27$, p<0.001, CFI=0.97, TLI=0.97, RMSEA=0.03 and SRMR=0.02. The Cronbach's alpha coefficient for the five factors was 0.91, 0.83, 0.90, 0.85 and 0.87 respectively. The overall alpha value was 0.97.

Control variables

A number of demographic variables have been found to be related to an employee's work attitudes and behaviour (Judge *et al.* 2001). As a result, teachers' age, gender and education were treated as control variables at the class level. Age was the actual age reported by teachers. Gender was coded as (1=male, 2=female). Education was coded as (1=diploma or under; 2=bachelor degree; 3=master degree or above). At the school level, the type of school classified by level (lowest to highest), was controlled for (1=primary; 2=junior middle; 3=senior middle; 4=vocational).

Analyses

As this study involved students nested in classes and classes nested in schools, the data collected were multilevel, or hierarchical, in nature. Failure to identify the nested nature of the data will lead to biased parameter estimation and it will affect the stability and validity of the research findings (Heck and Thomas 2009; Byrne 2012). Because multilevel data violate the assumption of independence of observations, traditional multiple liner regression approaches are not suitable (Preacher *et al*. 2011) as they are unable to capture any cross-level interactions that could assess the impact of an organisation on individuals or vice versa (Heck and Thomas 2009; Byrne 2012). Instead, a multilevel analysis technique is required for nested data. However, even though the data were collected from within a hierarchical structure, a multilevel analysis is not necessary if there is little or no similarity among individuals within groups and little variation between different groups (Heck and Thomas 2009; Byrne 2012). To test the suitability of the multilevel analysis, the intraclass correlation (ICC1) and the reliability of the mean (ICC2) were calculated. ICC1 illustrates the proportion of variance in different organisations and ICC2 shows the stability of means of organisational-level variables (Bliese 2000). As shown in Table 6.1, these values were greater than the cut-off rate of 0.12 for ICC1 and 0.70 for ICC2 (James 1982). These results provided support for the adoption of multilevel modelling analysis techniques for this study (Byrne 2012).

We used multilevel structural equation modelling, adopting Mplus software (version 7; Muthén and Muthén, Los Angeles, CA, USA) to test our hypotheses because it produces more accurate estimates (Preacher *et al*. 2010, 2011). In multilevel studies, it is crucial to clearly define the levels at which predictor variables operate (Mathieu and Taylor 2007). Even though HRM is derived from organisational policies that aim to shape various work relationships (Mossholder *et al*. 2011), individual employees might have different perceptions of the HRM practices (Nishii *et al*. 2008; Hartog *et al*. 2013). As such, employee-rated HPWS was

Table 6.1 Values of intraclass correlation and the reliability of the mean

Variable	HPWS	POS	IRB	OCB	QSL
ICC1	0.40	0.58	0.42	0.43	0.49
ICC2	0.92	0.91	0.83	0.84	0.97

ICC1, intraclass correlation; ICC2, reliability of the mean; HPWS, high performance work systems; POS, perceived organisational support; IRB, in-role behaviour; OCB, organisational citizen behaviour; QSL, quality of school life treated as a class level variable (level 2), which had both class level and school level impacts. This approach is consistent with Hartog *et al.* (2013). In the same way, POS, IRB and OCB were conceptualised as class level variables, as they all varied both at the class and school levels. Thus, relationships among HPWS, POS, IRB and OCB were modelled at both the school and class level. Student's QSL is a perceived variable measured at the student level that also can vary between individuals in the class level. Based on the approach of Preacher (2011), student's QSL was modelled at the class level.

It is suggested that 'having too many variables in the model may actually create problems in modelling and interpreting the meaning of the between-unit difference' (Heck and Thomas 2009: 65). Due to the large size of the full model in this study, it was not possible to run it in Mplus without performing parcelling of some factors. A homogenous parcelling approach was used, in which each parcel is the average of the items that load on the same first-order factor. This practice is 'the best choice of composite formation' (Landis *et al.* 2000: 190). Subsequently, four items that represented the four dimensions of HPWS were used for the estimation of structural equation models. QSL was measured by 31 items collected from students. There were five students per teacher. A summated score for the entire QSL scale for each student was created. Based on 'isomorphism between a random intercepts multi-level model and a restricted confirmatory factor analysis model with unit factor loadings' (Preacher 2011: 699), a restricted CFA with unit factor loading to bring the QSL to level 2 (class level) was subsequently conducted (see Preacher 2011).

In conducting multilevel analysis, rescaling or centring predictors is recommended because failing to do so might lead to uninterpretable results (Aguinis *et al.* 2011). Centring variables is a helpful way to counteract multicollinearity and multilevel models with centred variables are likely to be more stable (Field 2009). There are two ways of centring: grand mean and group mean centring. The grand mean is usually used for variables at the higher level (Enders and Tofighi 2007; Aryee *et al.* 2013). Following this logic, HPWS, POS, IRB and OCB were grand mean centred. QSL was group mean centred as this is suitable for exploring interactions between level 2 variables and can improve the power to detect the cross-level interaction effect (Enders and Fofighi 2007; Aguinis *et al.* 2011).

Results

The measurement models

To examine the discriminant validity of the variables, a series of confirmatory factor analyses were undertaken. The hypothesised five-factor model (HPWS, POS, IRB, OCB and QSL) was compared with various alternative models, namely, a four-factor model, where HPWS and POS were combined, another four-factor model with IRB and OCB combined and a three-factor model (HPWS combined with POS and IRB combined with OCB). The results showed that the default five-factor model had the best-fit indices and the best CFI, TLI, RMSEA and SRMR results (see Table 6.2). Thus, the hypothesised five-factor model was

Table 6.2 Model comparison

Model	Description	χ^2	df	χ^2diff	CFI	TLI	RMSEA	SRMR
Default model	Hypothesised 5-factor model	1,044*	131		0.91	0.91	0.05	0.07
Four-factor model	HPWS and POS combined	5,208*	859	4,164*	0.81	0.80	0.07	0.06
Four-factor model	IRB and OCB combined	4,853*	855	3,809*	0.82	0.81	0.07	0.09
Three-factor model	HPWS and POS and IRB and OCB combined	7,055*	862	6,011*	0.73	0.71	0.08	0.08

df, degree of freedom; χ^2diff, chi-square difference; CFI, comparative fit index; TLI, Tucker-Lewis fix index; RMSEA, root mean square error of approximation; SRMR, standardised root mean square residual. *Correlation is significant at the 0.01 level (2-tailed)

supported. The chi-square differences between the default model and the first four-factor model, the second four-factor model and the three-factor model were 4164, 3809 and 6011 respectively (p<0.001) showing substantial differences among these models. Therefore, the distinctiveness and construct validity of the variables was demonstrated.

Descriptive statistics

The means, standard deviations and correlations among all variables at the single level are provided in Table 6.3. The means and standard deviations were calculated with SPSS software (IBM Corp., Armonk, NY, USA) and the correlations of the full latent variables model (five-factor model) were undertaken with Mplus software. As shown in the table, HPWS, POS, IRB, OCB and QSL were positively correlated. The results provided preliminary support for the hypothesised model. As HPWS and POS were highly correlated (0.74), an average variance extracted estimate for HPWS and POS was calculated following the suggestion of Fornell and Larcker (1981). To fulfil the requirements of the distinctiveness of HRM and POS, the variance captured by HPWS and POS needed to be higher than 0.50 and the shared variance of both variables [squared correlation of HPWS and POS (0.74)=0.55]. The extracted average variance estimates for HPWS and POS were 0.57 and 0.59, which exceeded the benchmark of 0.50 and the shared variance of 0.55. Thus, the extracted variance estimate results and the previous model comparison parameters showed that HRM and POS were conceptually related, yet distinct.

Hypotheses testing

After the necessary preliminary steps to facilitate the analyses were performed, one full model that included all the hypothesised relationships at the specified theoretical levels was tested. This model fitted the data adequately: χ^2 (676)=1,757,

Table 6.3 Means, standard deviation and correlations of key variables

	Mean	SD	1	2	3	4	5	6	7	8
1. ST	2.51	0.82	–							
2. HPWS	5.29	1.45	−0.04	–						
3. Gender	1.63	0.48	−0.16**	.01	–					
4. Age	34.2	6.55	−0.12**	−0.06	−0.05	–				
5. Education	2.02	0.33	0.18**	0.01	−0.00	−0.11**	–			
6. POS	4.92	1.48	−0.06	0.74**	−0.02	−0.11*	0.03	–		
7. IRB	5.93	1.90	−0.03	0.50**	−0.01	−0.01	0.00	0.49**	–	
8. OCB	5.38	0.94	−0.03	0.24**	0.00	−0.01	0.00	0.29**	0.30**	–
9. QSL	5.71	1.40	−0.27**	0.32**	0.08*	0.03	0.03	0.35**	0.43**	0.19**

ST, school type; HPWS, high performance work systems. POS, perceived organisational support; IRB, in-role behaviour; OCB, organisational citizen behaviour; QSL, quality of school life. *Correlation is significant at the 0.05 level (2-tailed). **Correlation is significant at the 0.01 level (2-tailed)

$p < 0.001$, CFI=0.93, TLI=0.92, RMSEA=0.04, SRMR within=0.05 and SRMR between=0.11. Hypothesis 1 proposed that HRM would positively predict teachers' POS. HRM and POS were treated as within level variables that had impacts on both within and between levels. Consequently, these relationships were modelled at both within and between levels. HRM positively and significantly predicted teachers' POS (0.71 within and 0.92 between, $p < 0.001$) at both levels. Thus, in schools where the teachers rated HPWS more highly, POS was also higher. Similarly, when teachers' perceived higher levels of HRM, their POS was also higher. As such, hypothesis 1 was supported.

Hypothesis 2 proposed that teachers' POS would be positively related to their IRB (H2a) and OCB (H2b). The result showed that teachers' POS was positively and significantly related to their IRB (0.42 within and 0.64 between, $p < 0.001$) and OCB (0.18 within and 0.58 between, $p < 0.001$) at both the school and individual levels. The significant relationship at the individual level suggested that when teachers had higher levels of POS, their IRB and OCB were correspondingly higher. The significant relationship at the school level indicated that teachers' job performance was higher in schools where teachers experienced higher level of POS than that for schools where teachers perceived lower POS. As such, both H2a and H2b were supported. The result also showed that the impact of POS on IRB was found to be higher than that on OCB. This outcome indicated that teachers' POS was more related to their IRB than their OCB.

Hypothesis 3 suggested that HPWS would indirectly affect teacher's IRB (H3a) and OCB (H3b) through their POS. The previous results suggested that the indirect relationships were present at both the school and teacher levels. HPWS had a significant and positive impact on teachers' POS, which, in turn, positively and significantly predicted their IRB and OCB. The Sobel test showed that the indirect effects of POS was significant for IRB (0.30 within and 0.59 between, $p < 0.01$) and for OCB (0.13 within and 0.53 between, $p < 0.01$). As such, teachers' perceived

HPWS indirectly affected their IRB and OCB through the mediation of their POS. Therefore, H3a and H3b were supported. The significance of these indices at both teacher and school level suggested that if teachers perceived higher levels of HPWS and POS, their job performance would be better and schools would enjoy higher levels of employees' job performance.

H4a and H4b hypothesised a direct effect of teachers' IRB and OCB on their students' quality of school life. As outlined earlier, the analyses concerning students' quality of school life were modelled at the teacher level following the procedure of Preacher (2011). The result indicated that teachers' IRB positively and directly influenced their students' quality of school life. Thus, in classes where teachers demonstrated higher levels of IRB, their students' quality of school life was improved. As such, H4a was supported. The Sobel test indicated that the indirect effect of IRB between POS and QSL was significant for IRB (0.13, p<0.01). This finding, together with the indirect effect of HRM and IRB, indicated that HRM indirectly and positively affected teachers' in-role performance, which, in turn, influenced their student's QSL. However, contrary to H4b, the direct relationship between teacher's OCB and their students' QSL was not significant (0.06, p>0.05). As a result, H4b was not supported.

Given the non-significant direct effect of OCB on QSL, a *post hoc* model was run to test the indirect influence of OCB on QSL via IRB. This model also fitted the data well: χ^2 (676)=1,745, p<0.001, CFI=0.93, TLI=0.92, RMSEA=0.04, SRMR within=0.05 and SRMR between=0.12. As this model shared the same degrees of freedom with the hypothesised model, the chi-square difference test could not be computed. However, this *post hoc* model had slightly better fit indexes in terms of Akaike information criterion and Bayesian information criterion. Consequently, the *post hoc* model fitted slightly better than the hypothesised model. The result showed that OCB was positively related to IRB, which subsequently influenced students' QSL. The Sobel test showed that the indirect effect, even though not substantial, was significant (0.04, p<0.01). This finding suggested that teacher's OCB, which indirectly resulted from HRM, also influenced their students' QSL by contributing to their IRB.

Discussion

This study investigated the relationship between HPWS and students' QSL. It answered the call from Paauwe (2009), Richard *et al.* (2009) and Guest (2011) to adopt performance indicators that are more proximal and direct than other indicators such as financial or market performance (Paauwe 2009).

This study extended HR research to the education sector and provided empirical support in this setting for previous HR research. The majority of HRM research has been conducted in the manufacturing setting (Batt 2002; Sun *et al.* 2007; Liao *et al.* 2009) notwithstanding that education has been regarded as 'the cornerstone and pillar' of economic growth and development (Nguni *et al.* 2006: 145). Education exerts significant impacts on students, parents, local communities and even the competitiveness and stability of the whole society (OECD 2005b). Despite the education section being one of the largest professions in the world (Jimmieson *et al*. 2010), it has failed to attract any substantial interest from management scholars (Ouchi *et al*. 2005). The features of schools are considerably different from the characteristics of the manufacturing industry and the profit-driven service sector (Cochran-Smith and Fries 2001; Berry 2004). We argued that investigating the on-going and interpersonal employee–client relationships in the education sector might provide deeper insights than can be obtained from the transactional service sector (Jimmieson *et al*. 2010). As such, this study fills a significant research gap.

The HRM–performance link involves a cross-level impact which comprises HRM practices at the organisational level, which influences employees' work attitudes and behaviours at the individual level, and in turn, influence outcomes at organisational level (Paauwe 2009). For a better understanding of management and organisational phenomena, a multilevel framework is beneficial and necessary (Wright and Haggerty 2005; Richard *et al*. 2009; Nyberg *et al*. 2014). In particular, multilevel structural equation modelling is desirable and called for as it produces more accurate estimates (Preacher *et al*. 2010, 2011). This study contributes to a more sophisticated analysis by adopting multilevel structural equation modelling to analyse the data. This study is also innovative as it utilises three-level structural equation modelling and a large sample incorporating a variety of schools.

It has been argued that extensive research over the last 2 decades has been unable to prove a definitive link between HRM and organisational performance (Paauwe 2009; Guest 2011) and that the HRM–performance relationship remains uncertain (Guest *et al*. 2003; Wall and Wood 2005; Wright *et al*. 2005; Kehoe and Wright 2013), 'inconclusive' (Hesketh and Fleetwood 2006: 678) and 'should be treated with caution' (Wall and Wood 2005: 454). Conducted in the school system, where the relationship between employees and organisational outcome is more direct and proximal, this study furthers our understanding of the ambiguous HRM–performance relationship. It demonstrates that HRM does significantly contribute to organisational performance. Adopting a comprehensive model that simultaneously explored the employee and organisational outcomes, this study confirms the concept of sequential HRM–performance relationships: first on employees' attitudes and behaviours and subsequently on organisational outcomes (Becker *et al*. 1997; Kehoe and Wright 2013). It suggests that POS plays a significant mediating role in the relationship between HRM practices and work-related outcomes, which is consistent with the findings of Rhoades and Eisenberger (2002), Tremblay *et al*. (2010) and Allen *et al*. (2003).

In contrast to Wright *et al*. (2003) who suggested that HR practices were only weakly related to firm performance, this study demonstrated a relatively strong and positive relationship. This result also challenges Combs *et al*. (2006) who argued that a relatively low impact of HRM existed in the service sector when compared to the manufacturing sector. We suggest that the key reasons behind our findings are related to the characteristics of the school system. In the school system, the relationship between employees (teachers) and organisational outcomes (student satisfaction) is more direct and proximal. The teaching profession has high professional autonomy, high emotional demands and high levels of work stress (Hoy and DiPaola 2005; Jimmieson *et al.* 2010). As such, this finding confirms the argument of Rowan *et al.* (1997) that complex and non-routine autonomous work benefits from supportive organisational practices.

In this study, we found that teacher's OCB had no direct impact on students' QSL. One of the possible reasons for this finding is that the teachers' OCB scale was rated by supervisors who might not clearly understand the extent of teachers' OCB. However, given that a direct relationship was neither proposed nor evident in Jimmieson *et al.* (2010), which is the only notable study that has examined the examining OCB–QSL relationship, future research concerning the direct relationship is required.

Even though a direct relationship was not confirmed, an indirect relationship between teachers' OCB and students' QSL via their IRB was identified. This might be due to the ambiguous and uncertain boundary between teachers' IRB and OCB (Oplatka 2006; Jimmieson *et al.* 2010; Elstad *et al.* 2012; Sesen and Basim 2012). As a direct link between IRB and OCB has been seldom reported in the literature, future studies conducted in a wider context are recommended to test whether OCB contributes to IRB.

Conclusion

To establish the link between HRM and organisational performance has been one of the 'long-standing' goals of strategic HRM research (Jiang *et al.* 2012; 1265). This study addressed this goal and tested a comprehensive causal HRM–performance relationship model within the Chinese school system. It adopted QSL as the organisational performance indicator, which is a more direct and relevant measure than other more generally used indicators. Data from a large sample were collected from multiple sources and at multiple levels. It utilised a three-level structural equation model that is a significant advancement on most HR research. The study showed that HPWS led to improved employee job performance and customer (students) satisfaction.

7 Human resource management reform and its impact on teachers and students

Introduction

Education, as one of the fundamental elements of a society, is significant in the national economy and development, as well as national stability and competitiveness. In China, education has played, and will continue to play, a critical role in its transitional process. Chinese educational reforms focus on performance outcomes and quality improvements in order to build a prosperous, sustainable and harmonious society. Consequently, teacher management highlights performance, effectiveness and efficiency. Given the significant role of teacher management in education quality, this study provides insights as to how China has developed, and will continue to develop, its education system. Understanding the transformation of teacher management, to a large extent, helps grasp the essence of China in transition. As teacher management affects the quality of future generations, this study provides a glimpse of China's global competitiveness in the years to come.

To gain a systematic and comprehensive understanding of teacher management in the Chinese school system, this book: (i) explored the contextual factors shaping HRM policies and practice; (ii) examined the transitional HRM models; (iii) identified current HRM practices in terms of recruitment and selection, training and development, performance appraisal and reward management; and (iv) tested a conceptual model that links HRM with teachers' job performance and students' QSL. By undertaking such tasks, the research has been able to contribute to both theoretical developments in management and HRM policies and practices. The following sections will highlight these contributions.

Theoretical implications

Based on the key findings and the discussion on the transformation of HRM, this study has important theoretical implications in terms of institutional theory and the transitional management model.

Institutional isomorphism and diversification

Institutional isomorphism is evident in the Chinese school system. As schools are established, regulated, certified, financed and assessed under government legislation, the coercive isomorphism derived from government laws and regulations has been critical to the reform process. This supports DiMaggio and Powell's (1983) hypothesis that isomorphism is higher in organisations which are dependent on similar sources of support for vital resources. Normative isomorphism is demonstrated mainly due to the characteristics of the teaching profession such as formal education and training, as well as society's expectations. This finding also supports DiMaggio and Powell's (1983) proposition that the amount of institutional isomorphic change will be greater in organisations characterised by high professionalisation. Similarly, mimetic isomorphism is critical because of the pragmatic approach taken in China's transition to avoid uncertainties and to increase success rates.

At the same time, this study has found diversification of HR practices in Chinese schools: even though in the same region a variety of HRM practices exist. The diversification is demonstrated by three key issues. The first issue is the pragmatic approach that encourages education bureaus and schools to conduct their own experiments and have their own practices to reflect their unique strengths. The second issue is the adoption of the principal accountability system and the competitive mechanism that prompts schools to introduce innovative approaches to enhance effectiveness, efficiency and performance. The third issue is the enforcement of formal and informal institutions. In China, the reforms are underpinned by 'regulations from above and manoeuvres from below' and 'the mountains are high and the Emperor is far away' (Zhu 2007: 1510). These expressions suggest that laws and regulations in China may not be fully implemented as the enforcement of these laws and regulations at the local government level can be weak. Thus, alongside institutional isomorphism, institutional diversification is present to facilitate changes. However, the issue of whether institutional isomorphism outweighs institutional diversification is beyond the scope of this book. Further research is recommended to explore the interaction of institutional isomorphism and institutional diversification in the process of change.

Institutional horizontal and vertical interaction

This study provides support for the findings of North (1990, 1994) and Scott (2008b, 2010) that formal and informal institutions are interrelated and interdependent with one supplementing and enhancing the other. For example, the policy of prioritising educational development and building a highly effective teaching workforce is responsive to the interaction of both formal and informal institutions (see chapter 5). This interaction of both formal and informal institutions, which drives change, is found to be an on-going and convergent process across time – here referred to 'institutional horizontal interaction'. This is typified by the changing status of teachers from 'bourgeoisies' during the Cultural Revolution to be the insiders of the working class in the late 1970s and 1980s. However, at that time, teachers' incomes were still low and the teaching profession was among the least desired careers. In the 1990s and 2000s, with the increasing recognition of the significance of education in society, teacher management has become more enlightened and with a strong focus on managing teacher quality. Since 2006, the Chinese government has substantially increased educational investment to build a sustainable, prosperous and harmonious country. The substantial increase in education investment and teachers' salaries has changed the teaching profession into a highly desirable job choice. The increase of entry standards in the teaching profession and the need to build a highly qualified teaching workforce prompted the adoption of high performance work systems.

This study also found that in the horizontal interaction process, the role of different actors in different stages is distinct, with a combination of both top-down and bottom-up engagement. For example, in the early 1980s, the top-down approach was prevailing when the eminent leader, Deng Xiao-ping, who had overseas study experience, stressed the significant role of education in the Four Modernisations. Subsequently, the Compulsory Education Law, which proposed 9 years of free education, was enacted. In the 1980s and early 1990s, the bottom-up approach prevailed. With the opening of the Chinese domestic market, industry required and students wanted practical skills and teachers demanded higher remuneration. This bottom-up approach has driven the Chinese government to publish educational laws and to implement educational reforms to meet societal needs, which subsequently led to the return of a top-down approach.

In addition to institutional horizontal interaction, this study also identified 'institutional vertical interaction' that concerns interaction of different actors working at different levels. The concept of multilevel institutionalisation has been stressed in the literature, for example, Fujita and Krugman (2004) and Phillips *et al.* (2009). More recently, Scott (2010) calls for the exploration of the intermediaries to explain institutional change. This study has demonstrated that institutional interaction at the macro-level (political, economic, legal and sociocultural contexts) affected micro-level management (structure, finance, people and profession management), which subsequently affected HRM transformation. This finding, from an empirical point of view, fulfils Scott's (2010) goal to connect organisational studies to wider and more macro-structures.

As demonstrated in this study, the institutional horizontal interaction and institutional vertical interaction are not an either/or story. These two interactive directions are integrated to drive the transformation of HRM in the Chinese school system. As such, it is argued that institutionalisation can be conceptualised as the integration of both the horizontal and the vertical interactions that facilitates institutional change. The majority of researchers have to date focused too narrowly on either horizontal interaction or vertical interaction. Including both the horizontal and the vertical interaction in institutional research, particularly in empirical studies, allows an in-depth and comprehensive understanding of how various institutional driving forces interact at different levels to drive change.

An integrated pragmatic management model

This research extends previous studies on transitional HRM in the Chinese context. It not only confirms a hybrid or convergent model but also explicitly identifies a new and innovative management model: a pragmatic integrated transitional model. In this model, the essence of the Western and Chinese elements has been strategically integrated to achieve a high performance and high commitment workforce. The Western generated HPWS has been at the core of teacher management, enhanced and facilitated by traditional paternalistic and humanised management. Supporting this integrated transitional management model is pragmatic management that is a self-perfecting approach, constantly seeking gradual refinement and improvement. This transitional model is essential given schools are increasingly faced with performance pressure; therefore, they are proactively searching for ways to enhance their competitiveness.

Even though the management elements of Chinese culture have lost their dominance, their influences have not been entirely replaced, either in peoples' consciousness or in various management practices (Cheng *et al.* 2009). Rather, they mix and coexist with Western values and practices. This phenomenon reflects the Chinese government's ideology to build a country 'with Chinese characteristics' targeting a high rate of GDP growth and to cement social stability at the same time (Warner 2010). Additionally, traditional Chinese culture values the transcendence of dualism (Li 2008) and the core of Chinese traditional philosophy is to be moderate, trying to avoid imbalance and extremes (Cheng *et al.* 2009). Therefore, the Western and Chinese management approaches are integrated: there is not a clear-cut division between them.

The findings of this research challenges previous research that suggested that people management in China was in the process of converging to Western theories and practices with fewer Chinese characteristics (Ding *et al.* 2001; Björkman *et al.* 2008) or clear-cut models (Zhu *et al.* 2012). The identified pragmatic integrated transitional model found in this study supports Liang *et al.*'s (2012) contention that HPWS in the Chinese context needs to be seen as not only treating employees as valued long-term assets but also endeavouring to meet individual's personal needs and stressing family ties and obligations. The finding echoes the suggestions of Cheng *et al.* (2009) in that learning from the West is not substitutive but evolutional: melting Western values into the Chinese culture in the search for continuous improvement.

The identified new transitional management model in the Chinese school system demonstrates that China can be 'a fertile ground for the development of management theories' (Cooke 2009: 7). The rapidly changing economic and political context in China offers a 'unique opportunity' to explore the theoretical and empirical foundations in people management (Liang *et al.* 2012: 67). Research in the Chinese context enables the development of general theories that are applicable outside the Western context where organisational theories have generally arisen (Barney and Zhang 2009). Therefore, we recommended that new theories should be developed or tested in the context of a variety of indigenous cultural origins. Otherwise, the impact of the unique aspects of Chinese management will remain silent in the prevailing Western theories and thus interactions between management theories with different cultural origins will not occur (Cheng *et al.* 2009).

Practical implications

The findings of the interaction and impact of external, internal, formal and informal institutions in multiple layers on HRM transformation have a number of practical implications for policy makers. When designing HRM policy, policy makers are advised to take a thorough account of the related institutions, for example, the political, economic and sociocultural contexts at the macro-level and the structure, finance, people and profession management at both the macro and micro levels. In addition, for a sustainable effect, the policy and regulations must be consistent with the related political, economic and social norms, as well as cultural beliefs.

In many OECD countries, education systems are faced with the challenge of recruiting highly qualified graduates as teachers (OECD 2005a, 2011). The successful experience of the Chinese education sector in hiring the most qualified teachers suggests that pay matters. In this research, the pay of teachers was found to be over twice that of the local average income. Additionally, teachers, to a large extent, are now well regarded by society. The practices (rewards, social status and respects) have changed the teaching profession from the least wanted job to a highly desired career. Consequently, policy makers elsewhere should consider increasing teacher's rewards (including pay and associated benefits) and enhancing social status to tackle the teacher shortage problem.

The mixed feelings of school principals on PRP suggests that PRP is a two-edged sword. On one hand, PRP has been reported to have created a more performance-oriented culture. On the other hand, it has been found to have damaged teachers' relationships with their colleagues and to demotivate many teachers. This finding is consistent with previous studies, for example, Farrell and Morris (2004), Podgursky and Springer (2007) and Condrey (2012). As such, the introduction of PRP in the school context should proceed with caution.

This study also provides practical implications to new public management that has seen the introduction of market-oriented management approaches to improve effectiveness and efficiency (Walker *et al.* 2011). Most of the new public management schemes have failed largely due to their different values, ethos and nature to that which exists in the traditional public sector (Rhodes and Wanna 2007; Diefenbach 2009). The successful implementation of HPWS in Chinese schools suggests that new public management approaches need to be implemented with other management practices that provide additional care, support and respect, for example, paternalistic and humanised management.

The positive and significant impact of HPWS on teachers' job performance and students' quality of school life suggests that HRM does matter in the school context. As a result, education policy makers should consider the adoption of HPWS. The significant influence of HPWS on teachers' job performance found in this study suggests that schools would be well advised to consider implementing such bundles of practices. This study also indicates that schools' investment in HRM leads to improved students' QSL via mediating processes. This result shows that factors that can exert influence on the meditating variables are likely to impact on the HRM-student satisfaction relationship. Therefore, school principals should consider improving teachers' skills and motivation to improve school effectiveness. The indirect relationship between HPWS and school effectiveness also indicates that together with HPWS, organisational support is needed. Because the teaching profession is extremely stressful (Carton and Fruchart 2014) and teachers may transfer their feelings of mental and physical wellbeing to students, school principals should consider providing additional support and care to teachers. The finding that teachers' OCB contributes to their IRB, which subsequently significantly affects their students' QSL, suggests that principals should encourage higher levels of OCB to improve performance.

On-going challenges and the future development of the Chinese education system

Ever since China was forced to be more open in the mid-nineteenth century, the Chinese government and the Chinese people have attempted to rejuvenate the nation and develop a prosperous society. Education generally, although with some notable exceptions, has been perceived to be a significant force in achieving this goal under the strategy of 'rejuvenating the nation by education'. In the past two centuries, endless efforts have been made: from the Westernisation Movement, the Hundred Days Reform and the New Deal of the Late Qing Dynasty in the Qing dynasty through to the May Fourth Movement and the New Culture Movement in the republican era and to national development strategy based on science and education in the present market-oriented economy era.

Recently, under the leadership of President Xi Jin-ping, China named the goals of rejuvenating the nation and achieving happiness of its people as the 'China Dream' (People Net 2013). To achieve the 'China Dream' the Chinese government put forward 'Goals of Two Hundred Years' which, as the name suggests, sets the goals for the next 200 years. The first goal is to double the GDP and per capita disposal income of 2010 by 2021, achieving a moderately affluent society, when the Chinese Community Party will be celebrating its 100th birthday. Another goal is to build a prosperous, democratic, civilised and harmonious socialist modern country by the mid-twenty-first century when the People's Republic of China will have been established for 100 years.

To achieve the ambitious 'China Dream', education has been given a high priority. Educational investment by the Chinese government has been substantially increased (see chapter 3). Educational reforms, which aim to cultivate an innovation-oriented workforce, are a key part of this agenda. Teachers, regarded as the key to education quality, have been granted high social status and relatively high pay (see chapter 5). Teacher management approaches have combined some elements of essence of both Western and Chinese wisdom in order to build a professional and committed workforce with high quality (see chapter 4). The impact of teacher management reforms so far have been substantial (see chapter 6). Given the trend of its development, the future of China in terms of its education is promising. Yet, the government has encountered a number of challenges that need to be addressed if a sustainable, prosperous and harmonious society is to be built.

The first challenge is the unequal educational resources and provision of education due to the unequal development of the various regional economies. China has 22 regions, five autonomous regions and four municipalities. The economic development of these regions is diverse. For example, the highest GDP per capita are US$13,057 (Tianjin), US$12,782 (Shanghai) and US$12,447 (Beijing), whereas the lowest GDP per capita are US$2,541 (Guizhou), US$2,935 (Yunnan) and US$3,022 (Gansu) in 2011 (Wu 2013). The unequal development of regions results in unequal provision of education and thus raises concerns over education access and fairness. Because of the unbalanced economic development and education provisions, the poor in the poor regions remain poor (and perhaps get poorer) while the rich in better developed areas and regions get richer. This widening income and wealth gap has created substantial risks of social unrest and turmoil (The World Bank 2013). As such, how to tackle the problem of unequal economic and education development has become a key challenge for the Chinese government.

Second, the emphasis on the role of political ideology over education has limited the free development of education. As shown in the educational guiding principles, education must serve the social function rather than the individual function and must be under the CCP leadership (see chapter 2). The control over education by the government has resulted in the phenomenon of 'non-professionals in charge of professionals' and 'those who do not understand education in charge of education'. To some extent, education must satisfy the needs of the government and sometimes education in China is obliged to make sacrifices for the government. For example, one principal complained that she was forced to close the school for the whole day because the local government held a leadership vote and needed the school to be a voting site. Because the head of the education department was appointed from above (the government), they need to share a very good relationship with the local government. Most of the principals interviewed indicated that they had to attend 'dinner meetings' with officials to develop and maintain good relationships. The over-control of education by the government undermines the independence of education and the full focus and engagement in teaching activities.

Over the past 4 decades, the Chinese government has endeavoured to cultivate outstanding science talent. Yet this goal has been hampered by the inability of its scientists to get the highest science awards, for example, the Nobel Prize awards. In comparison, in the republican era where educational institutions enjoyed a high level of academic freedom and autonomy and were not subject to political pressure, the education system nurtured five Nobel Prize winners (see chapter 3). To change this situation, the Chinese government needs to balance the will for control and the need for educational freedom.

The third challenge is the limited capability of the current education system to nurture and develop an innovative workforce to meet social needs. The ever-changing global environment and the advancements in technology and science stresses the role of innovation. Since the open door policy, China has witnessed remarkable economic development mainly by becoming a global manufacturing powerhouse. Nevertheless, the spectacular high rate of growth is considered unsustainable as it brings severe environmental deteriorations and damage to natural resources. Realising the pitfalls, the Chinese government changed the previous 'world factory' developmental model to a sustainable 'laboratory of the world' (Johnson and Weiss 2011). Innovation has been identified as a key force to drive the transition and a national strategy to build an innovation-driven economy by 2020 has been launched (OECD 2008). Even though it is argued that 'China will be a dominant force in innovation for years to come' (Johnson and Weiss 2011: 198), the question of whether China will be able to succeed in making this challenging transition is still unanswered.

One of the key concerns is whether the Chinese education system can support the ambitious goal of establishing an innovative society. Being in a transition from a labour-intensive to knowledge- and technology-based economy, China is experiencing an acute shortage of skilled and innovative workers (Gu 2010). The *National Guideline for Medium- and Long-term Educational Reform and Development (2010–2020)* highlights the needs to cultivate students with innovative ability (State Council 2010). Nevertheless, the test result oriented education system constrains the ability to cultivate an innovative workforce. Students' test results not only determine the future of students, but also the fate of teachers, the schools and even officials in the education department and the government. Under this system, teaching activities focus on memorising and repetitive tasks. This can explain the reasons why Chinese students ranked first in the mathematics, science and reading assessments organised by OECD (Sharma 2011; OECD 2013). However, this short-term focused approach runs contrary to the long-term goals of the Chinese government to cultivate students' skills in creativity, problem-solving and independent inquiry. Changing the long-embedded and far-reaching test result oriented educational system is fundamental to building an innovative and sustainable society.

The fourth challenge is the nature of the educational reforms: the rapid pace of change in management practices. The pragmatic approach of 'crossing the river by feeling the stones' has helped the Chinese education sector make substantial improvements in teacher management and education quality. Some of the approaches are even more advanced than some Western countries in terms of teacher hiring, training, performance appraisal and performance-related pay schemes (OECD 2005a, 2011). However, because of the competitive mechanism, education leaders have to implement some innovative approaches in order to secure their positions and gain promotion. This practice has sometimes resulted in rapid implementation of changes without a full assessment and a proper trial period. In addition, the reforms are sometimes just like a campaign: implemented quickly and within a clear timeframe. Over time, the enthusiasm fades and the focus changes to other more innovative ideas. Principals indicated that teachers sometimes found it hard to keep pace with the rapidly changing regulations. Occasionally, when principals and teachers made substantial efforts and finally got used to the new regulations, they found that the new regulations were not in fashion any more. Given the substantial impacts of the educational reforms, the Chinese education sector should act more prudently and balance the pace of reforms.

Concluding remarks

Education has been regarded as 'the cornerstone and pillar' of economic growth and development (Nguni *et al*. 2006: 145). It exerts substantial impacts on students, parents, local communities and on the competitiveness and stability of the entire society (OECD 2005b). As education determines human qualities for the future, the education quality of the present predicts, at least in part, the competitiveness of a country for the future. Consequently, education has been one of the top concerns of national leaders, educational policy makers and a wide range of stakeholders in society. For example, the influential 1983 report of *A Nation at Risk* in the US raised considerable anxieties about the education quality and the future competitiveness of that country (Pil and Leana 2009). Despite the high level of investment and substantial efforts in various educational reforms, a number of Western countries are faced with declining student standards, particularly students' maths competency, which is deemed critical for the future competitiveness of a nation (OECD 2013). Moreover, management reforms that highlight effectiveness and efficiency in the education sector in some developed countries have been unsuccessful (Rhodes and Wanna 2007; Diefenbach 2009). The relatively successful reforms of China's teacher management system, as demonstrated in this study, can provide some pointers for developed countries that seek to maintain and enhance their competiveness and for developing countries that strive to narrow the gap with developed countries. The challenges that China currently faces can also shed some light on the transitional nature of a country and provide some direction for other developing countries undergoing transition.

Appendix 1 Key studies of transformational human resource management models in China

Studies	*Benchmark HRM model*	*Transitional HRM models identified*	*HRM functions explored*	*Research methods*
Ngai and Smith (2007)	Personnel management model	Dormitory labour regime in the mass production system	Recruitment and turnover, accommodation, management freedom and coercion	Comparative case studies (interviews with managers and workers in two manufacturing enterprises in Guangdong province in 2002 and 2003
Warner (2000)	General HRM model	Hard convergence and divergence, soft convergence and divergence with HRM practices		Documentary analysis and literature review focused on Asia-Pacific countries
Ding *et al.* (2001)	General HRM model	A transitional convergent model moving further from personnel management to western HRM with fewer Chinese characteristics.	Recruitment and selection, training and development, reward, employment contracts, PM, social security, labour turnover, dismissals and disputes plus three functions	Case studies based on semi-structured questionnaires and interviews with managers with township and village manufacturing enterprises in 2000 in Guangdong province.
Cooke (2004)	General HRM model	A mixture of soft and hard HR techniques	Recruitment and training, reward, labour flexibility, welfare provision plus five functions	Case study (14 interviews with managers and workers with one foreign-owned toy factory) in Guangdong province in 2002
Benson and Zhu (1999)	Modified version of Storey (1995)	Three paradigms of people management in transition: - Minimalist - Transitional - Innovative	Freedom in personnel selection, individual performance pay, continuous training, individual contracts plus 12 functions	Interviews with managers in six SOEs in Shanghai during 1997 to 1998

(Continued)

Appendix 1 (Continued)

Studies	Benchmark HRM model	Transitional HRM models identified	HRM functions explored	Research methods
Rowley and Benson (2002)	Modified version of Storey (1995)	A mix of both convergent and divergent models	Identical to the above but with four fewer functions	Interviews with managers in manufacturing SOEs and foreign-owned enterprises (1995 to 1998) in Japan, China, Korea and Thailand
Goodall and Warner (1997)	Poole (1997)	Four models: iron rice bowl; hybrid I and II mixing iron rice bowl and HRM practices; imported HRM model.	Reward systems, labour contracts, social insurance, labour-management relations and personnel policies	Interviews with managers with seven JV enterprises in Shanghai & Beijing (1995 to 1996)
Zhu *et al.* (2007)	European/US and Asian models	'Hybrid approach' mixing Chinese and Western models		Documentary analysis and literature review of seven Asia-Pacific countries
Björkman *et al.* (2008)	Hannon *et al.* (1995) and Rosenzweig *et al.* (1994)	From localised model to more convergent European models	Recruitment and selection, training, financial compensation and performance appraisal	Comparative studies (interviews with managers) (1996 and 2006) in European -owned multinational companies in industry
Zhu *et al.* (2012)	Rousseau (1989)	Three clear-cult models: - Paternalistic - Transactional - Differentiated	Paternalistic and transactional model	Three case studies with SOEs with managers and workers in south-east and south-west China and Jiangsu province
Warner (2010)	Traditional Chinese value and Confucian Model	Hybrid Confucian model (Confucian legacy, iron rice bowl and contemporary)	Training, harmony at work, vertical linkage, *guanxi*, leadership, work ethic, group	Documentary analysis and literature review

HRM, human resource management; PM, personnel management

Bibliography

Acevedo, A. 2012. Personalist business ethics and humanistic management: Insights from Jacques Maritain. *Journal of Business Ethics*, 105(2): 197–219.

Aguinis, H., Boyd, B. K., Pierce, C. A. and Short, J. C. 2011. Walking new avenues in management research methods and theories: Bridging micro and macro domains. *Journal of Management*, 37(2): 395–403.

Akhtar, S., Ding, D. Z. and Ge, L. G. 2008. Strategic HRM practices and their impact on company performance in Chinese enterprises. *Human Resource Management*, 47(1), 15–32.

Aktour, O. 1992. Management and theories of organizations in the 1990s: Toward a critical radical humanism? *Academy of Management Review*, 17(3): 407–31.

Allen, D. G., Shore, L. M. and Griffeth, R. W. 2003. The role of perceived organizational support and supportive human resource practices in the turnover process. *Journal of Management*, 29(1): 99–118.

Armstrong, M. 2011. *Armstrong's Handbook of Strategic Human Resource Management* (5th Ed.). London: KoganPage.

Arthur, J. B. 1992. The link between business strategy and industrial relations systems in American steel minimills. *Industrial and Labor Relations Review*, 45(3): 488–506.

Aryee, S., Walumbwa, F. O., Seidu, E. Y. and Otaye, L. E. 2013. Developing and leveraging human capital resource to promote service quality testing a theory of performance. *Journal of Management*, doi: 10.1177/0149206312471394.

Bach, S. 2000. From performance appraisal to performance management. In S. Bach and K. Sisson (Eds.), *Personnel Management: A Comprehensive Guide to Theory and Practice*. Oxford: Blackwell Business, pp. 241–63.

Barney, J. B. and Zhang, S. 2009. The future of Chinese management research: A theory of Chinese management versus a Chinese theory of management. *Management and Organization Review*, 5(1): 15–27.

Bartel, A. 2004. Human resource management and organizational performance: Evidence from retail banking. *Industrial and Labor Relations Review*, 57(2): 181–203.

Batt, R. 2002. Managing customer services: Human resource practices, quit rates, and sales growth. *Academy of Management Journal*, 45(3): 587–97.

Becker, B. E. and Huselid, M. A. 2006. Strategic human resources management: Where do we go from here? *Journal of Management*, 32(6): 898–925.

Becker, B. E., Huselid, M. A., Pickus, P. S. and Spratt, M. F. 1997. HR as a source of shareholder value: Research and recommendations. *Human Resource Management*, 36(1): 39–47.

Beer, M. 1997. The transformation of the human resource function: Resolving the tension between a traditional administrative and a new strategic role. *Human Resource Management*, 36(1): 49–56.

Beltrán-Martín, I., Roca-Puig, V., Escrig-Tena, A. and Bou-Llusar, J. C. 2008. Human resource flexibility as a mediating variable between high performance work systems and performance. *Journal of Management*, 34(5): 1009–44.

Benson, J. and Debroux, P. 1997. HRM in Japanese enterprises: Trends and challenges. *Asia Pacific Business Review*, 3(4): 62–81.

Benson, J. and Zhu, Y. 1999. Markets, firms and workers in Chinese state-owned enterprises. *Human Resource Management Journal*, 9(4): 58–74.

Berman, E., Bowman, J., West, J. and Wart, M. 2006. *Human Resource Management in Public Service*. London: Sage.

Berry, B. 2004. Recruiting and retaining 'highly qualified teachers' for hard-to-staff schools. *NASSP Bulletin*, 88(638): 5–27.

Bersin, J. 2004. *The Blended Learning Book: Best Practices, Proven Methodologies, and Lessons Learned*. San Francisco: Pfeiffer.

Bi, S. 2011. Sources and way out of teaching profession (jiaoshi zhisuolai zhisuoqu). *Shanghai Educational Research*, 12: 8–11.

Bian, Y. 2002. Chinese social stratification and social mobility. *Annual Review of Sociology*, 28: 91–116.

Björkman, I., Smale, A., Sumelius, J., Suutari, V. and Lu, Y. 2008. Changes in institutional context and MNC operations in China: Subsidiary HRM practices in 1996 versus 2006. *International Business Review*, 17(2): 146–58.

Blau, P. M. 1964. *Exchange and Power in Social Life*. New York: Wiley.

Bliese, P. D. 2000. Within-group agreement, non-independence, and reliability: Implications for data aggregation and analysis. In K. J. Klein and S. W. J. Kozlowski (Eds.), *Multilevel Theory, Research, and Methods in Organizations*. San Francisco: Jossey-Bass Publishers, pp. 349–81.

Boas, T. C. 2007. Conceptualizing continuity and change the composite-standard model of path dependence. *Journal of Theoretical Politics*, 19(1): 33-54.

Bogler, R. and Nir, A. E. 2012. The importance of teachers' perceived organizational support to job satisfaction: What's empowerment got to do with it? *Journal of Educational Administration*, 50(3): 287–306.

Bogler, R. and Somech, A. 2004. Influence of teacher empowerment on teachers' organizational commitment, professional commitment and organizational citizenship behavior in schools. *Teaching and Teacher Education*, 20(3): 277–89.

Borman, W. C. and Motowidlo, S. J. 1993. Expanding the criterion domain to include elements of contextual performance. In N. Schmitt, and W. C. Borman (Eds.), *Personnel Selection in Organizations*. San Francisco: Jossey-Bass Publishers, pp. 71–98.

Borman, W. C. and Motowidlo, S. J. 1997. Task performance and contextual performance: The meaning for personnel selection research. *Human performance*, 10(2): 99–109.

Boselie, P., Dietz, G. and Boon, C. 2005. Commonalities and contradictions in HRM and performance research. *Human Resource Management Journal*, 15(3): 67–94.

Brackett, M., Reyes, M. R., Rivers, S., Elbertson, N. and Salovey, P. 2011. Classroom emotional climate, teacher affiliation, and student conduct. *Journal of Classroom Interaction*, 46(1): 27–36.

Brockbank, W. 1999. If HR were really strategically proactive: Present and future directions in HR's contribution to competitive advantage. *Human Resource Management*, 38(4): 337–52.

Brodsgaard, K. E. 2012. Cadre and personnel management in the CPC. *China: An International Journal*, 10(2): 69–83.

Buley-Meissner, M. 1991. Teachers and teacher-education: A view from the People's Republic of China. *International Journal of Educational Development*, 11(1): 41–53.

Buller, P. F. and McEvoy, G. M. 2012. Strategy, human resource management and performance: Sharpening line of sight. *Human Resource Management Review*, 22(1): 43–56.

Burns, J. 1987. Civil service reform in contemporary China. *The Australian Journal of Chinese Affairs*, 18: 47–83.

Burns, J. and Wang, X. 2010. Civil service reform in China: Impacts on civil servants' behaviour. *The China Quarterly*, 201(1): 58–78.

Byrne, B. M. 2012. *Structural Equation Modeling with Mplus: Basic Concepts, Applications, and Programming*. New York: Routledge.

Caldwell, R. and Storey, J. 2007. The HR function: Integration or fragmentation? In J. Storey (Ed.), *Human Resource Management: A Critical Text*. London: Thomson, pp. 21–38.

Caprara, G. V., Barbaranelli, C., Steca, P. and Malone, P. S. 2006. Teachers' self-efficacy beliefs as determinants of job satisfaction and students' academic achievement: a study at the school level. *Journal of School Psychology*, 44(6): 473–90

Carton, A. and Fruchart, E. 2014. Sources of stress, coping strategies, emotional experience: Effects of the level of experience in primary school teachers in France. *Educational Review*, 66(2): 245–62.

Central Committee of the Chinese Communist Party. 1985. *Decision on the Reform of the Education System* (zhonggong zhongyang guanyu jiaoyu gaige de jueding), May. Beijing: Central Committee of the Chinese Communist Party.

Central Committee of the Chinese Communist Party. 2006. *Chinese Communist Party Central Committee's Resolution on Major Issues of Building a Socialist Harmonious Society* (zhonggong zhongyang guanyu goujian shehui zhuyi hexie shehui ruogan zhongda wenti de jueding), October. Beijing: Central Committee of the Chinese Communist Party.

Central Committee of the Chinese Communist Party and Ministry of Education. 1999. *Decision on Deepening Educational Reform and Promoting Quality Education on an All-round Way* (shenhua jiaoyu gaige, quanmian tuijin suzhi jiaoyu de jueding), Vol. 9. Beijing: Central Committee of the Chinese Communist Party and Ministry of Education.

Central Committee of the Chinese Communist Party and State Council. 1993. *Outline of Education Reform and Development in China* (zhongguo jiaoyu gaige he fangzhan gangyao), Vol. 3. Beijing: Central Committee of the Chinese Communist Party and State Council.

Central Quota Office, Ministry of Education and Ministry of Finance. 2001. *Suggestion on Compiling Quota for Teaching and Administrative Staff* (guanyu zhiding gongxiaoxue jiaozhigong bianzhi biaozhun de yijian), Vol. 74. Beijing: Central Quota Office, Ministry of Education and Ministry of Finance.

Chen, G. 2005. An analytical study of the educational objectives (jiaoxue zongzhi kaobian). *Journal of Hebei Normal University*, 7(6): 15–18.

Chen, X., Eberly, M. B., Chiang, T., Farh, J. and Cheng, B. 2014. Affective trust in Chinese leaders: Linking paternalistic leadership to employee performance. *Journal of Management*, 40(3), 796–819.

Chen, Z., Eisenberger, R., Johnson, K., Sucharski, I. and Aselage, J. 2009. Perceived organizational support and extra-role performance: Which leads to which? *The Journal of Social Psychology*, 149(1): 119–24.

Cheng, B. S., Chou, L. F., Wu, T. Y., Huang, M. P. and Farh, J. L. 2004. Paternalistic leadership and subordinate responses: Establishing a leadership model in Chinese organizations. *Asian Journal of Social Psychology*, 7(1): 89–117.

Cheng, B. S., Wang, A. C. and Huang, M. P. 2009. The road more popular versus the road less travelled: an 'insider's' perspective of advancing Chinese management research. *Management and Organization Review*, 5(1): 91–105.

Child, J. 1995. Changes in the structure and prediction of earnings in Chinese state enterprises during the economic reform. *International Journal of Human Resource Management*, 6(1): 1–30.

Child, J. 2009. Context, comparison, and methodology in Chinese management research. *Management and Organization Review*, 5(1): 57–73.

Choi, S. and Peng, Y. 2015. Humanized management? Capital and migrant labour in a time of labour shortage in South China. *Human Relations*, 68(2): 287–304.

Christensen, R. K. and Whiting, S. W. 2009. 'The role of task performance and organizational citizenship behavior in performance appraisals across sectors: Exploring the role of public service motivation'. Paper presented at the International Public Service Motivation Research Conference, Bloomington, IN, USA.

Chuang, C. H. and Liao, H. 2010. Strategic human resource management in service context: Taking care of business by taking care of employees and customers. *Personnel Psychology*, 63(1): 153–96.

Chubanshe, F. 2009. *Constitution on the People's Republic of China: Amendments Compared*. Beijing: Law Press.

Cochran-Smith, M. and Fries, M. K. 2001. Sticks, stones, and ideology: The discourse of reform in teacher education. *Educational Researcher*, 30(8): 3–15.

Cohen-Vogel, L. 2011. 'Staffing to the test': Are today's school personnel practices evidence based? *Educational Evaluation and Policy Analysis*, 33(4): 483–505.

Combs, J., Liu, Y., Hall, A. and Ketchen, D. 2006. How much do high-performance work practices matter? A meta-analysis of their effects on organizational performance. *Personnel Psychology*, 59(3): 501–28.

Condrey, S. E. 2012. Public human resource management: How we get where we are today. In N. M. Riccucci (Ed.), *Public Personnel Management: Current Concerns, Future Challenges* (5th Ed.). Boston: Longman, pp. 23–48.

Cooke, F. 2004. Foreign firms in China: Modelling HRM in a toy manufacturing corporation. *Human Resource Management Journal*, 14(3): 31–52.

Cooke, F. 2009. A decade of transformation of HRM in China: A review of literature and suggestions for future studies. *Asia Pacific Journal of Human Resources*, 47(1): 6–40.

Dacin, M. T., Goodstein, J. and Scott, W. R. 2002. Institutional theory and institutional change: Introduction to the special research forum. *The Academy of Management Journal*, 45(1): 43–56.

Dang, W. 2001. The reform movement of 1898 and modern education reform in China (maoxu weixin yu zhongguo jindai jiaoyu gaige). *Journal of Weinan Teachers College*, 17(3): 41–3.

Dawley, D., Houghton, J. D. and Bucklew, N. S. 2010. Perceived organizational support and turnover intention: The mediating effects of personal sacrifice and job fit. *The Journal of Social Psychology*, 150(3): 238–57.

Delery, J. E. 1998. Issues of fit in strategic human resource management: Implications for research. *Human Resource Management Review*, 8(3): 289–309.

Delery, J. E. and Doty, D. H. 1996. Modes of theorizing in strategic human resource management: Tests of universalistic, contingency, and configurations. *Academy of Management Journal*, 39(4): 802–35.

Deng, L. 2006. On the Sino-Japanese War of 1894–1895 and the Treaty of Shimonoseki (1895) (jiawu zhanzheng he maguan tiaoyue). *Journal of Hunan University of Science & Technology* 9(3): 78–80.

Deng, Z. and Treiman, D. J. 1997. The impact of the cultural revolution on trends in educational attainment in the People's Republic of China. *American Journal of Sociology*, 103(2): 391–428.

Diefenbach, T. 2009. New public management in public sector organizations: The dark sides of managerialistic 'enlightenment'. *Public Administration*, 87(4): 892–909.

DiMaggio, P. J. and Powell, W. W. 1983. The iron cage revisited: Institutional isomorphism and collective rationality in organizational fields. *American Sociological Review*, 48(2): 147–60.

Ding, D., Lan, G. and Warner, M. 2001. A new form of Chinese human resource management? Personnel and labour-management relations in Chinese township and village enterprises: A case-study approach. *Industrial Relations Journal*, 32(4): 328–43.

DiPaola, M. and Tschannen-Moran, M. 2001. Organizational citizenship behavior in schools and its relationship to school climate. *Journal of School Leadership*, 11(5): 424–47.

Dodgson, M. and Xue, L. 2009. Editorial innovation in China. *Innovation: Management, Policy & Practice*, 11(1): 1–5.

Dong, H. 1990. Discussion on educational guiding principles and education quality (jiaoxue fangzhen he suzhi jiaoyu zhi kaobian). *Liaoning Higher Education Research*, 6: 90–105.

Dong, H. 1992. A study of the socialism educational guiding principles with Chinese characteristics (guanyu you zhongguo tese de shehuizhuyi jiaoyu zhidaofangzhen de yantao). *Liaoning Higher Education Research*, 2: 11–18.

Dong, L., Christensen, T. and Painter, M. 2010. A case study of China's administrative reform. *The American Review of Public Administration*, 40(2): 170–89.

Druker, J., White, G., Hegewisch, A. and Mayne, L. 1996. Between hard and soft HRM: Human resource management in the construction industry. *Construction Management & Economics*, 14(5): 405–16.

Eisenberger, R., Armeli, S., Rexwinkel, B., Lynch, P. D. and Rhoades, L. 2001. Reciprocation of perceived organizational support. *Journal of Applied Psychology*, 86(1): 42–51.

Eisenberger, R., Huntington, R., Hutchison, S. and Sowa, D. 1986. Perceived organizational support. *Journal of Applied Psychology*, 71(3): 500–7.

Elstad, E., Christophersen, K. A. and Turmo, A. 2012. The strength of accountability and teachers' organisational citizenship behaviour. *Journal of Educational Administration*, 50(5): 612–28.

Enders, C. K. and Tofighi, D. 2007. Centering predictor variables in cross-sectional multilevel models: A new look at an old issue. *Psychological Methods*, 12(2): 121–38.

Epstein, J. and McPartland, J. 1976. The concept and measurement of the quality of school life. *American Educational Research Journal*, 13(1): 15–30.

Evans, W. R. and Davis, W. D. 2005. High-performance work systems and organizational performance: The mediating role of internal social structure. *Journal of Management*, 31(5): 758–75.

Farh, J. L. and Cheng, B. S. 2000. A cultural analysis of paternalistic leadership in Chinese organizations. In J. T. Li and A. S. Tsui and E. Weldon (Eds.), *Management and Organizations in the Chinese Context*. London: Macmillan, pp. 94–127.

Farrell, C. and Morris, J. 2004. Resigned compliance: Teacher attitudes towards performance-related pay in schools. *Educational Management Administration & Leadership*, 32(1): 81–104.

136 Bibliography

Feng, J. 2001. Pursuit of studying abroad: An imperial-financed system in times of Westernization Movement in the 19th Century of China (yangwu yundong shiqi de guanpai liuxuesheng zhidu). *Journal of Guangzhou University*, 15(3): 44–8.

Field, A. 2009. *Discovering Statistics Using SPSS*. London: Sage.

Fleisher, B., Li, H. and Zhao, M. Q. 2010. Human capital, economic growth, and regional inequality in China. *Journal of Development Economics*, 92(2): 215–31.

Fornell, C. and Larcker, D. F. 1981. Evaluating structural equation models with unobservable variables and measurement error. *Journal of Marketing Research*, 18(1): 39–50.

Forrester, G., Motteram, G. and Bangxiang, L. 2006. Transforming Chinese teachers' thinking, learning and understanding via e-learning. *Journal of Education for Teaching*, 32(2): 197–212.

Fryer, R. G. 2011. Teacher incentives and student achievement: Evidence from New York City public schools, *NBER Working Paper Series*, Vol. 16850. Cambridge: National Bureau of Economic Research.

Fujita, M. and Krugman, P. 2004. The new economic geography: Past, present and the future. *Papers in Regional Science*, 83(1): 139–64.

Fukumoto, T. and Muto, I. 2012. Rebalancing China's Economic Growth: Some Insights from Japan's Experience. *China & World Economy*, 20(1), 62–82.

Gan, C. 2002. Decline of the Imperial Examination System and the disintegration of institutional Confucianism (kejuzhidu de shuailuo he zhiduhua rujia de jieti). *Social Sciences in China*, 2: 107–207.

Ge, F. 2012. A historical survey of college teachers' remuneration during 1912–1949 (minguo gaoxiao laoshi de daiyu de lishi kaocha (1912–1949)). *Journal of Ningbo University*, 34(6): 38–42.

Goldhaber, D., Gross, B. and Player, D. 2011. Teacher career paths, teacher quality, and persistence in the classroom: Are public schools keeping their best? *Journal of Policy Analysis and Management*, 30(1): 57–87.

Goncalves, A. 1996. A paradigm of autonomy: The Hong Kong and Macau Sars. *Contemporary Southeast Asia*, 18(1): 36–60.

Goodall, K. and Warner, M. 1997. Human resources in Sino-foreigh joint ventures: Selected case studies in Shanghai, compared with Beijing. *Internatinal Journal of Human Resource Management*, 8(5): 569–594.

Gouldner, A. 1960. The norm of reciprocity: A preliminary statement. *American Sociological Review*, 25: 161–78.

Grant, A. M. and Mayer, D. M. 2009. Good soldiers and good actors: Prosocial and impression management motives as interactive predictors of affiliative citizenship behaviors. *Journal of Applied Psychology*, 94(4): 900–12.

Greenwood, R. and Hinings, C. R. 1996. Understanding radical organizational change: Bringing together the old and the new institutionalism. *Academy of Management Review*, 21(4): 1022–54.

Griffeth, R., Hom, P. and Gaertner, S. 2000. A meta-analysis of antecedents and correlates of employee turnover: Update, moderator tests, and research implications for the next millennium. *Journal of Management*, 26(3): 463–88.

Gu, M. 2010. A blueprint for educational development in China: A review of 'The National Guidelines for Medium- and Long-Term Educational Reform and Development (2010–2020)'. *Frontiers of Education in China*, 5(3): 291–309.

Guest, D. 2002. Human resource management, corporate performance and employee well-being: Building the worker into HRM. *Journal of Industrial Relations*, 44(3): 335–58.

Guest, D. E. 1987. Human resource management and industrial relations. *Journal of Management Studies*, 24(5): 503–21.

Guest, D. E. 2011. Human resource management and performance: Still searching for some answers. *Human Resource Management Journal*, 21(1): 3–13.

Guest, D. E., Michie, J., Conway, N. and Sheehan, M. 2003. Human resource management and corporate performance in the UK. *British Journal of Industrial Relations*, 41(2): 291–314.

Guo, S. 1999. Discussion on the imitation of the Japanese education system in the Late Qing Dynasty and Early Republic Era (pingshu qingmo minchu xinxuezhi dui riben xuezhi de mofang). *Journal of Shanxi University*, 2: 79–82.

Guthrie, D. 2009. *China and Globalization: The Social, Economic and Political Transformation of Chinese Society*. New York and London: Routledge.

Hall, P. A. and Taylor, R. C. 1996. Political science and the three new institutionalisms. *Political Studies*, 44(5): 936–57.

Hamilton, G. G. 1990. Patriarchy, patrimonialism, and filial piety: A comparison of China and Western Europe. *British Journal of Sociology*, 41(1): 77–104.

Han, A. G. 2008. Building a harmonious society and achieving individual harmony. *Journal of Chinese Political Science*, 13(2): 143–64.

Hargreaves, A. 1998. The emotional practice of teaching. *Teaching and Teacher Education*, 14(8): 835–54.

Hartog, D. N., Boon, C., Verburg, R. M. and Croon, M. A. 2013. HRM, communication, satisfaction, and perceived performance: A cross-level test. *Journal of Management*, 39(6): 1637–65.

Hasan, I., Wachtel, P. and Zhou, M. 2009. Institutional development, financial deepening and economic growth: Evidence from China. *Journal of Banking & Finance*, 33(1): 157–70.

Head, J. W. 2010. Feeling the stones when crossing the river: The rule of law in China. *Santa Clara Journal of International Law*, 7(2): 25–84.

Heck, R. and Thomas, S. 2009. *An Introduction to Multilevel Modelling Techniques* (2nd Ed.). New York: Routledge.

Hendry, C. and Pettigrew, A. M. 1990. Human Resource Management: An agenda for the 1990s. *International Journal of Human Resource Management*, 1(1): 17–43.

Hesketh, A. and Fleetwood, S. 2006. Beyond measuring the human resources management-organizational performance link: Applying critical realist meta-theory. *Organization*, 13(5): 677–99.

Hitt, M. A., Bierman, L., Shimizu, K. and Kochhar, R. 2001. Direct and moderating effects of human capital on strategy and performance in professional service firms: A resource-based perspective. *Academy of Management Journal*, 44(1): 13–28.

Holmes, R. M., Miller, T., Hitt, M. A. and Salmador, M. P. 2013. The interrelationships among informal institutions, formal institutions, and inward foreign direct investment. *Journal of Management*, 39(2): 531–66.

Hoy, W. K. and DiPaola, M. F. 2005. Organizational citizenship of faculty and achievement of high school students. *The High School Journal*, 88(3): 35–44.

Hu, L. and Bentler, P. M. 1999. Cutoff criteria for fit indexes in covariance structure analysis: Conventional criteria versus new alternatives. *Structural Equation Modeling: A Multidisciplinary Journal*, 6(1): 1–55.

Huang, G. 2009. Review of the educationists as presidents of universities and colleges in Republic of China (1920–1949) (minguo shiqi jiaoyu xuezhe churen daxue xiaozhang kaolun (1920–1949)). *Journal of Educaitonal Studies*, 5(3): 110–20.

Huselid, M. 1995. The impact of human resource management practices on turnover, productivity, and corporate financial performance. *Academy of Management Journal*, 38(3): 635–72.

Ilies, R., Nahrgang, J. D. and Morgeson, F. P. 2007. Leader-member exchange and citizenship behaviors: A meta-analysis. *Journal of Applied Psychology*, 92(1): 269.

James, L. R. 1982. Aggregation bias in estimates of perceptual agreement. *Journal of Applied Psychology*, 67(2): 219–29.

Jennings, P. A. and Greenberg, M. T. 2009. The prosocial classroom: Teacher social and emotional competence in relation to student and classroom outcomes. *Review of Educational Research*, 79(1): 491–525.

Jiang, K., Lepak, D. P., Hu, J. and Baer, J. C. 2012. How does human resource management influence organizational outcomes? A meta-analytic investigation of mediating mechanisms. *Academy of Management Journal*, 55(6): 1264–94.

Jimmieson, N. L., Hannam, R. L. and Yeo, G. B. 2010. Teacher organizational citizenship behaviours and job efficacy: Implications for student quality of school life. *British Journal of Psychology*, 101(3): 453–79.

Johnson, W. and Weiss, J. 2011. Into the heart of dragon: An introduction and agenda on innovation and educaiton towards innovation in China. *Journal of Technology Management in China*, 6(3): 196–202.

Judge, T. A., Thoresen, C. J., Bono, J. E. and Patton, G. K. 2001. The job satisfaction-job performance relationship: A qualitative and quantitative review. *Psychological Bulletin*, 127(3): 376–407.

Kandasamy, I. and Ancheri, S. 2009. Hotel employees' expectations of QWL: A qualitative study. *International Journal of Hospitality Management*, 28(3): 328–37.

Karatzias, A., Power, K. and Swanson, V. 2001. Quality of school life: Development and preliminary standardisation of an instrument based on performance indicators in Scottish secondary schools. *School Effectiveness and School Improvement*, 12(3): 265–84.

Keenan, C. B. 1974. Educational reform and politics in early Republican China. *The Journal of Asian Studies*, 33(2): 225–37.

Kehoe, R. R. and Wright, P. M. 2013. The impact of high-performance human resource practices on employees' attitudes and behaviors. *Journal of Management*, 39(2): 366–91.

Keng, K. 2006. China's unbalanced economic growth. *Journal of Contemporary China*, 15(46): 183–214.

Kim, S., Wright, P. and Su, Z. 2010. Human resource management and firm performance in China: A critical review. *Asia Pacific Journal of Human Resources*, 48(1): 58–85

Kong, C. 2008. Classroom learning experiences and students' perceptions of quality of school life. *Learning Environments Research*, 11(2): 111–29.

Kornai, J. 1992. *The Socialist System: The Political Economy of Communism*. Princeton: Princeton University Press.

Kravetz, D. J. 1988. *The Human Resources Revolution: Implementing Progressive Management Practices for Bottom-Line Success*. London: Jossey-Bass Publishers.

Kyriakides, L., Creemers, B. P. and Antoniou, P. 2009. Teacher behaviour and student outcomes: Suggestions for research on teacher training and professional development. *Teaching and Teacher Education*, 25(1): 12–23.

Lamie, J. M. 2006. Teacher education and training in China: Evaluating change with Chinese lecturers of English. *Journal of In-service Education*, 32(1): 63–84.

Landis, R. S., Beal, D. J. and Tesluk, P. E. 2000. A comparison of approaches to forming composite measures in structural equation models. *Organizational Research Methods*, 3(2): 186–207.

Landry, P. 2008. *Decentralized Authoritarianism in China: The Communist Party's Control of Local Elites in the Post-Mao Era*. Cambridge and New York: Cambridge University Press.

Lane, J. E. 2013. China at the crossroads. *International Journal of Social Economics*, 40(2): 169–80.

Lang, R. and Steger, T. 2002. The odyssey of management knowledge to transforming societies: A critical review of a theoretical alternative. *Human Resource Development International*, 5(3): 279–94.

Lau, R. 2000. Quality of work life and performance: An investigation of two key elements in the service profit chain model. *International Journal of Service Industry Management*, 11(5): 422–37.

LeBreton, J. M., Wu, J. and Bing, M. N. 2009. The truth (s) on testing for mediation in the social and organizational sciences. In C. Lance and R. Vandenberg (Eds.), *Statistical and Methodological Myths and Urban Legends: Doctrine, Verity and Fable in the Organizational and Social Sciences*. New York: Routledge, pp. 109–44.

Legge, K. 2005. *Human Resource Management: Rhetorics and Realities*. New York: MacMillan.

Legge, K. 2007. Networked organizations and the negation of HRM? In J. Storey (Ed.), *Human Resource Management: A Critical Text*. London: Thomson, pp. 39–56.

Lengnick-Hall, M. L., Lengnick-Hall, C. A., Andrade, L. and Drake, B. 2009. Strategic human resource management: the evolution of the field. *Human Resource Management Review*, 19(2), 64–85.

Leonard, C., Bourke, S. and Schofield, N. 2004. Affecting the affective: Affective outcomes in the context of school effectiveness, school improvement and quality schools. *Issues In Educational Research*, 14(1), 1–28.

Lewin, K. and Hui, X. 1989. Rethinking revolution: Reflections on China's 1985 educational reforms. *Comparative Education*, 25(1): 7–17.

Li, H. 1997. Discussion on the division of education history in Republic of China (lun minguo jiaoyushi de fenqi). *Journal of Shanghai Normal University*, 1: 126–32.

Li, H. 2004. Further elaboratoin on the 'High Qing Period' (guanyu 'kangqian shengshi' de zai sikao). *Journal of Shanxi Normal University*, 10(33): 189–90.

Li, J. 2012. Elementary school teachers' qualification in the Republic of China and its enlightenment (minguo shiqi xiaoxue jiaoshi de zige zhidu de kaocha jiqi qishi). *Teacher Education Research*, 24(3): 63–8.

Li, P. 2008. Toward a geocentric framework of trust: An application to organizational trust. *Management and Organization Review*, 4(3): 413–39.

Li, X. 1982. A study of Chinese overseas students in Japan in the Late Qing Dynasty (wanqing shiqi zai riben de zhongguo liuxuesheng de kaocha). *Literature, History & Philosophy*, 3: 28–30.

Li, X. and Wang, Y. 2011. An examination of teaching aims and goals and their historical impacts on Republic of China based on 'Education Journal' (cong 'jiaoyu zazhi kan minguo shiqi jiaoyu fangzhen de jingshi zhuzhi jiqi lishi yingxiang). *Journal of Inner Mongolia Normal University* (Educational Science), 24(4): 12–16.

Li, Z. 2009. *A Study of School Education Policy in the Late Qing Dynasty (wanqing shiqi jiaoyu zhengce de yanjiu)*. Hebei: Hebei University.

Liang, X., Marler, J. and Cui, Z. 2012. Strategic human resource management in China: East meets west. *Academy of Management*, 26(2): 55–70.

Liang, Z. and Chen, Y. P. 2007. The educational consequences of migration for children in China. *Social Science Research*, 36: 28–47.

Liao, H., Toya, K., Lepak, D. P. and Hong, Y. 2009. Do they see eye to eye? Management and employee perspectives of high-performance work systems and influence processes on service quality. *Journal of Applied Psychology*, 94(2): 371–91.

Lin, J., Cai, F. and Li, Z. 1996. *The China Miracle: Development Strategy and Economic Reform,* Hong Kong: Chinese University Press.

Liu, E. and Johnson, S. M. 2006. New teachers' experiences of hiring: Late, rushed, and information-poor. *Educational Administration Quarterly*, 42(3): 324–60.

Liu, H. and Qin, X. 2005. A study of teaching profession in the Republic of China (minguo shiqi jiaoshi zhiye tanxi). *Journal of Liaoning Educational Administration Institute* 22(12): 10–14.

Liu, Q. 1992. Sustaining the 'Four Cardinal Principles' as the basic principle for educating students (ba jianchi 'sixiang jiben yuanze' zuowei jiaoyu xuesheng de jiben sixiang). *Journal of Wuhan Educational Institute (Philosophy and Social Sciences)*, 41(11): 33–7.

Liu, S. and Teddlie, C. 2005. A follow-up study on teacher evaluation in China: Historical analysis and latest trends. *Journal of Personnel Evaluation in Education*, 18(4): 253–72.

Mathieu, J. and Taylor, S. 2007. A framework for testing meso-mediational relationships in Organizational Behavior. *Journal of Organizational Behavior*, 28: 141–72.

McNally, C. A. 2007. China's capitalist transition: The making of a new variety of capitalism. *Comparative Social Research*, 24: 177–203.

Mele, D. 2003. The challenge of humanistic management. *Journal of Business Ethics*, 44: 77–88.

Mello, J. 2010. *Strategic Human Resource Management* (3rd Ed.). Cincinnati: South-Western Publishing.

Meng, X. and Gregory, R. G. 2002. The impact of interrupted education on subsequent educational attainment: A cost of the Chinese Cultural Revolution. *Economic Development and Cultural Change*, 50(4): 935–59.

Messersmith, J. G., Patel, P. C., Lepak, D. P. and Gould-Williams, J. S. 2011. Unlocking the black box: Exploring the link between high-performance work systems and performance. *Journal of Applied Psychology*, 96(6): 1105–18.

Ministry of Education. 1999. *Regulation on Primary and Secondary School Teachers Continuous Education* (zhongxiaoxue jiaoshi jixu jiaoyu guiding), Vol. 7. Beijing: Ministry of Education.

Ministry of Education. 2002. *Suggestion on Teacher Education Reform and Development for 'the 10th Five-Year Plan'* (guanyu 'shiwu qijian' jiaoshi jiaoyu gaige yu fazhan de yijian), February. Beijing: Ministry of Education.

Ministry of Education. 2004. *Action Plan for Invigorating Education 2003 to 2007* (2003–2004 zhenxing jiaoyu xingdong jihua), February. Beijing: The Ministry of Education.

Ministry of Education. 2008. *The Guidelines on Teacher's Performance Appraisal of Compulsory Education Schools* (guanyu zuohao yiwu jiaoyu xuexiao jiaoshi jixiao kaohe gongzuo de zhidao yijian), Vol. 15. Beijing: Ministry of Education.

Ministry of Education. 2010. *Outline of China's National Plan for Medium and Long-term Education Reform and Development (2010–2020)* (guojia zhongchangqi jiaoyu gaige he fazhan guihua gangyao (2010–2020)). Beijing: Ministry of Education.

Ministry of Education. 2011. *Suggestion on Reinforcing Primary and Middle School Teachers' Training* (guanyu jiaqiang zhongxiaoxue jiaoshi peixun gongzuo de zhidao yijian), Vol. 1. Beijing: Ministry of Education.

Ministry of Education. 2013a. *Number of Higher Education Institutions.* Available at http://www.moe.edu.cn/publicfiles/business/htmlfiles/moe/s7567/201309/156873.html; accessed 13 November 2013.

Ministry of Education. 2013b. *Guideline on Deepening the Training Model Reforms and Increasing the Overall Training Quality*. Beijing: The Ministry of Education.

Ministry of Education and Ministry of Finance. 1999. *National Programmes for Education Reform and Development* (jiaoyu gaige yu fazhan peixun jihua). Beijing: Ministry of Education and Ministry of Finance.

Ministry of Education, National Bureau of Statistics and Ministry of Finance. 2014. *Report on Excuation of National Education Expenses* (guanyu 2013 nian quanguo jiaoyu jingfei zhixing qingkuang tongji gonggao), Vol. 4. Beijing: Ministry of Education, National Bureau of Statistics and Ministry of Finance.

Ministry of Education, National Development and Reform Commission and Ministry of Finance. 2012. *Suggestions on Deepening Teachers' Educational Reforms* (guanyu shenhua jiaoshi jiaoyu geige de yijian), Vol. 13. Beijing: Ministry of Education, National Development and Reform Commission and Ministry of Finance.

Ministry of Finance and Ministry of Education. 2006. *Temporary Ways to Manage the Administration Fund in Primary and Middle Schools in Rural Areas* (nongcun zhongxiaoxue gongyong jingfei zhichu guanli zanxing banfa), Vol. 5. Beijing: Ministry of Finance and Ministry of Education.

Ministry of Personnel. 2005. *Temporary Guidelines for Open Recruitment in Public Organizations* (shiye danwei gongkai zhaopin renyuan zanxing guiding), Vol. 6. Beijing: Ministry of Personnel.

Mok, K. H., Wong, Y. C. and Zhang, X. 2009. When marketisation and privatisation clash with socialist ideals: Educational inequality in urban China. *International Journal of Educational Development*, 29(5): 505–12.

Moorman, R. and Harland, L. 2002. Temporary employees as good citizens: Factors influencing their OCB performance. *Journal of Business and Psychology*, 17(2): 171–87.

Mossholder, K. W., Richardson, H. A. and Settoon, R. P. 2011. Human resource systems and helping in organizations: A relational perspective. *The Academy of Management Review* 36(1): 33–52.

Murphy, A. and Garavan, T. N. 2009. The adoption and diffusion of an NHRD standard: A conceptual framework. *Human Resource Development Review*, 8(1): 3–21.

National Bureau of Statistics of China. 2014. *China Statistical Yearbook 2014*. Beijing: Zhongguo Tongji Chubanshe.

Newman, K. L. 2000. Organizational transformation during institutional upheaval. *Academy of Management Review*, 25(3): 602–19.

Ngai, P. and Smith, C. 2007. Putting transnational labour process in its place the dormitory labour regime in post-socialist China. *Work Employment and Society*, 21(1): 27–45.

Nguni, S., Sleegers, P. and Denessen, E. 2006. Transformational and transactional leadership effects on teachers' job satisfaction, organizational commitment, and organizational citizenship behavior in primary schools: The Tanzanian case. *School Effectiveness and School Improvement*, 17(2): 145–77.

Nishii, L. H., Lepak, D. P. and Schneider, B. 2008. Employee attributions of the 'why' of HR practices: Their effects on employee attitudes and behaviors, and customer satisfaction. *Personnel Psychology*, 61(3): 503–45.

Niu, Z. 2009. Reforms on teachers' employment system and children's rights to education in China. *International Journal of Educational Management*, 23(1): 7–18.

North, D. C. 1990. *Institutions, Institutional Change and Economic Performance*. Cambridge: Cambridge University Press.

North, D. C. 1994. Economic performance through time. *The American Economic Review*, 84(3): 359–68.

Nyberg, A. J., Moliterno, T. P., Hale, D. and Lepak, D. P. 2014. Resource-based perspectives on unit-level human capital: A review and integration. *Journal of Management*, 40(1): 316–46.

OECD. 2005a. *Performance-related Pay Policies for Government Employees*. Paris: Organisation for Economic Cooperation and Development.

OECD. 2005b. *Teachers Matter: Attracting, Developing and Retaining Effective Teachers*. Paris: Organisation for Economic Cooperation and Development.

OECD. 2008. *Reviews of Innovation Policy: China 2008*. Paris: Organisation for Economic Cooperation and Development.

OECD. 2011. *Building a High Quality Teaching Profession: Lessons from around the World*. Paris: Organisation for Economic Cooperation and Development.

OECD. 2013. *Asian Countries Top OECD's Latest PISA Survey on State of Global Education*. Paris: Organisation for Economic Cooperation and Development.

Oplatka, I. 2006. Going beyond role expectations: Toward an understanding of the determinants and components of teacher organizational citizenship behavior. *Educational Administration Quarterly*, 42(3): 385–423.

Organ, D. W. 1988. *Organizational Citizenship Behavior: The Good Soldier Syndrome*. Lexington: Lexington Books.

Organ, D. W. 1990. The motivational basis of organizational citizenship behavior. *Research in Organizational Behavior*, 12(1): 43–72.

Organ, D. W., Podsakoff, P. M. and MacKenzie, S. B. 2006. *Organizational Citizenship Behavior: Its Nature, Antecedents, and Consequences*. Thousand Oaks: Sage.

Orlitzky, M., Schmidt, F. and Rynes, S. 2003. Corporate social and financial performance: A meta-analysis. *Organization Studies*, 24(3): 403–41.

Ouchi, W., Riordan, R., Lingle, L. and Porter, L. 2005. Academy of Management Journal editors' forum: Making public schools work: Management reform as the key. *Academy of Management Journal*, 48(6): 929–40.

Paauwe, J. 2009. HRM and performance: Achievements, methodological issues and prospects. *Journal of Management Studies*, 46(1): 129–42.

Paine, L. W. and Fang, Y. 2006. Reform as hybrid model of teaching and teacher development in China. *International Journal of Educational Research*, 45(4): 279–89.

People Net. 2013. *China Dream, China Strength (zhongguo meng, Zhongguo liliang)*. Available at http://theory.people.com.cn/n/2013/0105/c40555-20096083.html; accessed 18 August 2014.

Pepper, S. 1996. *Radicalism and Education Reform in Twentieth-century China: The Search for an Ideal Development Model*. Cambridge: Cambridge University Press.

Phillips, N., Tracey, P. and Karra, N. 2009. Rethinking institutional distance: Strengthening the tie between new institutional theory and international management. *Strategic Organization*, 7(3): 339–48.

Pil, F. K. and Leana, C. 2009. Applying organizational research to public school reform: The effects of teacher human and social capital on student performance. *Academy of Management Journal*, 52(6): 1101–24.

Podgursky, M. and Springer, M. 2007. Teacher performance pay: A review. *Journal of Policy Analysis and Management*, 26(4): 909–49.

Podsakoff, N. P., Whiting, S. W., Podsakoff, P. M. and Blume, B. D. 2009. Individual- and organizational-level consequences of organizational citizenship behaviors: A meta-analysis. *Journal of Applied Psychology*, 94(1): 122–41.

Posthuma, R. A., Campion, M. C., Masimova, M. and Campion, M. A. 2013. A high performance work practices taxonomy: Integrating the literature and directing future research. *Journal of Management*, 39(5): 1184–220.

Prabhakar, K. 2007. Exploring teacher education programs in China: Perspective of a visiting delegate. *The Delta Kappa Gamma Bulletin*, 73(2): 43–7.

Preacher, K. J. 2011. Multilevel SEM strategies for evaluating mediation in three-level data. *Multivariate Behavioral Research*, 46(4): 691–731.

Preacher, K. J., Zhang, Z. and Zyphur, M. J. 2011. Alternative methods for assessing mediation in multilevel data: The advantages of multilevel SEM. *Structural Equation Modeling*, 18(2): 161–82.

Preacher, K. J., Zyphur, M. J. and Zhang, Z. 2010. A general multilevel SEM framework for assessing multilevel mediation. *Psychological Methods*, 15(3): 209–33.

Qian, Y., Roland, G. and Xu, C. 2007. Coordinating changes in transition economies. In E. Berglof and G. Roland (Eds.), *The Economics of Transition: The Fifth Nobel Symposium in Economics*. New York: Palgrave Macmillan, pp. 518–46.

Qiao, K., Khiji, S. E. and Wang, X. 2009. High-performance work systems, organizational commitment and the role of demographic features in China. *The International Journal of Human Resource Management*, 20(11): 2311–30.

Rhoades, L. and Eisenberger, R. 2002. Perceived organizational support: A review of the literature. *Journal of Applied Psychology*, 87(4): 698–714.

Rhodes, R. A. W. and Wanna, J. 2007. The limits to public value, or rescuing responsible government from the platonic guardians. *Australian Journal of Public Administration*, 66(4): 406–21.

Richard, O. C., Ismail, K. M., Bhuian, S. N. and Taylor, E. C. 2009. Mentoring in supervisor-subordinate dyads: Antecedents, consequences, and test of a mediation model of mentorship. *Journal of Business Research*, 62(11): 1110–18.

Riggle, R. J., Edmondson, D. R. and Hansen, J. D. 2009. A meta-analysis of the relationship between perceived organizational support and job outcomes: 20 years of research. *Journal of Business Research*, 62(10): 1027–30.

Roan, A., Bramble, T. and Lafferty, G. 2001. Australian workplace agreements in practice: The 'hard'and 'soft'dimensions. *The Journal of Industrial Relations*, 43(4): 387–401.

Robinson, B. and Yi, W. 2008. The role and status of non-governmental ('daike') teachers in China's rural education. *International Journal of Educational Development*, 28(1): 35–54.

Romanowski, M. H. 2006. A changing nation: Issues facing Chinese teachers. *Kappa Delta Pi Record*, 42(2): 76–81.

Rowan, B., Chiang, F. S. and Miller, R. J. 1997. Using research on employees' performance to study the effects of teachers on students' achievement. *Sociology of Education*, 70(4): 256–84.

Rowan, B., Raudenbush, S. W. and Cheong, Y. F. 1993. Teaching as a nonroutine task: Implications for the management of schools. *Educational Administration Quarterly*, 29: 479–525.

Rowley, C. and Benson, J. 2002. Convergence and divergence in Asian human resource management. *California Management Review*, 44(2): 90–109.

Scott, W. R. 2004. Reflections on a half-century of organizational sociology. *Annual Review of Sociology*, 30: 1–21.

Scott, W. R. 2005. Institutional theory: Contributing to a theoretical research program. In K. G. Smith and M. A. Hitt (Eds.), *Great Minds in Management*. New York: Oxford University Press, pp. 460–84.

Scott, W. R. 2008a. Approaching adulthood: The maturing of institutional theory. *Theory and Society*, 37(5): 427–42.

Scott, W. R. 2008b. *Institutions and Organizations: Ideas and Interests* (3rd Ed.). London: Sage.

Scott, W. R. 2010. Reflections: The past and future of research on institutions and institutional change. *Journal of Change Management*, 10(1): 5–21.

Sesen, H. and Basim, N. H. 2012. Impact of satisfaction and commitment on teachers' organizational citizenship. *Educational Psychology*, 32(4): 475–91.

Settoon, R. P., Bennett, N. and Liden, R. C. 1996. Social exchange in organizations: Perceived organizational support, leader-member exchange, and employee reciprocity. *Journal of Applied Psychology*, 81(3): 219–27.

Sharma. 2011. How China is winning the school race. *BBC News Business*. Available at http://www.bbc.co.uk/news/business-14812822; accessed 18 February 2013.

Shi, K. 2013. Tracing education reforms of the North Song Dynasty from 'Wang Anshi Reforms' (cong 'wanganshi bianfa' tanxun beisong jiaoyu gaige de guiji). *Lantai World*, 30: 96–7.

Shore, L. M. and Shore, T. H. 1995. Perceived organizational support and organizational justice. In R. Cropanzano and K. M. Kacmar (Eds.), *Organizational Politics, Justice, and Support*. Westport: Quorum Press, pp. 149–64.

Simpson, R. L. 1985. Organizational structure. *Annual Review of Sociology*, 11: 425–36.

Somech, A. and Bogler, R. 2002. Antecedents and consequences of teacher organizational and professional commitment. *Educational Administration Quarterly*, 38(4): 555–77.

Somech, A. and Drach-Zahavy, A. 2000. Understanding extra-role behavior in schools: The relationships between job satisfaction, sense of efficacy, and teachers' extra-role behavior. *Teaching and Teacher Education*, 16(5-6): 649–59.

Spitzeck, H. 2011. An integrated model of humanistic management. *Journal of Business Ethics*, 99: 51–62.

State Council. 1999. *Action Plan to Revitalise Education for the 21st Century* (21shiji zhenxing jiaoyu xingdong jihua), Vol. 4. Beijing: State Council.

State Council. 2001. *Decision on Elementary Education Reform and Development* (guanyu zhongxiaoxue jiaoyu gaige yu fazhan de jueding), Vol. 21. Beijing: State Council.

State Council. 2002. *Suggestion on the Trial Employment System in Public Organizations* (guanyu zai shiye danwei shixing renyuan pinyong zhidu de yijian), Vol. 35. Beijing: State Council.

State Council. 2003. *Decision on Furthering Strengthening Education in Rural Areas* (guanyu jinyibu jiaqiang nongcun jiaoyu gongzuo de jueding), Vol. 19. Beijing: State Council.

State Council. 2005. *Notification of Deepening Reforms on the Funding Guaranteeing Mechanism of Rural Compulsory Education* (guanyu shenhua nongcun yiwu jiaoyujingfei baozhang jizhi gaige de tongzhi). Beijing: State Council.

State Council. 2006. *Guidelines on Addressing the Problems of Peasants' Workers* (guanyu jiejue nongminggong wenti de ruogan zhidao yijian). Beijing: State Council.

State Council. 2008. *Guidelines on the Implementation of Performance-related Pay in Elementary Education* (guanyu yiwu jiaoyu xuexiao shishi jixiao gongzi de zhidao yijian), Vol. 15. Beijing: State Council.

State Council. 2010. *National Guideline for Medium- and Long-term Educational Reform and Development (2010–2020)*. Beijing: State Council.

State Council. 2012. *Suggestion on Deepening the Balanced Development of the Compulsory Education* (guowuyuan guanyu tuijin yiwu jiaoyu junheng fanzhan de yijian), Vol. 48. Beijing: State Council.

Storey, J. 1992. *Developments in the Management of Human Resources: An Analytical Review*. Oxford: Blackwell Publishers.

Storey, J. 1995. Human resource management: Still marching on, or marching out. In J. Storey (Ed.), *Human Resource Management: A Critical Text*. London: Routledge, pp. 3–32.

Storey, J. 2007a. Human resource management today: An assessment. In J. Storey (Ed.), *Human Resource Management: A Critical Text*, 3rd Ed. London: Thomson, pp. 3–19.

Storey, J. 2007b. What is strategic HRM? In J. Storey (Ed.), *Human Resource Management: A Critical Test* (3rd Ed). London: Thomson, pp. 59–78.

Storey, J. and Sisson, K. 1993. *Managing Human Resources and Industrial Relations*. Buckingham: Open University Press.

Su, G. and Zhang, Q. 2009. The characteristics and implications of legislation in education in the Republic of China (shilun minguo shiqi jiaoyu lifa tese jiqi dangdai qishi). *Modern Education Science*, 1: 85–8.

Subramony, M. 2009. A meta-analytic investigation of the relationship between HRM bundles and firm performance. *Human Resource Management*, 48(5): 745–68.

Sun, L. Y., Aryee, S. and Law, K. S. 2007. High-performance human resource practices, citizenship behavior, and organizational performance: A relational perspective. *The Academy of Management Journal*, 50(3): 558–77.

Sun, S. 2009. Analysis and suggestion on problems of teachers' performance appraisal (jiaoshi pingjia fenti de fenxi jiqi jiejue duice). *School Management and Development*, April: 15–19.

Takeuchi, R., Lepak, D. P., Wang, H. and Takeuchi, K. 2007. An empirical examination of the mechanisms mediating between high-performance work systems and the performance of Japanese organizations. *Journal of Applied Psychology*, 92(4): 1069–83.

Tangen, R. 2009. Conceptualising quality of school life from pupils' perspectives: A four-dimensional model. *International Journal of Inclusive Education*, 13(8): 829–44.

The President of PR China. 1986. *The Compulsory Education Law of People's Republic of China* (zhonghua renmin gongheguo yiwu jiaoyufa), Vol. 38. Beijing: Central Government of PR China.

The President of PR China. 1993. *The Teacher Law of the People's Republic of China* (zhonghua renmin gongheguo jiaoshifa), Vol. 15. Beijing: Central Government of PR China

The President of PR China. 1995. *The Education Law of the People's Republic of China* (zhonghua renmin gongheguo jiaoyufa), Vol. 45. Beijing: Central Government of PR China

The President of PR China. 2006. *The Compulsory Education Law of People's Republic of China* (zhonghua renmin gongheguo yiwu jiaoyufa), Vol. 52. Beijing: Central Government of P. China

The World Bank. 2013. *China 2030: Building a Modern, Harmonious, and Creative Society*. Washington, DC: The World Bank Group.

Thien, L. M. and Razak, N. A. 2013. Academic coping, friendship quality, and student engagement associated with student quality of school life: A partial least square analysis. *Social Indicators Research*, 112: 679–708.

Thompson, P. 2011. The trouble with HRM. *Human Resource Management Journal*, 21(4): 355–67.

Thoonen, E. E., Sleegers, P. J., Oort, F. J., Peetsma, T. T. and Geijsel, F. P. 2011. How to improve teaching practices: The role of teacher motivation, organizational factors, and leadership practices. *Educational Administration Quarterly*, 47(3): 496–536.

Tong, C., Straussman, J. and Broadnax, W. 1999. Civil service reform in the People's Republic of China: Case studies of early implementation. *Public Administration and Development*, 19(2): 193–206.

Torrington, D. 1989. Human resource management and the personnel function. In J. Storey (Ed.), *New Perspectives on Human Resource Management*. London: Routledge, pp. 56–66.

Tremblay, M., Cloutier, J., Simard, G., Chênevert, D. and Vandenberghe, C. 2010. The role of HRM practices, procedural justice, organizational support and trust in organizational commitment and in-role and extra-role performance. *The International Journal of Human Resource Management*, 21(3): 405–33.

Truss, C., Gratton, L., Hope-Hailey, V., McGovern, P. and Stiles, P. 1997. Soft and hard models of human resource management: A reappraisal. *Journal of Management Studies*, 34(1): 53–73.

Tsang, M. 1996. Financial reform of basic education in China. *Economics of Education Review*, 15(4): 423–44.

Tsang, M. 2000. Education and national development in China since 1949: Oscillating policies and enduring dilemmas. *China Review*: 579–618.

Tsui, A. S. 2009. Editor's introduction – Autonomy of inquiry: Shaping the future of emerging scientific communities. *Management and Organization Review*, 5(1): 1–14.

Tsui, A. S. and Jia, J. 2013. Editorial calling for humanistic scholarship in China. *Management and Organization Review*, 9(1): 1–15.

Tsui, A. S., Schoonhoven, C. B., Meyer, M. W., Lau, C. M. and Milkovich, G. T. 2004. Organization and management in the midst of societal transformation: The People's Republic of China. *Organization Science*, 15(2): 133–44.

Ulrich, D. 1997. Measuring human resources: An overview of practice and a prescription for results. *Human Resource Management*, 36(3): 303–20.

Walker, R. M., Brewer, G. A., Boyne, G. A. and Avellaneda, C. N. 2011. Market orientation and public service performance: New Public Management gone mad? *Public Administration Review*, 71(5): 707–17.

Wall, T. D. and Wood, S. J. 2005. The romance of human resource management and business performance, and the case for big science. *Human Relations*, 58(4): 429–62.

Wang, G. G. 2012. Indigenous Chinese HRM research: Phenomena, methods, and challenges. *Journal of Chinese Human Resources Management*, 3(2): 88–99.

Wang, H. 1995. Humanism as the theme of Chinese modernity. *Surfaces*, 202(1). Available at http://www.pum.umontreal.ca/revues/surfaces/vol5/hui.html; accessed 10 April 2015.

Wang, J. and Wang, G. 2006. Exploring national human resource development: A case of China management development in a transitioning context. *Human Resource Development Review*, 5(2): 176–201.

Wang, L. and Du, H. 2006. On the guiding principles in education of the first 30 years of the founding of the People's Republic of China (jianguo 30 nianlai zhongguo jianyu sixiang de tantao). *Journal of Teachers College Qingdao University*, 23(2): 100–5.

Wang, X. 1999. Discussion on educational reforms in the late Qing dynasty (lun wanqing shiqi jiaoyu gaige). *Journal of Liaocheng Normal College*, 2: 27–31.

Wang, Y. 2011. Explorations on primary school teachers' welfare in Republic of China (minguo xiaoxu jiaoshi daiyu chutan). *Teaching and Management*, January: 25–7.

Warner, M. 1993. Human resource management 'with Chinese characteristics'. *The International Journal of Human Resource Management*, 4(1): 45–65.

Warner, M. 2002. Introduction: The Asia-Pacific HRM model revisited. *International Journal of Human Resource Management*, 11(2), 171–82.

Warner, M. 2008. Reassessing human resource management 'with Chinese characteristics': An overview. *The International Journal of Human Resource Management*, 19(5): 771–801.

Warner, M. 2009. 'Making sense' of HRM in China: Setting the scene. *The International Journal of Human Resource Management*, 20(11): 2169–93.

Warner, M. 2010. In search of Confucian HRM: Theory and practice in Greater China and beyond. *The International Journal of Human Resource Management*, 21(12): 2053–78.

Warner, M. 2011. *Confucian HRM in China: Theory and Practice*. London: Routledge.

Warner, M., Edwards, V., Polonsky, G., Pucko, D. and Zhu, Y. 2005. *Management in Transitional Economies: From the Berlin Wall to the Great Wall of China*. London: Routledge.

Warner, M. and Rowley, C. 2011. Chinese management at the crossroads: Setting the scene. In M. Warner and C. Rowley (Eds.), *Chinese Management in the 'Harmonious society': Managers, Markets and the Golbalized Economy*. London: Routledge, pp. 1–12.

Way, S. A. 2002. High performance work systems and intermediate indicators of firm performance within the US small business sector. *Journal of Management*, 28(6): 765–85.

Wei, Y. D. 2000. *Regional Development in China: States, Globalization and Inequality*. New York: Routledge.

Westwood, R. I. 1997. Harmony and patriarchy: The cultural basis for 'paternalistic headship' among the overseas Chinese. *Organization Studies*, 18: 445–80.

Whiting, S. W., Podsakoff, P. M. and Pierce, J. R. 2008. Effects of task performance, helping, voice, and organizational loyalty on performance appraisal ratings. *Journal of Applied Psychology*, 93(1): 125–39.

Williams, L. J. and Anderson, S. E. 1991. Job satisfaction and organizational commitment as predictors of organizational citizenship and in-role behaviors. *Journal of Management*, 17(3): 601–17.

Wright, P. M. and Haggerty, J. J. 2005. Missing variables in theories of strategic human resource management: Time, cause, and individuals. *Management Revue*, 16(2): 164–73.

Wright, P. M. and McMahan, G. C. 2011. Exploring human capital: Putting 'human' back into strategic human resource management. *Human Resource Management Journal*, 21(2): 93–104.

Wright, P. M. and Snell, S. 1998. Toward a unifying framework for exploring fit and flexibility in strategic human resource management. *Academy of Management Review*, 23(4): 756–72.

Wright, P. M., Dunford, B. B. and Snell, S. A. 2001. Human resources and the resource based view of the firm. *Journal of Management*, 27(6): 701–21.

Wright, P. M., Gardner, T. M. and Moynihan, L. M. 2003. The impact of HR practices on the performance of business units. *Human Resource Management Journal*, 13(3): 21–36.

Wright, P. M., Gardner, T. M., Moynihan, L. M. and Allen, M. R. 2005. The relationship between HR practices and firm performance: Examining causal order. *Personnel Psychology*, 58(2): 409–46.

Wu, P. and Chaturvedi, S. 2009. The role of procedural justice and power distance in the relationship between high performance work systems and employee attitudes: A multilevel perspective. *Journal of Management*, 35(5): 1228–47.

Wu, Y. 2013. *Regional Development and Economic Growth in China*. Singapore: World Scientific Publishing Company.

Xie, L. 2008. The implications from the education in the republican era (minguo jiaoyu de qishi). *Teachers Overview*, 1: 10–11.

Xiong, X. 1996. Discussion on the difficulties in and solutions to educational financing in the Republic of China (lun minguo shiqi jiaoyu jingfei de kunrao yu duice). *Journal of Hubei University*, 5: 94–100.

Xu, C. 2011. The fundamental institutions of China's reforms and development. *Journal of Economic Literature*, 49(4): 1076–151.

Xu, C., Wang, X. and Shu, Y. 2007. Local officials and economic growth. *Economic Research Journal*, 42(9): 18–31.

Xu, S. 1996. Discussion on the evolvement of new intellectuals in the Westernization Moverment period (lun yangwu yundong shiqi zhongguo xinshi zhishi fenziqun de xingcheng). *The Frontline of Social Science* 6: 206–13.

Xu, X. and Mei, W. 2009. *Educational Policies and Legislation in China*. New Jersey: Homa & Sekey Books.

Yan, Q. 2006. The reflection on the research on teachers' income and welfare in the Repulic of China (minguo shiqi jiaoshi shenghuo daiyu yanjiu de huigu yu fansi). *Journal of Nantong University*, 22(2): 55–9.

Yan, X. 2001. The rise of China in Chinese eyes. *Journal of Contemporary China*, 10(26): 33–9.

Yang, D. 2005. China's education in 2003: From growth to reform. *Chinese Education & Society*, 38(4): 11–45.

Yang, T. 2001. Discussion on educational guiding principles of late Qing dynasty (wangqing shiqi jiaoyu fangzhen de tantao). *Educational Study* 12: 70–4.

Yang, T. 2011. The problems and some suggestions in the current system reform of teacher education in China. *US-China Education Review*, B(1): 117–25.

Yang, T. 2012. The retrospection and elicitation of China's teacher education reform and opening-up more than 30 years. *US-China Education Review*, B(1): 88–98.

Yao, Y. and Yueh, L. 2009. Law, finance, and economic growth in China: An introduction. *World Development*, 37(4): 753–62.

Yeung, A., Warner, M. and Rowley, C. 2008. Guest Editors introduction – growth and globalization: Evolution of human resource management practices in Asia. *Human Resource Management*, 47, 1–13.

Yuan, Z., Wan, G. and Khor, N. 2012. The rise of middle class in rural China. *China Agricultural Economic Review*, 4(1): 36–51.

Zhang, H. and Chen, H. 2012. The economic transition in China at the crossroads: A perspective on three-gap analysis. *Journal of Cambridge Studies*, 7(1): 43–61.

Zhang, J., Liu, P. W. and Yung, L. 2007. The Cultural Revolution and returns to schooling in China: Estimates based on twins. *Journal of Development Economics*, 84(2): 631–9.

Zhang, X. 2006. Fiscal decentralization and political centralization in China: Implications for growth and inequality. *Journal of Comparative Economics*, 34(4): 713–26.

Zhang, X. 2010. The regulations and implications of Teachers' Certificate system in Repulic of China (minguo shiqi jiaoshi zigezheng xitong de guiding jiqi qishi) *Shiji Qiao*, 212(21): 92–3.

Zheng, C. and Lamond, D. 2009. A critical review of human resource management studies (1978–2007) in the People's Republic of China. *The International Journal of Human Resource Management*, 20(11): 2194–227.

Zhong, Q. 2006. Curriculum reform in China: Challenges and reflections. *Frontiers of Education In China*, 1(3): 370–82.

Zhou, C. 1996. Science, civil society and metaphysics. In B. Manuel, M. Wang and X. Yu (Eds.), *Civil Society in a Chinese Context*. Washington, DC: Council for Research in Values and Philosophy, pp. 67–75.

Zhou, H. and Shen, G. 2011. Elaborations and reflections on educational reforms in the 20th century in China (zhongguo 20 shiji jiaoyu gaige de huigu yu fansi). *Journal of Huazhong Normal University (Humanities and Social Sciences)*, 50(3): 132–8.

Zhou, J. and Reed, L. 2005. Chinese government documents on teacher education since the 1980s. *Journal of Education for Teaching*, 31(3): 201–13.

Zhou, W. 2001. Discussion on the High Qing Period (lun kangqian shengshi). *Social Science*, 10: 71–4.

Zhou, X. and Hou, L. 1999. Children of the Cultural Revolution: The state and the life course in the People's Republic of China. *American Sociological Review*, 64(1): 12–36.

Zhu, C., Zhang, M. and Shen, J. 2012. Paternalistic and transactional HRM: The nature and transformation of HRM in contemporary China. *The International Journal of Human Resource Management*, 23(19): 3964–82.

Zhu, Y., Warner, M. and Rowley, C. 2007. Human resource management with 'Asian' characteristics: A hybrid people-management system in East Asia. *The International Journal of Human Resource Management*, 18(5): 745–68.

Zhu, Y., Webber, M. and Benson, J. 2010. *The Everyday Impact of Economic Reform in China*. New York: Routledge.

Zhu, Z. 2007. Reform without a theory: Why does it work in China? *Organization Studies*, 28(10): 1503–22.

Zhuo, Q. 1994. Mao Zedong (1893–1976). *UNESCO: International Bureau of Education*, 24(1/2): 93–106.

Index